Olive Cook

English Cottages
and
Farmhouses

with 177 photographs, 14 in color, by

Edwin Smith

Thames and Hudson

To Norman Scarfe and Paul Fincham,
defenders of our heritage and dear friends

On the half-title page *The entrance hall of Mrs Borrick's cottage, Underhowe,*
Grasmere, in Westmorland. Fitted cupboards, on the left, divide it from the living room in
a way recalling the screen in a hall-house (see p. 90).

Frontispiece *The name of Newlands Hall Farm, Frosterley, Co. Durham, refers not to*
the 19th century, when the new house (far right) and barns were added, but to the time some
two hundred years earlier when the long-house (centre) was built on land reclaimed from the
waste.

First published in the USA in 1982 by Thames and Hudson Inc.,
500 Fifth Avenue, New York, New York 10110

Library of Congress Catalog Card Number 82–80247

Printed and bound in Great Britain by Jarrold and Sons Ltd, Norwich

Contents

Foreword and Acknowledgments

MUCH PROGRESS has been made in recent years in the understanding and appreciation of vernacular buildings, for inevitably the desire to cherish and record them has been quickened as they vanish from the scene. The Vernacular Architecture Group encourages the exploration and analysis of regional buildings and publishes an annual journal, and old farm implements and complete examples of the traditional structures of the farmstead are being collected and preserved by such bodies as the Museum of English Rural Life at Reading, the Acton Scott Farm Museum in Shropshire and the Abbot's Hall Rural Life Museum at Stowmarket. Those pioneer works, S.O. Addy's *The English House* (1898) and C.F. Innocent's *English Building Construction* (1916), which first established the homes of rural workers as part of architectural history, have been followed by more intensive studies. Professor M.W. Barley's *The English Farmhouse and Cottage* (1961) traces the changes in regional houses of the great flowering period of vernacular styles, the 16th and 17th centuries, and establishes a disciplined, archaeological approach to the subject. Cecil Hewett's *English Historic Carpentry* (1980) has thrown new light upon the whole study of medieval timber-framed buildings. Alec Clifton Taylor's *The Pattern of English Building* (1962) examines the variety and uses of native materials more exhaustively and with more perception than any previous account. Dr R.W. Brunskill's *Illustrated Handbook of Vernacular Architecture* (1970) and *Traditional Buildings of Britain* (1981) describe types of vernacular buildings and regional variations and suggest procedures for systematic recording and for studying in greater depth. Nigel Harvey's *A History of Farm Buildings* (1970), though addressed to those with farming rather than architectural interests, makes a valuable contribution because it brings the story almost up to the present day and lays particular emphasis on industrialized farm buildings. *The Development of Farm Buildings in Western Lowland Staffordshire up to 1880* by J.E.C. Peters is, like Dr Brunskill's *Vernacular Architecture of the Lake District* and Professor W.G. Hoskins's stimulating Devonshire and Leicestershire studies, among those specialized surveys of a single area which are opening up so many new aspects of the regional diversity of building types. Richard Harris's catalogue to the exhibition *Traditional Farm Buildings* organized by the Arts Council of Great Britain in 1979 provides an excellent and enthusiastic introduction to the study of these structures.

I owe a great debt of gratitude for many insights to all these writers, as well as to the authors of the books and papers mentioned in the text and listed in the bibliography. The present book offers a more general and simple-hearted picture of English farmsteads and cottages and their setting, in an attempt to put a complex and unwieldy subject into a perspective of human history and endeavour. It is an imperfect picture, for not only is the choice of examples personal, but the variety, the immense richness and above all the idiosyncrasy of the material must always elude efforts to classify and embrace it in its entirety. Even the distinction between farmhouse and cottage refuses to remain firm; manor house and farmhouse are continually changing places; and the patched and altered buildings of the farmstead seldom fit into a chronological arrangement. Nonetheless it is hoped that what is written and shown here may conduce to the further discovery and visual enjoyment of a unique heritage. The photographs at least need no justification. Taken over a long period, from 1950 to 1971, they record scenes and buildings which in a good many cases have either ceased to exist or have now lost their original atmosphere and character. So these illustrations are historical.

As this is the story of the material embodiments of a traditional way of life which has now come to an end it seemed appropriate in describing individual buildings to retain the traditional names and the traditional boundaries of the counties in which they stand. New county locations will be found in the index.

My warmest thanks go to all those owners and tenants of farms and cottages, too numerous to be named individually, who welcomed my husband into their homes and who in the past and more recently have so generously answered my questions and allowed me to go into their kitchens and parlours, their bedrooms and attics, their barns and their byres. I am specially grateful to Paul Gooderham of Saffron Walden for enabling me to see the catalogues of farmhouse sales conducted by his firm during the period of the Great Depression in the 19th century; to Paul Beck for bringing to my notice documents relating to land tenure in Shropshire; to Sheila Robinson for very helpful suggestions; and to the late Reginald Lambeth, Rural Industries Organizer for Cambridgeshire, for much fascinating information about ancient beliefs and practices in East Anglia. I am grateful above all to the staff of Thames and Hudson for their support and patience, and in particular to my editor, Emily Lane, whose untiring efforts have saved me from many a blunder and have done much to improve the manuscript, and to Pauline Baines, the designer of the book, for her appreciation of the visual material.

Introduction

THE CHANGELESS CYCLE of the seasons and the rhythm of ploughing, sowing, harvesting and the breeding of cattle and sheep impose the same immutable conditions on the modern farmer as upon his Iron Age and Saxon forebears and would seem an assurance of a comforting sense of continuity. But during the quarter of a century which separates this book from its predecessor, also called *English Cottages and Farmhouses*, published in 1954, the whole structure of farming and village life has undergone a revolution which is destroying that sense of continuity as surely as it has already destroyed many of the traditional buildings celebrated in that volume. None of the upheavals of the past, not even the break-up of the manor, the long process of enclosure, or the gradual transformation of agriculture after the close of the Middle Ages from a self-supporting industry into a profit-making business, has so drastically altered the landscape of farm and field and the character of rural life.

It is sometimes said that the uprooting of the hedges, which engendered such a feeling of intimacy and contributed so much to the rich detail of the domestic English landscape, has restored the aspect of the open fields of the Middle Ages. The resemblance, even where it can be said to exist, is superficial. It must always be taken into account that open-field England was a tiny area in a vast expanse of waste, moor and forest; in the 13th century the royal forest alone is estimated to have covered one third of the whole country. The history of the Essex parish in which my own house lies and of the fields on which I look as I write is well documented, and a brief comparison of the present character and disposition of the land and buildings with their past appearance and usage sufficiently illuminates the contrast between the slow organic change of earlier centuries and present disruption, even though the visual comeliness of this particular corner of East Anglia still gives pleasure. The view from my window embraces a sweep of vast cornfields, rarely defined by a hedge or a row of self-sown saplings, sloping down to the Cam valley, then rising to pale chalky uplands on which crops grow sparsely and which might be taken for Sussex downland. Spring and autumn gales blow the topsoil from these heights so that it settles as a thick dust on sills and ledges. Here and there a copse, last vestige of once extensive forests, survives as a game preserve. Along the ridge, but invisible from here, runs a motorway and monster pylons bestride the gentle contours.

Down by the river a village of clunch, brick and half-timbered farms and cottages, a church and a mill appears at a casual glance to look much as it must have done for generations, though a scattering of council houses on the outskirts, each with its attendant car, proclaims the age, and it is symptomatic also of the age that the original villagers live in these council houses, and work for the most part in a factory a few miles away, while the cottages in which they grew up are now, sometimes smartened and 'modernized' beyond recognition, the homes of commuters or the retreats of weekenders. Like the farmhouses alongside them which have become residences instead of places of work, they have lost their connection with agricultural life. A 15th-century barn serves as an occasional theatre and social centre, other barns are used as garages, and yet another shows the tattered ribs and rotten, sagging thatch of dereliction as it sinks into a bed of nettles and rubbish.

The fields stretch in every direction enlivened only by one or two isolated farmsteads and by streams and tracks which, though their banks and verges have been impoverished by modern farming methods, are still those of the medieval landscape. One of the farms, a 17th-century rectangular house, stands on the site of an important messuage of the Middle Ages. A short straight path leads to the porch from the track, on the other side of which flint walls enclose the yard round which the traditional barn, stables, granary and pigsties were once grouped. The barn fills the whole end of the yard but now it is sheathed in corrugated iron, roofed with asbestos and linked to two huge metal silos. The granary has become a garage and beside it rises one of those enormous, windowless concrete structures which are typical of industrial 'indoor farming' and which take as little account of locality and the scale of the countryside as the silos. Behind the barn amid the debris of decaying carthouses and an old Nissen hut fragments of waggons and cartwheels, pieces of mouldering harness, an ancient rusted coulter blade and part of a light harrow with wrought-iron tines speak as plainly as the new buildings of fundamental change on the farm.

Twenty years ago hedges sheltered the fields on the western uplands and divided the undulating expanses to the east and north into numbers of smaller and more irregular fields. The varieties of trees and shrubs growing in several of these hedges – hazel, spindle, holly, oak and blackthorn – testified to their antiquity. The coverts were thicker and more widespread, a greater diversity of crops gave richer colour to the landscape and in the pastures by the river cattle grazed in the open. The splendid plenitude of nature, the countless species of birds, insects and wild creatures and the seasonal progress of plants in the hedgerows, along the paths and invading the crops, proclaimed the exquisite and precarious equilibrium between this highly evolved, mature and humanized countryside and the wilderness from which it had gradually been wrested. Neither pylons nor motorway intruded on a scene which except for the clearing of woodland, some 18th-century planting and some Victorian cottage building, had altered little since the 17th century, by which time all the fields are described as 'inclusus' – enclosed. The prospect was indeed readily recognizable as a modification of the early 15th-century landscape which was made up of a mesh of small open fields, hedged pastures and large hedged fields set amid a densely wooded terrain. The crops then included wheat, barley, peas, beans and oats. There were more scattered cottages and farmsteads at that time and more farm animals were to be seen than in this later predominantly corn-growing region: pigs, cows, horses, geese and sheep in flocks of from six to three hundred were owned by all classes of peasantry.

The fields then, as they were until quite recently, were the scene of busy human and animal activity for most of the year. Ploughing (with oxen in the early Middle Ages, later with horses), drilling and sowing, haymaking and harvesting, threshing, stone-picking, muck-spreading, hedging and ditching followed each other in quick succession during the inexorable farming year. When machines were first introduced in the last century they lightened the farm labourer's toil without immediately detracting from the animated life of the fields. Although the cutting and binding of corn were done by machines, the sheaves were still, a quarter of a century ago, collected by hand and put up in shocks or stooks in long rows down the field to create a time-honoured image of golden abundance. The threshing-machine, a big red box on wheels, took the place of men armed with flails beating out the grain on the barn floor, but men still pitched the sheaves into the machine and carried away the straw as it dropped out at the back. And the existence of the barn itself was not at once threatened; sometimes indeed the threshing-machine was kept in the big central bay. The barn was still needed for straw, and very often it provided shelter for horses and cattle.

But as technology advanced it rendered nearly all old farm buildings, old farm implements and early forms of machinery obsolete. The internal combustion engine above all, the ousting of the horse by the tractor and the huge self-propelled combine, transformed farming and the rural scene. The revolution was preparing in the 19th century when a new commercial plutocracy who had never lived from agricultural rents and were no more than superficially connected with the land played the part of traditional squires on money drawn from industry and investment. The eventual break-up of large estates, the high cost of manpower and the pressure of overpopulation accelerated the process.

By means of the new machinery corn can be threshed as it is reaped and the grain transported directly to the silos. The full catastrophic consequences of this innovation were slow to be felt owing both to a long depression during the first half of this century and to the conservatism of farmers, especially in the remoter districts. Now it has become obvious that no traditional farm building can be used for cattle and pigs where modern methods have been fully adopted and that the threshing barn, stable and carthouse are completely redundant. Farmers must always satisfy market requirements and they cannot in general preserve useless buildings representing an obstacle to profitable husbandry and a drain on resources for the sake of historic or aesthetic interest.

Similarly, because much larger fields are needed for economic working farms have been thrown together to form huge arable units, hedges have been uprooted and boundaries altered more than at any other time. Even where hedges have been allowed to survive they are brutally cut back by a machine which maims if it does not always destroy the green life tended with such skill and care for so many generations by the craftsman plashing and weaving with his billhook. The introduction of fertilizers and herbicides has freed the farmer from the discipline of the traditional rotational system, the object of which was to check disease and weeds and ensure fertility, and this has not only disrupted much of the former patchwork effect of different crops but has taken its toll of plant and wild life. An unnatural silence has fallen on the land. The giant machines visit the fields two or three times a year, devoting no more than a few days to each of the processes of ploughing, sowing and harvesting. Because the field is no longer fed on foldyard muck and because of the new methods of housing livestock, the modern farmer has little use for straw, so a few days after the combines have harvested the crops, the fields are fired. This is generally done at dusk, thus heightening the drama of an event which turns the landscape into a spectacle of calamity recalling John Martin's lurid fantasies. Sometimes every field within sight blazes, filling the evening sky with a fierce glow and the air with a menacing crackle louder than any other sound. The towering flames lap the scant remains of hedges and the few mature trees on the margins of the fields, and the following day their scorched and blackened forms exacerbate the desolation of the charred land. The former sweet wild flowers of the stubble fields, small plants which, hidden among the roots of the growing corn, only came into their own after harvest, are seen no more. The devastated earth lies bleak and abandoned until the next appearance of the machines. It was the driver of such a machine who remarked to George Ewart Evans: 'The trouble with farming today, it's such a lonely job. When I started as a back'us boy thirty years ago at least you had plenty of company!'

Though agriculture must always remain a vital factor in the life of the nation and change on the farm is in itself nothing new, the change that has taken place in the last two decades and is still going on is unlike anything which has previously transformed the landscape of Britain. It is not evolution but a complete break with tradition. Today's concrete and metal farm buildings cannot be considered either aesthetically or socially as developments of the barns and byres, the stables, granaries and carthouses of the past. So it is against a background of disintegration that the subject of this book is set. It is inevitably a celebration of the past; the present can do no more than enhance by contrast the interest of what a short time ago was still a living tradition and a manifestation of the enchanting variety of the English landscape. These pages seek to recall and record before they have gone forever some of the vernacular buildings of this country, as memorials both of the rural craftsmen who fashioned them and of the life unfolded within and without their walls during centuries of organic growth and change. They bear witness to ways of living which had altered little when most of the photographs in this book were taken, but which now, together with an older generation of farmers and farm labourers who remembered and talked to the photographer and his collaborator about the techniques and customs displaced by the machine, have ceased to be.

I
Origins and Patterns

WE DO NOT KNOW EXACTLY when our forebears began to till the soil of this island and grow crops, but the earliest traces of their fields and farms, found upon the chalk downs and high moors – remarkable patterns of cultivation such as the lynchets seen on the vast limestone expanse of Malham in Yorkshire or on Swallowcliffe and Fyfield Downs in Wiltshire – probably commemorate farmers of the Bronze Age. Excavations and aerial photography have shown that the basic traditional types of rural homestead were already established in Britain in the centuries preceding the Roman Occupation, and that they occurred in the same situations in which they were found later – in villages, in scattered hamlets, or isolated.

It is always stimulating to the imagination to come upon traces of man's earliest attempts to turn the wilderness into fruitful fields, for such gentle remodelling of the earth's surface can be seen as a continuation of the stupendous natural creative processes which have shaped the substance of the land during untold millions of years. But when, as sometimes happens, a farm, rebuilt and altered over the centuries, stands on the actual site of an Iron Age steading, its fabric as expressive as the original structure of the rock and earth beneath it, the evidence of the flow of generation after generation devoted to the raising of crops and the rearing of cattle and sheep, going on and on in that particular place despite wars and plagues and all the vicissitudes of history, takes on a significance of symbolic proportions. W.G. Hoskins describes such a farm at Bosignian in Cornwall and writes convincingly of the Iron Age beginnings of Bartingdale Farm on the east Yorkshire wolds. A little farm which in the 1960s still punctuated the immensity of the chalk undulations near Deptford, Wiltshire, presenting the typical farm image of a fort, compact and square, with thatched barn, thatched, pillared shelter for cattle, cart sheds and a haystack ranged round a foldyard within the security of thatched walls, may well have been the latest manifestation of the homestead of the many earlier generations of cultivators and herdsmen, Bronze Age, Iron Age and Romano-British, whose marks can still be made out on the surrounding plains. It may well have been the descendant of a farm like the nearby and well-known Iron Age Little Woodbury, where house, barns, byres, corn-drying racks and storage pits were similarly grouped within an enclosure. Johnson's Farm in Anstey, Hertfordshire, rises, like many another in this region of heavy clay, on a site moated for drainage as much as for protection. Excavations have revealed continuous occupation from the time of the Iron Age.

1

2

Opposite
1 Evidence of a long tradition of farming at Malham, Yorkshire, where the terraces of ancient cultivation, almost certainly of prehistoric origin, usually called lynchets, are clearly visible.

13

In the granite country of the south-west the impressive remains of Iron Age farming villages stand above ground to evoke the distant past and invite comparison with their successors. The tiny hamlets scattered amid the Celtic fields of a parish such as Morvah are movingly recognizable versions of the pattern created by such prehistoric settlements as Porthmeor and Chysauster. Heather mats the ruins of Chysauster and unites them with the surrounding fields and moorland, but this is the most superficial source of the obvious harmony between the eight roofless homesteads and their setting. Like all traditional rural buildings they translate the most integral component of the landscape into ordered shapes. In this case fragments of the Cornish granite, called 'moorstones', have been skilfully piled without mortar to form oval dwellings, which thus represent a stage in the evolution of the most rudimentary type of house, the round hut, from the circular to the rectangular plan.

Traces of round huts occur in many regions but usually there is nothing substantial to draw the eye. It is on Dartmoor in the vicinity of Grimspound and especially between Widecombe, Shapley and Haytor that this primitive way of living becomes a reality. Some of the countless rough shelters go back to the Bronze Age and are overshadowed by mysterious standing stones and burial chambers, others lurch among the vestiges of prehistoric fields, but all figure forth the essence of the stony waste and fill it with spectral life. It is known from the existence of post holes that timber counterparts of such round huts were common in stoneless regions during the Iron Age, and at West Harling in East Anglia a considerable farmhouse of the period has been excavated. It was circular with an internal circular yard.

The West Harling farmhouse sheltered men and animals under the same roof, and at Chysauster the single-roomed dwellings also housed animals as well as men. In a primitive society it would seem a natural and convenient solution to the problem of providing cover for animals to put them under the same roof as their owners, but the custom of sharing the house with the cow, which persisted to the present century in the wilder and predominantly pastoral country of the north and west, may also owe something to ancient beliefs. The cow helped to warm the house, and it was thought to be unlucky if she was unable to catch a glimpse of the fire. The fire protected the animal from evil spirits and encouraged a greater yield of milk.

On Dartmoor, as in the Lake District and the north, the long rectangular shape of a house occupied by men and farm animals was sanctioned by tradition and preserved by superstition, for a house more than one room wide was thought to be ill-fated. The 'long-house' was one of the basic forms taken by the farmstead. It can yet be seen, in a shape as primitive as that of the Chysauster houses, in the windowless crofters' cottages of the Hebrides and the Shetlands, and, until it finally disintegrated in the early 1970s, a farmhouse of this rudest type, ivy-clutched, its cyclopean dry-stone walls still entire, but with the mouldering thatch retreating from its rafters, stood, a Methuselah of a house, and haunted, so the villagers said, in the bleak fields on the edge of Broomley, Northumberland.

The plan of a narrow rectangle divided by a cross passage into house and

2 Barn, open-fronted shelter and stable at Deptford, Wiltshire, form a compact rectangular enclosure within thatched walls of chalk lump, and perpetuate an arrangement known on these downs at least as far back as Roman times.

3 The Iron Age village of Chysauster, Cornwall, consists of single-roomed dwellings each of which sheltered animals as well as men, a custom which persisted until the present century.

Opposite
I Lower Brockhampton
Manor, near Bromyard,
Herefordshire. The hall
block, left, is unaisled and
so less steeply roofed than
at St Clere's (Pl. II). Part
of the gatehouse appears
on the right.

II *Overleaf* St Clere's, at
St Osyth in Essex
(originally built *c.* 1355),
shows that H-shaped
arrangement composed of
two two-storeyed units
and an aisled hall which
was crucial for the
development of
farmhouse and cottage.
The hall chimneystack is a
later addition replacing an
open hearth. (See p. 44.)

147

shippen was probably originally favoured in regions other than those with which it became particularly associated. Such a house figures in the reconstruction of the Iceni village at Cockley Cley, Norfolk, and it seems likely that at least one of the farmsteads in Anglo-Saxon Thetford was of this type. A long-house still breaks the rhythm of the street at Willersey, Gloucestershire, and an engraving of Bermondsey (then a village south of London) in Holinshed's *Chronicle* of 1585 shows a man leading a horse from a long-house. By the Elizabethan period such farmhouses were only rarely being built in the lowlands, but in the West Country the plan lingered on and in the north it became the commonest type of steading. The continuing overwhelming influence of the plan is there expressed in countless versions of that long, horizontal accent which never fails to satisfy the eye in an irregular, craggy terrain of fell and mountain. The idyllically pastoral farm in Cotterdale, Yorkshire, where the former shippen has become part of the house and another cowshed with a hayloft above it has been added to the opposite end of the building, and the low, graceful sweep of whitewashed sandstone at Dufton, Westmorland, where maroon-painted quoins, mere decoration on the expanse of wall, mark the division between human and animal quarters – both farmsteads with separate entrances for men and beasts – elaborate the inchoate theme of the Chysauster dwellings. But the archaic character of the communal roof for farmer and livestock can perhaps be even more sharply apprehended in the stark landscape of Hebden Moor, Yorkshire, where the isolated farms, which only came into being during the course of late 18th-century enclosures, are juxtaposed to shelters for sheep, wild stones heaped against the boulders of the field walls in just the same form as the Cornish Iron Age houses.

4 This farmstead at Cotterdale, Yorkshire, of the same material as the terraced landscape of limestone, sandstone and dark shale, retains the cross passage which once gave access to both house and cowbyre, and despite rebuilding is still expressive of the long-house tradition.

A tradition perhaps more important than the long-house plan for the evolution of the farmstead and cottage is to be sought in the obscure origins of timber construction. Medieval timber-framing survives in two basic forms, cruck and post-and-truss construction, the sources of both of which can only be surmised. Crucks (a word of common occurrence in early building records, found, for instance, in the accounts for the construction of a kitchen at Windsor Castle in 1236 and in the contract for a bakehouse at Harlech in 1278) are pairs of long, heavy timbers set opposite each other directly in the earth, or on a stone base, or embedded in the lower part of stone walls, and curving to meet at the ridge. The more developed crucks were made by splitting a bent trunk, thus achieving symmetry, and each pair was steadied by a horizontal tie-beam pegged into the members. Cruck construction often presents so rude an aspect that it seems as though it must embody a far more ancient practice than post-and-truss building. It does not seem too fanciful to trace its origins, as C.F. Innocent did, to primitive forms of shelter consisting of a covering of sods supported by pairs of inclining timbers connected by a ridge-pole – or 'first' (from *festum*), as the ridge-piece is called by Anglo-Saxon writers such as the author of *Beowulf*, and as it is still called in parts of Shropshire and Cheshire. The house at Thetford already mentioned was built on crucks and divided into five bays by these essential structural features. That simple early timber building was thus as firmly ordered by the idea of the bay as were the great masterpieces of architecture of the succeeding centuries and as the steel and concrete farm buildings of today still are. Bays were not uniform in size, and S.O. Addy's interesting and often repeated suggestion that their length was determined by the accommodation needed for the stalling of two pairs of oxen does not seem to be confirmed by fact. The bay lengths, for instance, in a cruck barn at Esthwaite, Lancashire, vary from 9 to 14 feet.

This atmospheric barn exhibits the form which cruck construction usually assumed from the later Middle Ages onwards. The framing of walls and roof is no longer continuous, as it must have been in the earliest examples. The crucks rise from the base of the dry-stone walls; spurs, running now into the masonry, mark what was probably the original height of the walls. Further spurs take the place of the cross tie-beams, thus providing much greater headroom, and the crucks are held together by two collars, one at the level of the second purlin, the other just under the ridge-piece. With its crudely jointed timbers and pointed arches, inevitably recalling the Middle Ages, this Esthwaite interior looks like a venerable survival. In fact it probably dates from no earlier than the 16th century, and its air of antiquity is characteristic of northern barns. Crucks had been used with more sense of design – even with a feeling for a drama – before this barn was built, as a number of late medieval cottages at Weobley, Herefordshire, show. As the carpenter's art developed the primitive curved tree principle was to inspire him with some of his happiest inventions.

Timber buildings with separately framed walls and roof may have evolved from cruck construction. In the barn at Esthwaite rudimentary principal rafters are fixed to the backs of the crucks and this could represent a stage in the gradual assumption by the principal rafters of the original

Opposite
III A half-timbered cottage with square-panelled framing at Hampton Lucy, Warwickshire. The thatched roof is extended in a steep catslide (reminiscent of an aisled hall) to cover an outshot.

7

6

5

5 The cottage in the foreground of this street at Weobley, Herefordshire, is built on the same cruck principle as the barn at Esthwaite (*right*).

6 *Right* Cruck constructed barn, Esthwaite, Lancashire.

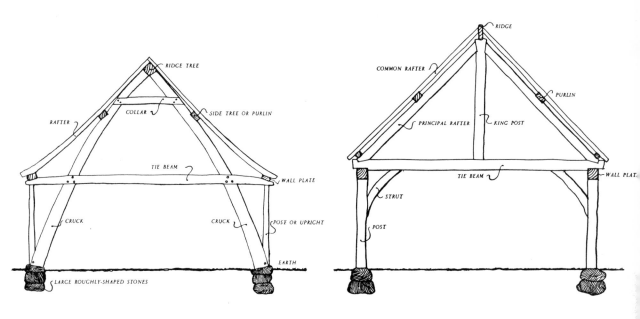

Labels in left diagram: RIDGE TREE, COLLAR, SIDE TREE OR PURLIN, RAFTER, TIE BEAM, WALL PLATE, CRUCK, CRUCK, POST OR UPRIGHT, EARTH, LARGE ROUGHLY-SHAPED STONES

Labels in right diagram: RIDGE, COMMON RAFTER, PURLIN, PRINCIPAL RAFTER, KING POST, TIE BEAM, WALL PLATE, STRUT, POST

function of the crucks. The possibility of such a connection between crucks and principal rafters is supported by a drawing in the 1899 volume of *Archaeologia Cambrensis* of a remarkable single-roomed farmhouse near Strata Florida in Cardiganshire. Of roughest rubble and unshaped timbers, it was thought to have stood since the Middle Ages; and like his medieval predecessors the farmer shared his home with cow, pigs and poultry, separated from them only by a flimsy wattle screen. The principal rafters were entirely cruck-like in form, but rose from the wall plates instead of the ground; they supported purlins and ridge-tree and were strengthened by a tie-beam. The tie-beams rested on gnarled posts, thus creating a rude arcade and aisles, and there was also a central post going up from the floor to carry the ridge-tree. In developed buildings of this type, this central post is set not on the ground but on the tie-beam and turns into a king-post; if it rests on the tie-beam and supports a collar, it becomes a crown-post.

Whether or not the two forms of timber construction were related in this way or emerged independently, it is known that aisled halls were familiar sights in Roman Britain. No remains of such structures can be seen above ground, but archaeologists have shown that they had much in common with the work of medieval carpenters. Dr I.A. Richmond unearthed farmsteads which incorporated aisled halls whose walls were framed and filled with wattle and daub and whose roofs were of the king-post and tie-beam type. As conclusive evidence is wanting it cannot be said that Roman methods survived the Dark Ages. Roman monuments, as the poem *The Ruin* so movingly reveals, filled the Anglo-Saxon settlers with fear as the

7 Diagrams showing cruck framing and post-and-truss framing.

7

work of supernatural beings. But the settlers were farmers and it would have been strange if they had not availed themselves of some of the arrangements of the Roman cultivators. The log huts and log halls excavated and reconstructed at West Stow in Suffolk, which the Saxons already inhabited before the departure of the Romans, exhibit none of the sophistication of the Roman tradition and proclaim their preference for the solid walls of split oak to which they were accustomed rather than the timber frame. But the use of the barn for living accommodation in Roman Britain may have contributed to the establishment of a similar structure as the most characteristic dwelling of the later Saxon and medieval farming landowner. A barn on one side of the quadrangular yard of the Romano-British farm discovered at Ditchley, Oxfordshire, closely resembled the later English barn with nave and aisles divided by timber pillars. Just as in the later hall-house, the aisles were used for both storage and sleeping quarters, in this case those of the farm workers. At Ditchley labourers and master were separately housed, but on simpler farms, perhaps managed by a tenant farmer, as at Clanville in Hampshire or East Denton in Wiltshire, the barn housed both farmer and workers. It is known that some of the more modest Romano-British farmsteads, such as Llantwit Major in Glamorganshire, with its barn dwelling, and Ditchley itself (except for the main house which fell into decay), remained active centres of rural labour until the late 4th and 5th centuries.

The aspect of the single-roomed farmhouse of the pre-Conquest period is still preserved in the interiors of the many aisled barns found particularly in southern England, East Anglia and parts of Yorkshire. Immediately on stepping into a barn such as that at Caldecote, Hertfordshire, the remote past becomes a living experience as it never quite does in a reconstructed building or when little of the original fabric can be seen above ground. Here at Caldecote part of one aisle has been enclosed with wattles as it might have been in the Saxon farmhouse, for storage or for livestock. The two doors confronting each other across the barn resemble those of the early hall, where one of the openings was used for animals, and at the far end of the building another door repeats that which in the hall led to a detached kitchen. Both the main doors were left open so that the draught might fan the central fire and send up its smoke to the rafters.

Looking up now in the dim interior, smoke-like shadows give substance to the image of the fire and movement to the intricate pattern of diagonal, zigzagging and upthrusting timbers overhead, a pattern which emerges as a logical arrangement following ancient practice. The great span of the sharply sloping roof must be supported not only by wall plates but by arcade plates resting on heavy posts and thus creating aisles. The posts have been shaped from tree trunks and a glance shows that they have been set inverted. According to some authorities this custom preserved the timber by allowing the sap to dry out, but the real advantage of the convention was that the butt end of the tree was thick enough for the tie-beam and arcade plates to be laid upon it, jointed to it and coupled with each other. The principal rafters meet the arcade plate at its junction with the tie-beam, thus forming a triangular structure known as a truss. In a building of this kind it is the space between two trusses which constitutes a bay. In the narrow

8

Opposite
8 Post-and-truss framing at Caldecote, Hertfordshire. This barn interior conveys something of the aspect of the earliest aisled halls.

upper stages of the roof between the arcade plates and the ridge the principal rafters are tied together by collars supported by two posts standing on the tie-beam precisely at the point where it is braced by a strut slanting up from the arcade post. So an emphatic repeating pattern strengthens the rhythmic order of the bays, while down below aisle tie-beams running from the wall plate and tenoned to the arcade posts, and diagonal struts rising from the aisle tie-beam to carry a purlin over the aisle, echo and enrich that pattern.

The hall which stemmed directly from the barn-like dwelling of Saxon and earlier periods is the most significant element in the development of the medieval house. It was, however, only one of a number of types of house which had already made their appearance at the time of the Norman Conquest. In late Saxon Thetford there were small houses with a basement, which may have evolved from dwellings of the kind excavated at Sutton Courtenay, Berkshire, which were of one storey only with the floor as much as two feet below ground level. The Bayeux Tapestry shows three astonishing tiny one- or two-roomed rectangular cottages, each with a door in the middle, like a child's drawing of a house, thus achieving a symmetry which does not occur in surviving cottages before the close of the 17th century at the earliest. Little houses of this basic design can still sometimes be seen in village streets, at Digby in Lincolnshire, for instance. It may be that although no early examples of cottages like those in the Bayeux Tapestry have survived they do represent a continuing tradition. The Tapestry cottages are also unexpectedly sturdy in structure. Two of them are fashioned of horizontal planks, one is of stone and all are roofed with stone slates or wooden shingles. Like the grander houses with a first-floor hall which figure in the Tapestry, prototypes of the two-storeyed stone houses which were to be conspicuous in both town and country after the Conquest, these little cottages may be based on French example, since they must have belonged to the time immediately before the Battle of Hastings when under Edward the Confessor French influence was strong.

The Anglo-Saxons used the so-called Belgic plough, which had been brought to Britain before the Roman Occupation but was not widely known. It was a heavy implement which required eight oxen to pull it and it was capable of making a longer furrow than could easily be accommodated by the small Celtic fields or the similar fields of the Romans. This was one important reason for the establishment of the open field system. The Saxons also introduced the tradition of working the land co-operatively by means of the strip unit. A parcel of strips varying in size from about one-third to half an acre made up what was known as a furlong, and the open field comprised diverse numbers of furlongs. It is thought that the arrangement was imposed on the landscape in every region where the Anglo-Saxons settled, but many moorland, mountainous, forest and fenland territories lay outside the open field area. Cheshire, Lancashire, Cumberland and Westmorland and the dense woods of Essex and Kent knew little of the system.

The ploughing of the long narrow stretches with the eight-oxen teams threw the soil towards the centre of the strip, producing a high ridge. Each strip was separated from its neighbour by a double furrow, making a pattern of ridge and furrow which is still visible today in many parts of the country, as on the windy heights between Thwaite and Keld in Yorkshire and at South Middleton in Northumberland, a county abounding in 'lost villages', the result of the conversion of arable to cattle and sheep pastures. On a winter day when snow lies in the ancient furrows, or in the slanting light of a summer evening – such as on the occasion of my only visit there threw into relief every detail of the expanse of Goldsborough Pasture, Yorkshire – the design of long forgotten arable springs to the eye, not the straight lines of modern ploughing but graceful curves swelling in gentle waves across the immemorial fields.

9 The two-storeyed Norman house at Boothby Pagnell, Lincolnshire (see pp. 40–41).

2

The Carpenter's Art

THE OPEN STRIP CULTIVATION of the Anglo-Saxons remained the most characteristic method of farming throughout the Middle Ages, and was indeed still going on as late as the 18th century side by side with the most advanced agricultural practices in enclosed fields. Each farmer was allotted a certain number of strips, which were not adjacent to each other, so that no man had better soil than another. Even the land of the lord of the manor lay scattered among the fields of his men. Across the strips, to prevent cattle from straying into the growing crops, the farmers set hurdles. The village craft of hurdle-making was probably established before the Conquest, and it was not until after the Second World War that mass production put an end to it. Hurdle-makers, one of them a woman, were still working at Barrow in Suffolk in the early 1950s as their predecessors had done for centuries, splitting the ash to the requisite lengths and thicknesses, making the morticed holes and assembling the hurdles by hand. At that time the hurdles were destined for sheep farms in Lincolnshire and Yorkshire, for flocks had largely vanished from Suffolk. The mention of them recalls, however, the very great importance of sheep farming in the Middle Ages: without the image of the shepherd and his flock the picture of medieval agricultural life would be wanting. Wool was a major source of the country's wealth and it was at this period that the woolsack became the symbolic seat of England's Chancellor. Sheep were not confined to the specifically pastoral regions of the north, the Cotswolds and the Sussex Downs but were found on arable farms in abundance; and it was not only powerful lords, bishops and abbots who owned sheep but the peasants of humble manors who by the reign of Edward III were rearing more animals than their landlords.

Already in Anglo-Saxon England rural society was hierarchical: by the time the Norman clerks of William I were compiling Domesday Book the manorial system, which was the name they gave the social order, was completely developed. The manor comprised the whole estate; village and manor house did not necessarily coincide and sometimes the lands of a village might be attached to more than one manor. All the tenants on an estate were bound to the lord and his demesne farm (the home farm): the free tenants, later known as yeomen, paid rent for their land, the unfree tenants or serfs did weekly labour service, and all of them attended the lord's court of justice, his 'hall moot', for the settlement of their disputes and communal affairs.

Opposite
10 The carpenter's precision and fine sense of proportion impart grandeur and elegance to the most commonly occurring form of post-and-truss construction in the 13th-century barn interior at Court Farm, Great Coxwell, Berkshire.

The duties and payments demanded of tenants by their lords are sometimes described in medieval surveys or 'Inquisitions', which give lists of tenants and state the conditions under which they held properties. For instance in 1293 a certain Roger de Cheles of Lawton Baskerville in Shropshire rented nine acres, a little meadow and a cottage from Sir Roger Baskerville, lord of the manor, by service of 'riding with him on his own horse but at the charge of his lord'. The payment asked often seems arrestingly strange to a 20th-century reader: documents for the same Shropshire village for the year 1251 refer to rents in the form of a white rose or a white glove. The exaction of one pound of pepper is less bizarre, for in the 13th century pepper was a rare and expensive luxury and the peppercorn rent was by no means merely nominal as it is today.

The most revealing detail about the services and rents required of farmworkers is found in surveys made for ecclesiastical lords, for it was in the early Middle Ages, in the 12th century especially, that most of the great religious houses were founded and richly endowed with land. It is significant that the commonest names of farms, apart from Manor Farm, Hall Farm and Home Farm, are Abbey Farm and Priory Farm. The *Peterborough Chronicle* (published in translation by the Camden Society in 1849) contains such a record, written by Walter the Archdeacon at the time of the Abbot of Peterborough's death in 1125. Walter's account of the village of Pytchley in Northamptonshire preserves the life of that far-off time with meticulous detail:

> There are there 9 full villeins and 9 half-villeins and 5 cottagers. The full villeins work 3 days a week up to the feast of St. Peter in August and thence up to Michaelmas every day by custom, and the half villeins in accordance with their tenures; and the cottagers one day a week and two in August. Altogether they have 8 plough teams. Each full villein ought to plough and harrow one acre at the winter ploughing and one at the spring, and winnow the seed in his lord's grange and sow it. The half villeins do as much as belongs to them. Beyond this they should lend their plough teams 3 times at the winter ploughing and 3 times at the spring ploughing and once for harrowing. And what they plough they reap and cart. And they render 3 shillings at Christmas and 5 shillings at Easter and 32 pence at St. Peter's feast. And Agemund the miller renders 26 shillings for his mill and for one yardland. And the villeins render 20 eggs and the half villeins 10 eggs and the cottagers 5 eggs at Easter. Viel renders 3 shillings for one yardland and Aze 5; the priest, for the church and 2 yardlands, 5 shillings. Walter the free man pays 2 shillings for a half yardland. Leofric the smith pays 12 pence for one toft. Aegelric of Kettering pays 6 pence for the land he rents and Aegelric of Broughton 12 pence and Lambert 12 pence. And Ralf the sokeman lends his plough 3 times a year. Martin gives a penny and Azo a penny and Ulf and Lambert a penny. On the home farm there are 4 ploughteams with 30 oxen and 8 oxherds who each hold a half yardland of the home farm. There are 2 draught horses, 220 sheep, 20 pigs, and 10 old sheep in their second year.

A 'yardland' varied in acreage according to local custom between 30 and 40 acres scattered over the village fields. If the details in this account of services and rents are of exceptional interest, the names of the villagers are no less intriguing, for with the exception of Lambert they are all still Saxon and Scandinavian names.

The system illustrated by Walter the Archdeacon's survey bound the villagers together as a community and gave the humblest a voice in the agricultural policy. To a romantic like William Morris it seemed to offer a model of successful communal life. And as long as the object of each farmer was to raise food for his family rather than for the market it was economically sound. But like all human institutions it was imperfect. The feudal power of the lord of the manor pressed ever more heavily on the peasant cultivators as the Middle Ages advanced.

Although the farmworkers together formed a self-governing community their relationship to their lord was that of serfs. They could not legally leave their holdings, they could not even give their children in marriage without the lord's consent; and this system of servile tenure obtained throughout the country. Such a situation could not endure and during the 14th century the manorial economy began to disintegrate. The collapse was foreshadowed as early as the 12th century when some manorial lords adopted the custom of commuting the forced services due on the home farm for money rents, and the demesne was worked by hired men labouring all the year round instead of by farmers called off from their own strips on certain days of the week. Services were thus beginning to be regulated by money, and as money became more plentiful from the latter half of the 14th century and expanding commerce created new markets for farm produce, so land came to be regarded as a source of income rather than of feudal and military power. Revolutionary change was hastened by the Black Death. For whereas a surplus of peasant cultivators had strengthened the position of the manorial lords in the 13th century, there was now a shortage of men to till the land and the natural consequence was an acceleration of the practice of commuting labour services for money payments and a sharp increase in wages. The relation between the feudal lord and his retainers was turning into that between employer and employed, landlord and tenant.

One result of this development was that the lords of the manor gradually began to withdraw their demesnes from the village lands and to enclose them. Sometimes a lord would let the entire manor to one or more tenants, reserving only the manor house for himself. That is what Sir William Clopton did in 1410 when he let all the land of the manor of Hawstead in Suffolk to Walter Bone. Sometimes the lord would build himself an entirely new house, and the original manor house would become the home farmhouse inhabited by a tenant farmer with hired servants living in. Manorial lords also began to encourage their tenants to forego their common rights over the cultivated land they occupied and to consolidate their individual holdings and till them as separate farms.

In his *English Farming Past and Present* (1912) Lord Ernle illustrates the transformation of the manorial system by quoting the history of the manor of Castle Combe in Wiltshire from documents published in 1852. This account casts so clear a light on the process that it seems worth giving a shortened version of it. At the time of the Domesday Survey the manor consisted of 1,200 acres of arable land of which 480 acres were part of the lord's demesne. They were worked by thirteen serfs and the labour of the five villeins and the twelve bordars who occupied the remainder of the

11 A 15th-century tithe barn of Glastonbury Abbey at Manor Farm, Doulting, Somerset, seen from an open-fronted shelter. The building material – grey limestone – was quarried near Shepton Mallet.

12 This impressive early 14th-century dovecote at Sibthorpe, Nottinghamshire, originally stood near a manor house of which the only trace is a depression marking the site of the moat.

arable land. All these men were bondmen. By 1340 the village lands had increased to 1,000 acres and there were ten freemen among the tenants who held their land at fixed money rents. The rest were still bondmen. Eight of them were given cottages in return for labour services; fifteen of them farmed holdings of from 30 to 60 acres in return for some labour services and some money rents; and eleven others held 15 acres each in return for labour on the demesne. The thirty-four bondmen could, if the lord consented, buy their freedom by paying the cash value of their services as shown in the steward's book. In 1352, immediately after the visitation of the Black Death, the whole manor was divided into separate farms and let for money rents.

The pace of change was rarely as rapid as this, but by the beginning of the 16th century the relation between owners, tenants and cultivators of the land had fallen into a recognizable form of the pattern it was to assume over much of the country for the next three hundred years and more.

It is only occasionally in places such as those mentioned in the previous chapter that we can still faintly descry across centuries of taming and despoliation the landscape in which the medieval farmers toiled: it is the buildings they erected which most vividly recall their lives. Of actual farm buildings the commonest medieval survivals are barns and dovecotes. It is unlikely that a single livestock shelter of that period can now be seen, although their existence is well documented in manorial records. A farm belonging to the Knights Templars at Rothley in Leicestershire, for instance, is recorded as boasting a cattle shed that housed 24 oxen, 11 cows, a bull, 9 bullocks and 4 calves. The fine open-fronted shelter shed facing the 11 15th-century tithe barn at Doulting, Somerset, an arcade of segmental arches echoing the shapes of the barn porch arches and springing from massive cylindrical columns, may preserve the form of a medieval structure although it was built in the 17th century.

32

The Normans introduced dovecotes to Britain and numbers of squat, sturdy, tower-like little buildings of the early Middle Ages, either circular 12 or square, still symbolize the forgotten privilege of the lord of the manor who alone enjoyed the right to keep pigeons. The birds grew plump on the peasants' corn until they were fit for the lord's table, a welcome alternative during the winter months to a monotonous diet of salted beef. The thick walls of the dovecotes were lined with tiers of nesting boxes, sometimes gracefully arched (like those in the plaster walls of a square, half-timbered structure at Steeple Bumpstead, Essex), sometimes consisting merely of holes opening off ledges like those making a dizzy pattern of diminishing circles inside the cylinder of the dovecote at Sibthorpe, Nottinghamshire. The pigeons reached their nests through a lantern, as at Richards Castle, Herefordshire, where later dormers also gave access, or through a louver, as at Sibthorpe. The impressive girth and simplicity of this Nottingham-shire building, the starkness of the rubble masonry relieved by but a single stringcourse, are enhanced by the isolation of the site in flat fields.

The main crop during the Middle Ages was corn and the rites connected with the harvest were among the most expressive of the festivals, public holidays and fairs which enlivened the scant leisure of the farmworker. The Harvest Supper, of which the whole farming community partook, remained an annual event in many parts of the country even after machines had replaced the sickle, and the superstitions and observances pertaining to the cutting of the last sheaf are still commemorated in some villages by the custom of bringing a corn dolly to the parish church and setting it on the screen or pulpit, on a pew or in the porch during Harvest Festival. There was no man who did not fear to cut the last sheaf, for it was the ultimate refuge of the Corn Spirit and the one who destroyed it was doomed. The sum of money awarded to him who achieved this undesirable distinction was no comfort. But once gathered the sheaf was carried, originally not to the church but to the farmhouse, tied up, decorated and sometimes dressed as a woman to preside over the Supper and guarantee the fruitfulness of the fields in the coming year. The traditional corn dolly assumes a different shape in each region, all reflecting aspects of harvest custom. Sometimes it takes the form of a miniature sheaf of corn; sometimes it figures forth the Goddess of the Harvest, the Corn Spirit; in Cambridgeshire it becomes a bell, recalling the bells of the ringers who walked in the procession headed by the harvest 'Lord' and his 'Lady' after the last load had been taken to the stockyard; in Herefordshire, Shropshire and Northamptonshire it celebrates the animals most closely associated with the harvest and appears as a mare or the horns of oxen, while the beautiful Devonshire Cross embodies the Christian imagery which was inextricably bound up with pagan memories in medieval lore.

The most important building relating to the harvest was the barn. Countless examples have survived because the design of the barn and the work that went on in it remained unchanged for so many centuries. It was as essential to the corn-growing farmer as to the stockman: the work done in the building provided the yard with straw for litter and the animals in the stockyard provided the fields with manure and so contributed to the contents of the barn. Sheaves of corn or straw were stored in the two ends of the building while in the central bay, called the middlestead, entered by double doors high and wide enough to allow the corn-laden wagons to enter, the corn was threshed during the winter months, either on a raised wooden floor of elm or poplar or on the hard earthen floor of the barn itself. The tool used for threshing was the flail, a symbol of the corn harvest, consisting of two sticks, one, the handle, fashioned of ash, and one, the swingle, half as long, made from holly, yew or blackthorn, joined by a flexible knot so that the flail would swing in any direction. Men born before the turn of the century who had used the flail and were still alive in the 1950s spoke to me of the deadly monotony and gruelling character of the work; they used to lighten the tedium by continually varying the rhythm of the swinging, sometimes achieving a subtlety rivalling that of change-ringers on the village bells.

After the corn had been threshed it was winnowed. The big double doors and the smaller doors opposite were opened wide and the grain, cast up into the draught, was separated from the chaff and bits of straw mixed with it. The men used a special wooden shovel for this process so that the grain should not be injured. A wooden sieve or basket was also used to sift out dust and small seeds from the grain. The winnowing basket was triangular in shape with a handle on either side of the apex. Such baskets have vanished except for rare examples in one or two of the new museums of rural life, but their aspect is perfectly preserved on the brass at Chartham, Kent, of Sir Robert de Septvans, a 14th-century Essex farmer.

The dusty, mealy smell of grain still pervades the dim interiors of abandoned barns, even in decay, and still proclaims the skill and endurance of the men who laboured in them. The huge dimensions of many medieval barns, sometimes, like the one at Abbotsbury in Dorset, surpassing those of the parish church, affirm their profound significance in the life of the people. The most dramatic of these medieval buildings were either monastic in origin, like the barns at Abbotsbury, at Glastonbury and Pilton 16 in Somerset, and at Tisbury in Wiltshire, or they were parochial tithe barns, 15,8 like those at Cherhill in Wiltshire, Caldecote in Hertfordshire and Great 10,13 Coxwell in Berkshire. From the 9th century the tenth part of the annual produce of agriculture was exacted for the support of the clergy, the fabric of church buildings and the poor; and every tenth sheaf was carried off to the tithe barn. After the Dissolution many monastic barns became tithe barns.

Though the design of all barns is determined by the use to which they were put and a basic instantly recognizable plan is common to them all, they exhibit much diversity in detail and all the individuality of local craftsmanship both within and without. The austere proportions of the 10,13 vast and noble stone barn at Court Farm, Great Coxwell, accentuated rather than relieved by the extremely chaste ornament, the chamfering of the porch arches, the restrained moulding of the buttresses and the unexpectedly irregular pattern of the ventilation holes, are animated by a totally different spirit from that which radiates from the decorative barn at Abbotsbury, where the slender angle buttresses and the stepped buttress in the centre of the gable end are adorned with gay little battlements conveying a feeling of exhilaration which is irresistibly encouraged by the

quick rhythm of the closely set wall buttresses. The stone barns at Pilton and Glastonbury, carved with figures of angels and evangelists, embellished with sculptured finials, traceried windows and cruciform openings and with porches like transepts, emphatically declare their ecclesiastical origin. They are also eloquent of the easily worked limestone of the region in which they stand, just as the timber frames of the barns at Cressing Temple in Essex and the black geometry of the barns at Abbess Roding and Wendens Ambo in the same county reflect the character of East Anglia. The fronts of the last-mentioned buildings are interrupted by two or three porches, and exceptionally large structures such as these and the barn at Doulting are often furnished with more than a single entrance on the front. When barns are aisled, as they almost invariably are in East Anglia, the south-east, Hampshire, Berkshire and Buckinghamshire, and as they frequently are in Somerset, Wiltshire and Gloucestershire, the entrance inevitably takes the form of a lofty, jutting porch with a hipped or gabled roof to accommodate the harvest wagons. But in those places where cruck construction was traditional, such as Herefordshire, Shropshire and the north, the aisled barn is hardly known and then the entrance is not necessarily marked by a porch.

Though the external images of the great medieval stone barns rank in recollection with those of parish churches and monastic ruins, their stone fabric was a rare sight on the medieval farm: timber was the customary material for working buildings except in absolutely treeless lands, and in the context of this book it is the internal timber structure of barns which excites the keenest interest. Here are revealed the elements of the rapidly developing carpenter's art on which the evolution of the plan and structure of the medieval farmhouse and cottage most depended.

13 *Above left* The huge transept-like porch of the barn at Court Farm, Great Coxwell, opened onto the threshing floor and accommodated the harvest wagon. The entrance at the gable end is an unusual feature, more often found in Continental barns, where the threshing floor was longitudinal.

14 *Above* A thatched, timber-framed barn with three entrances at Wendens Ambo, Essex, built in the 15th century. The later weather-boarding protects the wattle-and-daub infilling of the framework. The wagon-sized porch doors open outwards.

The carpentry of the precisely ordered interior of the Great Coxwell barn presents a refined version of the design already seen at Caldecote. It is one found in barns of all periods. The vigorous repeating pattern created by the pairs of diagonal struts rising from the arcade posts to support the chamfered tie-beams and the purlins, the pleasing contrast between the abrupt movement of these struts and the smooth curves of the aisle tie-beam braces, the proportion of the tall stone bases of the posts and above all the nicety of the jointing transform function into art. The Barley Barn at Cressing Temple discloses a less harmonious and consistent design for it was twice altered and rebuilt after it was first reared at the incredibly early date of about 1200. But enough of the initial conceit remains to show its sophistication. It was based on an ingenious play upon parallels and saltire crosses, which surely must have been deliberately intended to allude to the carpenter's patrons, the Knights Templars. Even today the interior is dominated by the great crosses made by long straight braces running from the arcade posts to the tie-beam and short diagonally set struts connecting the tie-beam with a parallel beam below it. Formerly double tiers of aisle tie-beams echoed the two tiers of main tie-beams and from the lower of these rose great timbers duplicating the slope of the principal rafters and crossing just below the apex of the roof. But now crown posts rest on the upper tie-beams to support the longitudinal beam beneath the collars.

The crown-post roof is found as commonly as the type of structure seen at Great Coxwell, generally where there is no ridge-piece. The design was
once splendidly represented in the celebrated barn at Cherhill which, long in ruins, was allowed to collapse in the mid-1950s. Like the Cressing Temple barns this building was of timber throughout, the walls comprising heavy vertical studs filled with wattle-and-daub panels and recalling the stave walls of the Saxons. The effect of the wall timbers inside was to heighten the skeletal character of the giant cage of pale oak. The structure at Cherhill was shored up by a massive long timber curving from the wall footing up to the outer side of the arcade post, which immediately recalled a cruck. The same use of the cruck shape occurs in the 14th-century barn at Lenham in Kent and in the barn at Lordship's Farm, Writtle, Essex. The builders must have been familiar with the cruck tradition although in none of these instances is the timber fully integrated into the design.

In some late medieval barns, at Netteswell and at Little Easton, both in Essex, posts and tie-beams consort with crucks in powerful compositions, the cruck assuming the role of a gigantic brace passing from the wall footing across the arcade post to the tie-beam. It used to be thought that cruck construction was only found north and west of a line running from Flamborough Head in Yorkshire through Sheffield down to the Hampshire coast. But the tradition was evidently part of the repertory of the medieval carpenter. C.A. Hewett has discovered instances of ingeniously used crucks and forms deriving from them in the church at Mountnessing, at Southchurch Hall and in the barn at Ladylands, Good Easter, all in Essex. This should not perhaps cause surprise in a period when great architectural enterprises attracted craftsmen from diverse regions and brought them into contact with customs and methods to which they were strangers.

Some of the most characteristic features of developed timber
construction seem to have been inspired by the cruck. In the Cressing
Temple Barley Barn, for example, one of the tie-beams is supported by big
curving braces which are conspicuously cruck-like. The possible
connection between crucks and principal rafters has been alluded to. The
roof of the barn at Place Farm, Tisbury, appears as a glorious confirmation 16
of this suggestion. For just as the famous roof of Needham Market church
in Suffolk takes the fantastic shape of an aisled post-and-truss building
hovering over the nave, so the roof at Tisbury assumes the form of an
entire, superbly organized cruck fabrication 200 feet long raised aloft and
set on top of the walls. The arched braces of the tie-beams again repeat the
cruck configuration, though each is composed of two timbers jointed
together to make a curve.

37

16 *Left* The tithe barn at Place Farm, Tisbury, Wiltshire, unaisled and with an arch-braced roof.

17 *Right* The arch-braced roof of the hall of Woodlands Manor, Mere, Wiltshire. Tiered cinquefoiled windbraces support the rafters.

18 *Far right* Looking upwards in the early 14th-century hall of Tiptofts, Wimbish, Essex. The arcade post can be seen at the bottom, the later Elizabethan brick chimneystack on the right (p. 96).

Crucks, through the arched braces to which they gave rise, were the source of one of the most ornamental features of unaisled buildings, the windbrace. For the windbrace is the arched brace swung round through ninety degrees and set against the rafters, to give lateral stability. Simple windbraces, crude miniature crucks, placed so that they meet to form arches below the purlin, create a decorative overhanging arcade in the tithe barn at Henley, Suffolk.

The domestic interior of the later Middle Ages, when the hall had become a status symbol, gave the carpenter an opportunity to elaborate the device. The tiered windbraces in the hall at Ashbury Manor, Berkshire, are so delicately cusped that the effect is of a narrow ribbon rippling along the edges of the arches. At Woodlands Manor, Mere, in Wiltshire, boldly cinquefoiled windbraces branch in alternating directions in three tiers to make a gigantic, wavy criss-cross pattern; while at Chapel Farm, Lingen, Herefordshire, cusped and foiled braces arch across the rafters with wild spontaneity like the antlers of a leaping stag.

17

The halls of these three houses, like the barns with arched braced roofs to which they are akin and like all cruck-based interiors, such as the arresting hall at Lower Brockhampton, Herefordshire, the whole character of which is determined by the giant central cruck truss, are clear of aisles and posts. It remained for the carpenter to invent a means of dispensing with the arcade posts in the aisled hall. The overwhelming, cramping inconvenience of the arcade posts in a domestic interior can still be experienced in St Clere's, at St Osyth in Essex, one of the least altered of aisled halls. The elephantine octagonal piers and vigorous arched braces, those supporting the tie-beams

meeting to form powerful arches, seem to fill the room with their tremendous presence, dwarfing and crowding out the household gods of later ages. In the Middle Ages this interior must have been yet more overwhelming, for the now open spandrels were then filled to create the impression of solid arches.

The carpenter's solution to the problem was the device known as the hammerbeam, a short horizontal timber projecting from the wall plate, supported by a brace springing from the wall post and itself carrying the post on which the tie-beam rests. This contrivance, which is characteristic of the most advanced timber roofs, makes a surprising appearance in the hall of the modest mid-14th-century manor farmhouse of Tiptofts at Wimbish in Essex, only a few years after its first occurrence in England in the Strangers' Hall at Winchester. Only one hammerbeam truss remains, for the hall has lost one of its original three bays, and this truss is blackened by the smoke and soot of the open fire which once burned where now the bulk of an inordinate Elizabethan brick chimneystack thrusts its way through the lofty room.

At the service end of the hall at Tiptofts the old aisled plan is preserved in 18 a single arcade post, once matched by another on the opposite side of the room where the former arcade has been replaced by a wall. These posts were deliberately retained to hold the 'speres' or short fixed screens which protected the main body of the hall from the draught from the doors. The speres developed into a continuous screen creating a passage – the 'screens passage' – between the hall and the doors leading to the buttery (where drink was kept), pantry (for dry stores) and detached kitchen. In spite of drastic alterations ruining the proportions of the room and exaggerating its height, the elegance of the carpentry at Tiptofts informs that bare hall with an enchanting air of spring-like freshness as potent and as palpable as that which emanates from paintings of the period, such as the Wilton Diptych, in which Richard II wears a collar of broom above his embroidered dress of gold tissue and the accompanying angels wear collars of the same broom with chaplets of white roses in their hair. Graceful roll and fillet moulding embellishes the cambered tie-beam and the capitals of the hexagonal crown posts, the arcade pier is a slender quatrefoil in section with a richly moulded capital, and cusps and wave moulding decorate the spandrels. The pier is an accomplished and perhaps intended replica in wood of the stone piers in the north arcade of Wimbish church, which had been standing for at least half a century when the Tiptofts carpenter was at work.

We have seen that many different types of houses had already evolved before the end of the 11th century. Of these the most significant for the development of the farmhouse and cottage were the long-house and the hall-house. The character of the former was implicit in the most primitive examples; the latter, chiefly owing to the carpenter's ingenuity, became the principal element in the most fruitful of domestic plans.

The two components which contributed most to the evolution of the English house, in addition to the hall-house, were the donjon keep and the type of two-storeyed stone house (with a hall on the upper floor) associated with the Norman Conquest. The tower image of the keep, whether conjoined to the two-storeyed house as at Little Wenham Hall, Suffolk, and at Markenfield Hall, Yorkshire, or set alongside the open hall, as at Longthorpe Tower, Northamptonshire, does not play a major role in the design of the farmhouse even though two of the manor houses just named were always farmsteads. Towers are often, however, conspicuous features of northern farmhouses where defence for so long remained a vital consideration. At Burneside Hall, Westmorland, a 14th-century tower rises on a tunnel vault at the northern end of a two-storeyed block with a first-floor hall, which is set at right angles to a two-storeyed south wing. A decaying gatehouse with broken, roughly repaired doors of sear oak, vertical boards and strap hinges of medieval or Tudor workmanship, yields a moving view of this once grand and now half derelict farmhouse, the stone and rubble tower rent, roofless and ivy grown, the house itself encased in cement, the cusps of the mullioned windows picked out in dark red and the whole set behind the Victorian railings of a little flower garden separating the house from the triangular farmyard.

19

Two-storeyed Norman houses, the type of building from which both the two-storeyed blocks at Burneside Hall derived, still stand; and three of them at least, built by manorial lords, were directly connected with farming: Boothby Pagnell Manor in Lincolnshire, Hemingford Manor in Huntingdonshire (the home of Payne de Hemingford in about 1150 and continuously inhabited ever since), and the mysterious Merton Hall in Cambridge (headquarters of the King's Sheriff, lord of Bourne and several other Cambridgeshire manors). Each of these houses displays the same plan of a first-floor hall with a smaller apartment leading from it, set above a vaulted ground floor used for storage and perhaps, in the case of

Hemingford Manor, for the shelter of animals. With their striking and
sophisticated architectural detail, massive fabric, external stair – still intact
at Boothby Pagnell – leading up to the great chamber with its wall fireplace,
and two-light windows contained in the round emphatically moulded
arches of their period, they present an astonishing visual contrast to the
hall-house and a totally different arrangement.

Certain features of these little houses reappear in the plans of farmhouses
and cottages of much later centuries. The bastle houses of the Border
country, built for defence (the word is related to 'Bastille'), like those of the
early 17th century at Glassonby and Ainstable in Cumberland, repeat the
design of the Norman house in almost every particular. An external stair
leads to first-floor domestic quarters consisting of two rooms, the larger
displaying a wall fireplace, while the ground floor originally housed cattle.
Only the windows – tiny, square, heavily barred apertures in the case of the
bastle house – marked the distinction between the two structures. Outside
stairs in northern cottages built as late as the 19th century, and the stairs
leading up to the first-floor entrance of some granaries built over cart sheds
or animal shelters, as at Bibury in Gloucestershire, also recall the Norman
house.

Burneside Hall is one of many examples of the elaborations in stone of
the Norman plan which appeared during the 14th and 15th centuries. But
such houses were generally built only by the nobility and the dignitaries of
the Church and were considered sufficiently remarkable to be named in
deeds to indicate boundaries. They are more important for the story of the
country house than for the development of the farmhouse and cottage, and

41

20 Blackmoor Farm, near
Cannington, Somerset.

only three of them will be mentioned here. Ashbury Manor, Berkshire, the
hall roof of which has already been described, and the Manor House at
Meare, Somerset, have both been farmhouses since the Dissolution of the
Monasteries. Blackmoor Farm, near Cannington in Somerset, a late 15th-
century manor house, has always been associated with husbandry. Abbot
Adam de Sodbury of Glastonbury built the Meare house as a summer
retreat in about 1330. It unites two two-storeyed houses set at right angles
to each other; a projecting porch on the main front resembles that which by
this time usually sheltered the entrance to a hall-house and is placed in the
position which in a hall-house marked the screens passage. The figure of an
abbot rising from the gable of this porch still announces the ecclesiastical
origin of the farmhouse and mossed buttresses dividing the bays, the ghost
of a huge Gothic window emerging from the blotched masonry of the
façade, and the tall, cusped lights of the noble windows of the rear heighten
the disparity between the early and more recent history of this gaunt relic.
The great upper hall illumined by those Decorated windows, where the
Abbot and his attendants lived in splendour, served the farmer's wife of the
1950s as a lumber room. On entering it one looked towards the magnificent
fireplace with its tall five-sided moulded hood and swelling corbels across a
surreal assortment of junk – discarded toys, among them a headless baby
doll; an old pram; parts of bicycles; one or two broken farming tools; a pile
of apples; a heap of rags; and a decrepit, sagging upholstered armchair.

Ashbury Manor was the creation, more than a century later, of another Glastonbury prelate, Abbot Selwood. The builder started with an older house and added another range in line with it containing a lower and an upper hall. An almost centrally-placed porch led into a screens passage between the new range and the original building, which became the pantry, buttery and kitchen. This is a very early instance of the incorporation of the kitchen in the domestic plan. A short arm at the rear consists of a small chamber on each floor, a garderobe or lavatory (a feature which is only found in grand houses), and a spiral stair, a form of staircase which was introduced by the Normans and is essentially connected with stone buildings.

Blackmoor Farm consists of three two-storeyed blocks and the patched and weatherstained exterior remarkably preserves its medieval aspect: the windows with their ogee-headed lights survive unaltered and the projecting porch is still furnished with its original outer and inner doorways. The house has slightly changed inside; it had a central double hall, one on each of the two floors, while one of the cross blocks comprised a tall chapel and a two-storeyed antechapel (the upper floor of which was reached by a spiral staircase), and the other, projecting at the rear of the house, contained the kitchen with a chamber above it. So Blackmoor Farm already embodies the plan which was to emerge from the fusion of the Norman house and the open hall.

21 *Above left* The upper floor of the two-storeyed manor house at Ashbury, Berkshire, is reached by a stone spiral staircase with a newel column at the narrow end of the steps.

22 *Above* The rear of the 14th-century manor house, Meare, Somerset.

21

20

43

It was this combination of the two-storeyed house and the single-storeyed hall in the commonest of structures, the timber-framed house, that led to the most significant developments in the plans of farmhouses and cottages. At Little Chesterford Manor, Essex, a replica of Hemingford Manor was built of flint rubble and clunch in about 1225 and an aisled hall was set at right angles to it some seventy years later. During the 14th century a two-storeyed cross-wing, similar to the original stone house in shape but timber-framed, appeared at the opposite end of the hall, turning the design into the H-plan which was to dominate farmhouse building for II generations. The house at St Osyth, the hall of which has been described, is timber-framed throughout and is a classic example of the early H-shaped house comprising a one-storeyed hall flanked by two-storeyed cross-wings. The ground floor of the wing to the right of the screens passage (marked by the entrance) was used as buttery and pantry and the room above it, reached by a simple ladder, served for storage. The ground-floor room at the other end of the hall was called the 'bower' or 'chamber', although both terms might also be applied to the upstairs room, which was also known as the 'solar'. By the last quarter of the 14th century, about twenty-five years after St Clere's was built, the word 'parlour' had come into use for the lower room. When Pandarus visits his niece in Chaucer's *Troilus and Criseyde*, written in about 1380, he finds her with two ladies in her 'paved parlour'. When, in the same poem, Chaucer refers to the 'chambre' it is of a bedroom he is speaking.

Bower and hall, again according to Chaucer, seem to have been as much part of the poor cottage as of the manor farmhouse. In the *Nun's Priest's Tale* the poet says of the widow's 'narwe cotage', 'ful sooty was hir bour and eek hire halle'. Poor though she was this widow had three large sows, 'three keen and eek a sheep that highte Malle', and

> Hir bord was served moost with white and blak, –
> Milk and broun breed, in which she found no lak;
> Seynd bacoun and somtyme an ey or tweye.

Even in such a humble dwelling the animals were separately housed and shared a yard with Chaunticleer the cock and his seven hens.

At St Clere's a lean-to adjoins and enlarges the service wing. This modest addition to the plan became part of the idiom of farmhouse and cottage building in most regions. In 16th- and 17th-century cottages and often in much later examples it constituted the only service room. Variously known as the 'outshot' or 'outend', or, in some parts of Kent (according to inventories in the Maidstone Record Office), the 'cove', the form of the lean-to may have been suggested by the hall aisle.

The heavy timbers of houses such as St Clere's were framed on the ground, the timbers being marked with Roman numerals, and then 'reared' into position, a formidable task in which the help of neighbours was essential. Records refer to payment for meat and drink to villagers for their pains. In 1420 twopence for drink was given to each of the men of Alford in Somerset who had assisted at the 'reryng' of a house in that village. (Framed houses could, if necessary, be easily dismantled and moved. In 1377 a hall-house with two chambers was taken in Surrey from Wimbledon

to Shene, and in the 15th century a hall was moved from the manor of Thundersley and re-erected at Rayleigh Park, Essex. In our own century Sir Edwin Lutyens transferred the hall of a house at Benenden, Kent, to Northiam in Sussex, where it became part of Great Dixter, and in recent years the magnificent abandoned barn at Wherstead, Suffolk, was removed to another county and converted into a house.) The spaces between the timbers were commonly filled with wattle and daub, the daub composed of a mixture of clay, dung and chopped straw, laid on rods fixed horizontally in grooves in the sides of vertical, closely set timbers or, when the panels are wider, on a basketwork of upright staves, usually of oak, and horizontal rods of hazel or ash. The panels were often finished on each side with a thin coat of plaster composed of lime, sand and cow hair, which offered more resistance to the weather than daub. If left uncovered, the daub tended to shrink.

The strong influence of the traditional plan of a hall with one or two cross-wings can be detected in the streets of most of the villages and small country towns in regions where timber-framing survives. Again and again groups of two or more cottages catch the eye which clearly started life as halls with cross-wings. Sometimes the former hall may remain one-storeyed, sometimes – as in a house at Linton, Cambridgeshire, now divided into two cottages – a dormer window shows that a floor was

23 Cottages at Linton, Cambridgeshire, once part of a single house, the design of which is recognizably the same as that of St Clere's (Pl. II) despite later alterations, the most important of which was the lateral division of the hall to create an upper storey, lit by a dormer.

23

inserted at a later date. Houses built at the end of the 16th and during the 17th centuries and designed as two-storeyed structures from the beginning still conform to the familiar plan of a central block either with a single or with two cross-wings. Anyone walking or even driving through almost any East Anglian village will encounter several examples, each now generally become two or more cottages or perhaps a little shop and cottages. In some of these houses the ridge of the two-storeyed hall block rises above the ridges of the cross-wings, thus reversing the arrangement seen at St Clere's and in other early hall-houses, where the cross-wings considerably overtop the hall.

Very often it is the side wall of a single cross-wing which fronts the street, while the former hall is at the rear. A number of houses at Weobley, Herefordshire, present their cross-wings to the street, and the conspicuous front, decorated with carving, of a house in Saffron Walden, Essex, now the Eight Bells inn but once a farmhouse, is the wall of a cross-wing attached to a one-storeyed hall built under the same roof as a barn, like a long-house, and facing what was the stockyard.

The projection of the cross-wings of the house at Linton is noticeably slight by comparison with those of an early house like St Clere's, and the roof line is continuous. The carpenter was making continual modifications in the conception of the timber-framed house to bring it ever more in line with the two-storeyed stone houses of the wealthy. His endeavours were prompted by the growing needs of tenant farmers, whose welfare was a special concern of Henry VII after two centuries of agricultural unrest, but who could rarely afford to build in any material but wood. An important step towards the achievement of a compact design had been taken when the hall was cleared of its aisles, for the pitch of the roof then became less steep and the eaves line much higher. A comparison of the exterior of St Clere's with that of Lower Brockhampton Manor illustrates the way in which this change began to reduce the original sharp differentiation between hall and cross-wings.

The next stage in the development of the timber-framed house was to align the walls of hall and cross-wings. To this end, the ground-floor walls were commonly brought into line, while the cross-wings were marked only by their gables and an upper projection depending on a feature known as the jetty, which became popular during the 15th century. A number of explanations have been put forward to account for this development: it has been described as a means of enlarging the upper room, as a method of preventing the floor joists from sagging, and as a protection for the foundations of the house. The most obvious advantage of the device is that it strengthens the timber framework by providing two places instead of one for jointing the ground- and upper-floor posts with the first-floor sill beam. Yet it seems unlikely that the carpenter was consciously striving for any of these advantages. In all creative activities new ideas arise spontaneously in the course of the work, and probably it was when laying the joists to support the floorboards of an upper storey that the visual as well as the practical possibilities of the jetty sprang to the carpenter's mind. It was a way also of marking the existence of what had become important rooms. The decorative opportunities afforded by the oversail must have made a

24 Jetty with moulded fascia board and corner post supporting the dragon beam at Clavering, Essex.

special appeal in an age when the carpenter's craft had become a superb art, transfiguring the roofs of East Anglian churches with visions of flying angels, quickening the mystery of sanctuary and chapel with the delicate filigree of vigorously branching screens, and animating choir stalls, benches and bosses with teeming imagery as expressive of the pageantry of nature as of the abiding influence of the supernatural.

The jetty was not only ornamental in itself: the timber sill of the upper wall above the jetty (the bressumer) provided a splendid expanse for a running motif. At Baldwin's Manor, Swaffham Prior, Cambridgeshire, the bressumer of the cross-wing, which faces the street with the hall at the rear, is embellished with a scroll-and-fillet ornament; and examples at Saffron Walden show battlements and vines and rose tendrils with birds of the fields and hedges peeping from the leaves. Sometimes the projecting ends of the beams of a jetty are covered by a fascia board and this again may be carved, as in a row of cottages, once a single building, at Clavering in 24 Essex. If the upper storey oversails the lower along the façade and on an adjacent side, as it does at Clavering, two sets of joists must be set at right angles to each other and to this end a stout beam called the dragon was fixed diagonally across the floor. Where it projected at the corner of the house it was supported by a corner post, an obvious place for the display of the woodcarver's talent. The sensitive shaping and moulding of the reeded shaft, tall gently curving bracket, and square capital of the bleached, silvery post at Clavering remain tremblingly alive after five centuries of attrition.

Another feature of the timber-framed house which the carver found irresistible was the bargeboard, a late 15th-century innovation, fixed to the ends of a gable a short distance from the face of the wall to protect the roof timbers from the effects of the weather. The bargeboards of the gatehouse and cross-wing at Lower Brockhampton are enlivened by firmly carved trailing vines, and at Weobley the bargeboards flaunt bold quatrefoils, undulating ribbons and scallops.

When the bay window or oriel made its first appearance in the later Middle Ages, to indicate the presence of a solar in more substantial farmhouses, it was supported by a wooden bracket which gave the carver sufficient space for a figure composition. At Newport, Essex, where the base of an oriel is corbelled out of a single balk, the craftsman's chosen theme was the crowned Virgin holding the Child and brandishing a sceptre between two angelic musicians (an organist and a harpist), cut in deep relief with an eager rapture stronger than erosion, cracks and weather stains.

This house at Newport is noticeable by comparison with all the others so far seen for the absence of gabled cross-wings. The eaves line of the oversailing storeys is continued over the recessed hall by means of braces curving from the wings. This compact form of hall-house is known as the 'Wealden' type, and is popularly associated with the Weald of Kent and Sussex. A particularly complete and polished example stands at Goudhurst – Pattenden Manor, named after its first owner who built it in about 1470. Although the hall of Pattenden was open to the roof in the 15th century

25 Oriel in the jettied upper floor of one wing of a 'Wealden' house at Newport, Essex.

48

the front and back doors and the screens passage between them were not in the hall but in the north wing, under the floor of the upper room; thus the screen did not project into the hall at all but stood flush with the wall above it. The space had already in fact become what in much later plans is known as the 'hall', that is the entrance hallway. The Newport house is proof that the Wealden plan was not peculiar to the Weald. Groups of cottages in Bridge Street and Castle Street, Saffron Walden, were built as single houses to this design; and a house as far away as Stratford-on-Avon, Warwickshire, takes this form.

The end of the story of the metamorphosis of the hall-house into a dwelling which was two-storeyed throughout belongs to the following chapter and to the period when chimneys became an essential feature of domestic building. That period also saw the full flowering of vernacular styles. Of course where builders could only resort to local materials differences became manifest from the beginning. The stone slates, for instance, which cover the vast roof expanses of the barns at Great Coxwell and Pilton are as eloquent of the limestone of their regions as is the fabric of their walls. And the distinction in style between the aisled barns found eastward from Wiltshire and in the south-east, and the unaisled barns of the west, has been observed. But even though in their homeland crucks give aggressive individuality to some houses of the late Middle Ages, as at Weobley, there were few sharp distinctions before the 16th century in the most widespread of all forms of medieval farm and domestic building, the timber-framed. The cross-wing at Lower Brockhampton does indeed hint in a rudimentary way at the special decorative tradition of this part of the country, which was to reach its amazing culmination in the Elizabethan age. A roundel fills the apex of the gable and closely set studs consort with

26 At Pattenden Manor, Goudhurst, Kent, a typical 'Wealden' house, the three units of the hall-house are still distinct but, covered by a single roof, they begin to assume a rectangular plan.

25 square panels. But closely set studs distinguish not only the gatehouse of
26 Lower Brockhampton but the houses at Newport in Essex and Goudhurst in Kent just examined. And square panels were common in districts other than the West Midlands in the Middle Ages. They can be seen, for instance, at Biddenden in Kent, Fittleworth in Sussex, Cerne Abbas in Dorset,
51 Dorchester in Oxfordshire and even at Banks Green in Essex. Timber-framed houses pictured in contemporary manuscripts, such as the Bedford Book of Hours, are invariably square-panelled, and this must surely indicate that idiosyncrasies of style had yet to develop.

Very little has been said about the dwellings of the lord of the manor's poorest tenants, and for good reason, for no medieval peasant's cottage survives. Many of them were doubtless so insubstantial that they could be erected or demolished as readily as tents, for it was a common cause of complaint in the Middle Ages that villeins absconding from their manors would take down their houses and carry off the fabric to set it up in their place of refuge. But writers like Chaucer and the author of *Piers Plowman* tell us something of village homes in the Middle Ages, and tax assessments which were based on personal property throw light on the size and contents of the humblest houses of some areas. M. W. Barley quotes the assessments for the town and neighbouring villages of Colchester in Essex for the years 1296 and 1301. Peasants' houses seem to have consisted of one or at most (like that of Chaucer's widow) two rooms, and the contents appear not to have amounted to more than one or two beds and a few cooking implements such as an andiron, a brass posnet (a forerunner of the saucepan, fitted with short legs) and a tripod. A trestle table known as 'the board' and a cradle are mentioned in *Piers Plowman*.

More is known of the furniture, goods and chattels of wealthy households. Inventories of well-appointed farmhouses like that of the Pastons at Hellesdon in Norfolk list trestle tables, benches, stools, cushions, a principal bed with a headpiece and canopy, truckle beds which in the daytime were kept under the big bed, chests for clothes, a cupboard for food called the 'aumbry', pewter and brass pots and pans, gridirons, candlesticks, silver spoons, marble pestles and mortars and one or two spits. A stool with a jug on it and a chair (which was a rare article of furniture) with large carved leaves bursting from the supports occur on a misericord in Screveton Church, Nottinghamshire, where a man is shown warming himself at a wall fireplace.

The hangings in the Pastons' house were of a fine cloth called 'say', resembling serge. A cheap and popular form of wall decoration was the painted cloth, a canvas stretched on a wooden frame. Such hangings came into fashion at the end of the Middle Ages as a substitute for the tapestries of the nobility, and by the mid-16th century even a farm labourer living in a two-roomed cottage might boast of one. They must have been the work of itinerant painters. The cloths are now rare and no medieval example can be seen. A late 16th-century set in the Luton Museum, Bedfordshire, religious in subject-matter, shows the affinity with tapestry design; and a series of Elizabethan wall paintings from Hill Hall, Theydon Mount, Essex (now in the Victoria and Albert Museum, London), is executed in the manner of cloth paintings and is also clearly intended to imitate tapestry.

Opposite
27 Wall paintings at Piccott's End, Hertfordshire, discovered in 1953.

Opposite
IV Thatched cottage
made of chalk lump at
Little Sampford, Essex.
Oak shingles above and
below the dormers may
indicate that the entire
roof was once shingled.

V *Overleaf* Thatched and
clapboarded cottage,
Anstey, Hertfordshire,
recalling the small
farmhouses recorded in
16th- and 17th-century
inventories. (See
pp. 84–85.)

Paintings done directly on the plastered walls were as much favoured as cloth paintings in the late Middle Ages and the vogue persisted until the mid-17th century. A painted room of about 1500 was discovered under layer upon layer of wallpaper in the upper room of a wing of a very modest house at Piccott's End, Hertfordshire. The subjects, as might be expected, are religious, and those which are best preserved are reminiscent of a triptych, the panels of which are divided by the studs of the timber frame, though the artist has carried his background design of coiling vines of great size right over the timbers. A full-length figure of the Salvator Mundi fills the central panel; to the left is a Pietà and to the right the Baptism. The huge ochre cross behind the Virgin of the Pietà bears the word 'FÜRST', which suggests a German source for the paintings. Perhaps they were based on a German woodcut of the period. Crude though the work is, its coarseness accentuated by the lumpiness of the wattle-and-daub infilling under the plaster, the dynamic indigo outlines, the expressionist drawing and the white, ochre and vermilion of the colour scheme convey an extraordinary vehemence of feeling. These paintings in these unpretending domestic surroundings bring us abruptly into contact with an attitude of mind to which we have long become strangers, an attitude which pervaded all the activities of the Middle Ages but which at the very time the painter was at work on these panels was rapidly changing to embrace horizons far beyond the confines of the medieval world and to bring about electrifying developments and mutations even in the traditional, rural buildings of which I am writing.

3
A Vernacular Art at its Zenith

WHEN THE 16TH CENTURY OPENED the landscape looked much as it had done a hundred years earlier: the population, still barely 3 million, was thinly scattered in the north and for the most part lived in the belt of country lying between the Wash and the Thames and running in a south-westerly direction to the Severn. Fell and forest, moor and marsh covered many more square miles than field and farm, spicing the life of town and village with a sense of mystery and adventure. But the profound change in outlook which divided medieval from Renaissance England, a change symbolized by the Dissolution of the Monasteries, the establishment of the Church of England and the translation of the Bible, was soon reflected in the aspect of the countryside and in attitudes to farming. The 18th century was the great age of revolution in farming practices, but that revolution was set in motion two hundred years earlier. The glimpse of conditions in the later Middle Ages afforded by the previous chapter showed that the almost static organization of medieval agriculture, so deeply expressive of the religious experience of the period, was already undergoing a transformation. But now, at a time of which every manifestation bears the impress of extraordinary, irresistible impetus, the transition to a form of agriculture based on money and markets rather than on services was rapid and concentrated. The medieval village and manor farms supplied the wants of their own communities: the aim of Tudor and Elizabethan farmers and their successors was not merely to satisfy their own needs but to raise cattle and crops for profit and to accumulate industrial wealth.

The new lively interest in farming and the growth of the conscious desire to improve methods led to the appearance of an agricultural literature and of manuals of instruction. *The Boke of Husbandry* by John Fitzherbert, a Catholic of Derbyshire and an expert breeder of horses, was published in 1523 and reprinted a number of times during Elizabeth's reign. It describes the writer's own procedures and practical experience, with frequent reference to old sayings and country lore:

> He that hath both sheep, swine and hive
> Sleep he, wake he, he may thrive.

Fitzherbert exhorts the farmer to oversee everything himself and to keep in his purse a pair of tablets on which to write down anything amiss when on his rounds. If he cannot write 'let him nicke the defautes uppon a sticke'. The young farmer is advised to 'gette a copy of this presente boke', learn it by heart and 'according to the season of the yere, rede to his Servants what chapter he will'.

Opposite
VI A thatcher at work, Sheepwash, Devon. (See p. 104.)

Thomas Tusser, better known today and in his own time more popular, was a musician, trained as a choir boy in the chapel of Wallingford Castle, but he farmed all his adult life at Brantham in Suffolk, where the house he lived in still forms part of Brantham Hall Farm. It was there that he introduced the cultivation of barley, hitherto not grown in that district, and there that he wrote his *Hundred Points of Good Husbandry*, expanded sixteen years later, in 1573, to *Five Hundred Points of Good Husbandry*. Tusser uses hypnotically jogging rhymes and rhythms which seldom betoken a musical ear:

> Take verjuice and heat it, a pint for a cow,
> Bay salt, a handful, to rub tongue ye wot how;
> That done with the salt, let her drink of the rest,
> This many times raiseth the feeble up beast.

Nevertheless the whole book springs from the writer's personal knowledge of farming and great love of the land and reveals a most endearing character – kindly, tolerant and generous, fond of old traditions, rejoicing in the festivals which enlivened the farmer's year, and yet, like so many Elizabethans, always mindful of the brevity and uncertainty of life.

Tusser tells of the farmer's skills and of his seasonal labour. He informs us when crops should be sown, and points out that different grains should not be grown together though they may be mixed before being sent to the miller. So indeed they were in the 16th century, for the most commonly eaten bread, called 'maslin', was baked from a mixture of wheat and rye which in times of dearth might be diluted with barley, peas, beans and lupins. The land must be prepared for winter crops, says Tusser, by three ploughings, in autumn, spring and summer. Apples must not be gathered until after Michaelmas; in autumn rams and young bulls must be gelded and stable and cowhouse put into good repair; and at that season too Cisley, the dairy wench, must clean out the boar's pen 'for measling [tapeworms] and stench'. In October the thresher must begin work in the barn and sloes are gathered. From November onwards beasts are occasionally killed and beef, bacon and mutton are all hung in the chimney to dry in the smoke of the fire. Green peas must be sown at Hallowtide, runcivals (marrowfat peas) at Candlemas. Hedging and ditching are the chief outdoor work of December, and this month is cheered by the great Christmas festival of fire and light, of new beginnings and lengthening days. Tusser's homely picture of the twelve days of rejoicing, of the thronged hall decked with holly and ivy, of the bringing home of the yule log, the play of the mummers, the dancing and singing, the zest of the instrumentalists and the feasting, puts one in mind of the marvellous celebration of the season's rites, unaltered after more than three hundred years, in Thomas Hardy's *Under the Greenwood Tree* (1872). Both descriptions have an affinity with the earthy paintings of the Dutch School.

> Beef, mutton and pork, shred pies of the best,
> Pig, veal, goose and capon, and turkey well dres't,
> Cheese, apples and nuts, jolly carols to hear
> As then in the country is counted good cheer.

Tusser does not mention Christmas puddings, for they did not make their

Opposite
28 Coln Rogers, Gloucestershire. The size and importance of the barn denote a farming cycle dominated by arable husbandry.

appearance until about 1670. Turkeys had only been introduced into England about ten years before the publication of Tusser's 1557 edition.

The routine of the 16th-century arable farmer in a region remote from East Anglia is minutely recorded by a contemporary of Tusser's, a Cornishman, William Carnsew of Bokelly, who kept a diary for the year 1576–77. It is naturally a more personal account than Tusser's, but the routine of the two farmers is remarkably similar. Yet another writer, Leonard Mascall, a Sussex man, compiled the *Government of Cattell* in 1591, dealing with the diseases of animals. In the following century Gervase Markham not only wrote a number of instructive volumes about all branches of husbandry but provided plans for a convenient farmhouse which was to include a great hall, a dining parlour with an 'inward closet' for the mistress's use, a stranger's lodging 'within the parlour' and a buttery, kitchen with room for brewing, a dairy and a milk house. Henry Best specialized in the farming methods of his native Yorkshire and Sir Hugh Platt and Edward Maxey concentrated on ways of sowing seed other than by hand broadcasting.

Special crops were grown for the market. The huge London market – the capital numbered about 200,000 by the end of Elizabeth's reign and by the time of the Restoration included almost a tenth of the $5\frac{1}{2}$ million inhabitants of England – commandeered butter from Suffolk, cheese from Cheshire, cider from Devon and Hereford, and cattle from the north. The best flax and hemp came from Lincolnshire; madder and saffron for cloth dyeing were concentrated in Essex; hops, introduced from the Low Countries, were being cultivated by the middle of the 16th century, not just in Kent, with which they were particularly associated later on, but in Worcestershire, Essex, Yorkshire and Cornwall. Tudor farmers used improvised maltkilns as drying rooms for the hops, sometimes built in the back of a chimney, but early in the 17th century the group of traditional farm buildings was invaded in the areas mentioned by the conspicuous shape of the tall, rectangular oasthouse with a brick drying floor.

The devotion of different regions to the crops they grew best instead of to subsistence farming was one small instance of the delight in diversity and individuality which marked the inquiring energetic spirit liberated by a changed habit of mind. And this was not the only way in which it found expression in the practical world of farming. Certain localities began to be known for special breeds of farm animals, described by the Rev. William Harrison in 1577 (in his *Description of the Island of Britayne*) as unrivalled for size and beauty, and hardly recognizable as the same species as the scrawny, stunted sheep and cattle of the Middle Ages depicted in such manuscripts as the Luttrell Psalter. Long-horned oxen, black with big white horns tipped with black, were raised in Yorkshire, Derby, Lancashire and Staffordshire, while the ancestors of the modern shorthorn, pied with white and with crooked horns, were bred in Lincolnshire. Leicestershire and Northamptonshire became famous for their cattle. Small-boned, black-faced sheep were associated with Herefordshire and Shropshire; the Cotswold breed, which gave its name to the hills – 'the wolds of the sheepcotes' – was already long-woolled and distinct; and the sheep of Yorkshire and the north were satisfying an increasing demand for coarser wool. The 'great horse' which was to give rise to the mighty shire horses of later ages occasionally found its way into the farmyard, after stallions imported from Naples, Germany, Hungary, Friesland and Flanders had encouraged the breed. But it was only after body armour was finally discarded in the 17th century that the really heavy horse was able to show its mettle on the farm.

Familiar crops were enriched by new varieties. Wheat might be white, red, main (a mixture of white and red), Turkey or Pinky, grey, flaxen, pollard, English or peak; barley was of three kinds: sprot, longear and bear or big; oats were red, black or rough; and there were white, green, grey and runcival peas. A new crop, buckwheat, was introduced from Russia and North Germany: it was described in the *Four Books of Husbandry* by the Dutchman Heresbach, translated into English in 1577 by Barnaby Googe, a Lincolnshire farmer and poet. Googe was the first person to recommend the growing of trefoil and clover for pasture. He also stressed the importance of manure and designed a novel reaping machine. In the mid-17th century a Worcestershire farmer, Andrew Yarenton, grew clover and wrote a manual about it, *The Great Improvement of Lands by Clover*. Some thirty years earlier Sir Richard Weston had grown turnips on his Surrey farm as a field crop and had thus inaugurated the cultivation of root crops which, developed by the Georgian pioneers of improved farming, led to entirely new systems of husbandry. Robert Loder, a yeoman who lived in Berkshire at Prince's Manor Farm overlooking the Vale of the White Horse, experimented with different manures, including malt dust; by ploughing in a crop of autumn corn that had failed, he got a yield as high as the national average in the first half of the present century.

Robert Loder's innovations and something of his vigorous, determined character and his eagerness for financial gain are revealed in his fortuitously preserved farm accounts. There were no doubt many others of like energy and resourcefulness, especially among the new and prosperous class of yeomen farmers who were responsible for more than a hundred acres. Yeomen were defined by Bacon as 'the middle people between gentlemen and peasants'. They constituted a class which had come into being as a result of the social changes which followed on the Black Death. Among them were not only freeholders such as Robert Loder but lessees for lives and copyholders, who paid a nominal yearly rent and a fine when the land passed from father to son. They were called 'copyholders' because the transfer of their property was entered in the Court Roll of the manor and their title was secured by their copy of the Roll. Latimer's father was a yeoman of this kind: he had no land of his own and rented his farm at £4 a year. Harrison describes the yeomen as 'for the most part farmers to gentlemen' that by attention to their business 'do come to great wealth insomuch that many of them are able and doo buie the lands of unthriftie gentlemen'. Harrison also says that they 'commonlie live wealthilie, keepe good houses' and had 'learned also to garnish their cupboards with plate, their joined beds with tapistrie and silke hangings, and their tables with carpets and fine naperie'.

The importance of the yeoman farmer is underlined by such specialist authors as Tusser and Fitzherbert, for their concern is not the great manorial estate but the individual farm managed by the owner or tenant with the help of his wife and a few hired servants. The custom of hiring farm servants at Statute Fairs, which continued until the present century and is so graphically described by Hardy in *Far From the Madding Crowd* (1874), is first heard of in the reign of Elizabeth I. The hiring fairs were held for ten days or a fortnight before Martinmas, 11 November, when the rates of wages for the district were given out publicly. The labourers offering themselves for engagement would stand in a row wearing the signs of their trade, a crook or a tuft of wool for a shepherd, a whip for a carter, a straw for a cowman. Many farmhouse inventories mention a servants' chamber, and the regular farmhands also lived in. They were usually the bailiff (on a wealthy farm), the foreman or 'chief hind', the ploughman and the carter, the shepherd and the 'common hind'. In addition to these servants there were the day labourers who were sometimes given meals and whose wages varied according to the season. At the busiest time of the year the farmer also employed 'task workers', who were paid by the acre.

The specialization and innovations attempted by Tudor and Stuart farmers would not have been possible in the open fields. Enclosure was advocated by both Fitzherbert and Tusser:

> The country enclosed I praise,

wrote the latter,

> The other delighteth me not
> For nothing the wealth it doth raise
> To such as inferior be.

and

> More plenty of mutton and beef
> Corn, butter and cheese of the best,
> More wealth anywhere (to be brief)
> More people, more handsome and prest
> Where find ye (go search any coast)
> Than ther, where enclosures are most.

The enclosure of land with permanent hedges for agricultural purposes had been going on throughout the Middle Ages. The landscape towards the west below the Trent and towards the east and south-east was already a patchwork of small hedged fields, scattered farms and meandering lanes. When John Leland (the first of the great Tudor topographers and antiquarians) was travelling between 1534 and 1543 he noticed that much of Devon was hedged by high banks crowned with ash, oak and hazel and that most of Somerset had been enclosed. A decade later, with a growing population, widespread interest in farming methods, and huge tracts of land changing hands after the suppression of the great abbeys, enclosure was proceeding at a faster rate than ever before. It took several forms. First, forest and waste land were enclosed. This was the traditional way of increasing arable and pasture, and a spectacular example of it was the reclamation by the middle of the 17th century of the watery solitudes of the vast fen that stretched from Cambridge to Lincoln and from King's Lynn to Peterborough. Secondly commons were enclosed to prevent haphazard breeding. And thirdly open field strips were transformed into hedged fields, often for grazing, especially in the Midlands. In the process villages and hamlets were sometimes wiped off the face of the earth: in Leicestershire as many as sixty villages had vanished by 1600 and cattle and sheep were feeding on grass which covered the foundations of deserted homesteads.

Both foreign and native travellers in Tudor England stood amazed at the numbers and sizes of the flocks of sheep they saw. Fleeces rather than corn were stored in the great red brick barn at Crows Hall, Debenham (Suffolk), when it belonged to Bassingbourn Gawdy, and a ram's head of moulded brick looks out from the wall to commemorate that usage. According to an act passed in 1534 to limit the number of sheep that might be owned by a single individual, some farmers possessed as many as 24,000 animals. Sheep were the commonest source of wealth and their importance is reflected in the vitality and power of the pastoral theme in the poetry of Spenser, Shakespeare and Herrick and later of Milton. The animals which produced the finest wool, the most valuable in the world, fed on the thin upland pastures which alternate with the clay valleys in the geological structure of the island. They were leaner than the sheep that enjoyed more succulent fields but, owing to some peculiarity of the soil, they grew the best fleeces.

The conversion of arable land to pasture aroused deep resentment. 'Where forty persons had their livings, now one man and his sheep hath all', cried Latimer, preaching against commercial landowners. And in Norfolk Kett and his followers slaughtered 20,000 sheep in 1549 – although enclosure for grazing could scarcely have caused serious hardship in that part of East Anglia where, when the antiquary William Camden visited it in 1586, hardly any open fields had been hedged. No, Kett's violence must have been an instinctive reaction to inevitable change and an understandable protest against the injustice which in some measure was bound to accompany the metamorphosis of the peasant into farmer or landless labourer. It was in the hope of enabling farmworkers to become independent of common and arable land that the famous statute of 1589 ordered that no new cottage was to be built unless it was surrounded by 4 acres of land. Nor was more than one family to occupy a single dwelling. The act was seldom enforced. Records of parishes in north-west Essex and parts of Suffolk in the 16th century disclose that though a cottage plot might be 80 feet square it was not unusual for a plot of half that size to be let; and on several occasions two tenants are named as occupying one cottage, each of them paying the full rent. This situation was not peculiar to Essex and Suffolk, for in his absorbing *History of Myddle*, written towards the end of the 17th century, Richard Gough tells of a cottage in that Shropshire parish which in the early years of Charles I's reign was shared by William Vaughan, a weaver, and Adam Dale, a mason.

The Act speaks of the 'erection of great numbers of cottages which are daily more increased in many parts of this Realme'. The numbers can be imagined when one learns that in the small Lincolnshire parish of Epworth alone one hundred additional cottages were built during the last quarter of the 16th century. The principal reason for so much new building was to provide shelter for the rapidly increasing population. I have already referred to the growth of London; in the country the increase is thought to have been more than fifty per cent in two generations. Domestic building was also affected by the tremendous social changes of the Tudor period. Parish records of progressive areas such as Bedfordshire, Nottinghamshire, Leicestershire and Lincolnshire show that the population was continually changing during the second half of the 16th century. This mobility was accompanied by changes in the relations of the social classes. The nobility were becoming less important; some yeomen farmers were moving into the ranks of the gentry and acquiring manors on which their fathers had been tenants. At the same time the numbers of their own 'middle' class were swelling. Vast traffic in land was going on and houses were everywhere needed on the growing estates of new owners and their tenants.

Richard Gough continually mentions the building of cottages on the commons by forebears of the parishioners of his own day, rural labourers who for the most part had come from other parts of the country. Ellice Hamner had erected a cottage in Myddle Wood in 1581; some time later John Wagge 'incloased some peices out of Myddle Wood and made it a small tenement'; Evan Jones – 'he couald speake neither good Welsh nor English' – built 'a lytle hutt upon Myddle Wood near the Clay lake, att the higher end of the towne and incloased a peice out of the Common'. Evan's son William also enclosed land in Myddle Wood and built a cottage.

Countless more substantial farmhouses were also making their appearance on the newly reclaimed wastelands. Among them were the gaunt and forbidding Pit House Farm, afterwards a Cromwellian stronghold, a landmark on the high, inclement expanse of Tow Law, Co. Durham; Pizwell, which grew into a tiny hamlet on the louring slopes of Dartmoor; North Lees Hall, the romantic, towered home of the Eyres on the wild fell above Hathersage in Derbyshire; and Moorhays Farm, near Cruwys Morchard in Devon, where William Zellecke had acquired the lease of a 'parcell of waste ground'. Existing farmhouses were undergoing alteration to provide comforts unknown to their builders; sometimes they were enlarged, sometimes entirely or partially rebuilt in more durable materials, sometimes divided into two or more dwellings. Whole villages of timber-framed dwellings on the limestone belt and in the uplands of Lancashire and the Yorkshire Dales were replaced by stone-built farmsteads and cottages. The spate of building slackened during the Civil War and was slightly interrupted by outbreaks of plague, but its impetus defied all checks, and certainly by the end of the 17th century the numbers of new houses had wrought a greater change in the landscape than the increased extent of hedges and walls.

So extraordinary is the wealth of houses left by the 16th and 17th centuries that thousands still testify to the energetic spirit of that period. The most obviously remarkable of these houses are the great Elizabethan and Jacobean mansions, ostentatious and ebullient, flaunting their strapwork parapets, their pillared porches and their ranges of huge intricately leaded windows from prominent sites. But the farmsteads and cottages of this wonderful age are no less satisfying to the imagination and no less ravishing to the eye. Unsophisticated though they may be they inhabit the same domain of fantasy and high romance as Hardwick and

63

Wollaton. For what image could appear stranger than Houchins, at Feering 68
in Essex, with its grotesquely exaggerated cross-wing, what more
improbable than the heavy black devices on the white walls of Oak Farm, at 65
Styal in Cheshire, what more bewitching and more visionary than the
combination in the fabric of humble Hammoon Manor of Dorset thatch
and a pedimented stone porch lit by a Tudor window and entered between
ringed and swelling Baroque columns? They and their like belong to the
countryside of Shakespeare and still, however altered, evoke the
Shakespearean world of rich pastoral and adumbrate the old rural
certainties.

Farming and farm buildings

Now, for the first time, no doubt because they were constructed of more
durable materials than in earlier periods, we encounter farmsteads which
include all the familiar structures. Owing to the conservative character of
farm buildings and the continued use for so many centuries of local
materials for their construction it is not easy to date them, but the year of
building or alteration so often proudly recorded on the farmhouse itself –
in the arabic numerals which became popular after the Reformation – may
sometimes give an indication of the age of the adjacent cattle and cart sheds,
granaries and barns.

The two most commonly occurring forms of layout of the farmstead, the
courtyard and the linear, were noted earlier; but 16th- and 17th-century
groups reveal many variations on these two themes. The linear
arrangement remains typical of the north and the south-west. At Blencarn 29
in Cumberland haylofts, cowbyres and stables of coarse dark red sandstone 40
and primitive aspect make a low L-shape about a midden a little distance
from the farmhouse, now called Pleasant View because it overlooks
Dufton Fell. At Redgate Farm, Wolsingham, Co. Durham, the house and 30
outbuildings form a narrow courtyard of sombre masonry pressed down,
under the brow of a hill (or 'wray' as the farmer calls it), by the huge stone
slates which roof the whole farmstead defying winter and tornado winds to
do their worst. At Blentarn, Easedale, a Westmorland farm well known to
Dorothy and William Wordsworth, the hayloft and stable stand parallel
to the long line of the farmhouse and cowbyre, while at Brimmerhead the
little farm buildings are scattered. At Newton, Yorkshire, a pond village
established despite its name before the Conquest, a 19th-century farmhouse
adjoins the long-house it replaced, and a 17th-century barn carries the line
of these buildings beyond a row of structures set at right angles to the long-
house, the whole creating a half-H pattern.

Farms farther south show as much diversity in arrangement. A farmhouse and farm buildings at Clenston, Dorset, make an irregular U
design; farmsteads at Coln Rogers, Gloucestershire, and at Heytesbury, 28
Wiltshire, conform loosely to the quadrangular model; while at Field Farm,
Bibury, in Gloucestershire, the farm buildings stand in line away from the 31
farmhouse, and at Abbess Roding, Essex, the farm buildings, now all 32
sheathed in tarred weatherboarding, are gathered into a courtyard to one
side of the farmhouse.

29 *Right* Long-house, Birk Howe, Little Langdale, Westmorland. The chimneys, plastered and protected by slate ridges, and the sturdy porches are characteristic of the region. The central porch leads into the house, the opening on the right into the animal shelter, of rougher masonry (see p. 89).

30 *Below* Redgate Farm, near Wolsingham, Co. Durham. Dark millstone grit is covered by huge roof slates.

31 *Opposite, above* Barn, granary, hayloft with outshot, and stable at Field Farm, Bibury, Gloucestershire.

32 *Opposite, below* A 16th-century farm at Abbess Roding, Essex. Tarred barns and white houses are a distinctive feature of the Essex landscape.

The barns and dovecotes which are almost the only relics of medieval farming remained conspicuous objects in the steading despite the appearance of other buildings. Pigeon keeping was no longer the monopoly of the lord of the manor: John Norden (whose lifelong endeavour was to make a complete survey of the country shire by shire, the *Speculum Britanniae*) estimated that there were as many as 26,000 dovecotes in England in his day. Nesting boxes for pigeons might be incorporated in the walls and gables of farmhouses and even cottages. They make a band of ornament under the porch eaves of a small farmhouse at Widecombe, Devon; they pattern a cottage gable at Little Rissington, Gloucestershire; dot the front of a porch at Southrop nearby; and spread in three broad tiers across the gable of a farmhouse at Little Milton, Oxfordshire. Dovecotes of the 16th and 17th centuries tend to be square or rectangular rather than circular in shape; they are emphatic products of their region and can on occasion rival the craziest 18th-century folly in the freakish humour of their architecture. The toy-like dovecote at Luntley, Herefordshire, parodies the ponderous stone slating and the bizarre square-panelled black-and-white style of the West Midlands with its miniature scale. Sir John Gostwick's dovecote at Willington, Bedfordshire, built in about 1540 of local limestone rubble and stone from two nearby priories demolished a few years previously, is an eyecatcher with the force of a thunderbolt. It starts up abruptly from an absolutely flat landscape, a preposterously tall narrow rectangle in the form of a fantastic nave and aisles with openings for the pigeons along the clerestory and with stepped gables exaggerating the plunging lines of the roof slopes, not just at either end but in the centre of the roof as well to mark the division between the two nesting chambers within. Tiers of windbraces both support and adorn the trimly carpentered high queen-post roof above the nesting boxes, many hundreds of them, set in the masonry in orderly rows.

The interiors of barns such as those of Parsonage Farm, at Stebbing in Essex, which like others of this period has a single aisle, and the ones at Yelling and St Ives in Huntingdonshire (the latter belonging to the East 36 Midlands Marketing Association and so preserved), strongly recall the barns of the Middle Ages but are distinguished from them by greater severity and economy in the organization of the roof and also, where the building itself is of timber, of the frame. But a thatched, timbered barn at Etchingham in Sussex does give a hint of that sudden leap of the 35 imagination which irradiates so many everyday products of the 16th century. The long cruck-like braces which at Cherhill passed from the base 15 of the wall right across the aisle to support the arcade posts branch out from the centre of the barn floor at Etchingham, sustaining the stout wall plates of the unaisled structure and creating the spectacular visual effect of a great inverted cruck.

The Etchingham barn is unique; but if the Yelling interior – like the 36 majority of 16th- and 17th-century examples – shows no striking constructional developments there is one aspect of this building which is altogether novel: its walls are of brick. Bricks were not made in England after the departure of the Romans until the end of the 13th century, when they were used in the fabric of Little Wenham Hall, Suffolk. Three hundred years went by before a barn was built of brick and the site of it was, significantly, also in East Anglia, partly because of the relative shortage of stone in an area where timber was becoming scarce and partly because of the trading connections of this region with the Netherlands, where brick building had long been established. The vast early 16th-century barn of Hall Farm, at Hales in Norfolk, glows with a colour nearer vermilion than 34 terracotta, varied here and there by a header of cinder hue vitrified in the firing. Bricks depend for their colour on the local clay, which in most of Norfolk contains a high proportion of iron staining it a rich red when fired. The strong colour of this immense barn, the largest in the county, and the outlandish proportions of the stepped gables outlined by mouldings and marked by the crumbling remains of the gablets with which they were once furnished, leave, like the Willington Dovecote, an impression of 33 strangeness and excitement, revealing for a moment the unfamiliar habit of mind which made such a composition possible. A brick barn at Great Gransden, Huntingdonshire, built more than a hundred years later, is by contrast of sober design and subdued rose colour, articulated by the calm rhythm of large regular ventilation slits; while the red madder bricks of a hay barn at Mottram St Andrew, Cheshire, impart a dark intensity to the building. There the simple omission of headers, leaving precise square little openings in the wall, produces an attractive geometric decoration and ventilates the building at the same time.

Tudor and Stuart barns are not usually seen in isolation, as some of their medieval counterparts are, but as part of the farmstead group. All over the country very modest outbuildings can be seen, lean-to shelters for animals, poultry or implements, stables or byres for a single cow or horse, such as those at Brimmerhead in Easedale, the wild valley between Helm Crag and Silver How in Westmorland, and at Widecombe, in a luxuriant declivity in 37 the Devon moors, which differ from each other sharply in setting and fabric

34 *Above* A 16th-century brick barn with Netherlandish crow-stepped gables at Hales, Norfolk.

35 *Left* Barn at Etchingham, Sussex, also of the 16th century.

36 *Below* Interior of the 17th-century brick barn at Church Farm, Yelling, Huntingdonshire.

37 *Above* Widecombe-in-
the-Moor, Devon. On the
left cowbyre and hayloft,
in the foreground a
humble stable, all of
granite, slatestone and
lava – as is the house, in
the background, with a
row of dove-holes below
its porch roof.

38 *Left* Former lodge of
Campden House serving
as a shelter for livestock
at Chipping Campden,
Gloucestershire.

Opposite
VII Brick nogging at
Water Stratford,
Buckinghamshire.
(See p. 111.)

but scarcely at all in form. And many farms include makeshift buildings, like the Nissen huts mentioned at the beginning of this book, or buildings which had another use when they were first erected. Esthwaite Hall in Lancashire sank to the rank of stable and hayloft when it was replaced by a large pretentious mansion in the 19th century, and pigs and livestock took over the ashlared lodges of Sir Baptist Hicks's house at Chipping Campden, Gloucestershire, after it was destroyed in the Civil War.

In general whatever their size farms comprise the same categories of buildings – barn, stable, granary, cowhouse, cart shed and perhaps a piggery. The emphasis, however, differs according to the type of farming the buildings serve. Where arable farming predominates the barn remains the most important and conspicuous structure. In pastoral country, on the other hand, barns are small, and the long two-storeyed range with stable and byre on the ground floor and a hayloft or perhaps a granary above, usually entered by an outside stair, becomes the principal building. In Gloucestershire at Coln Rogers the gigantic barn dwarfs even the farmhouse with its lofty chimneys, and at Field Farm, Bibury, where the linear arrangement of the farm buildings, characteristic of the north rather than of the Cotswolds, has been remarked, the towering proportions of the barn and its gabled door give the group a dramatic accent and totally distinguish it from any assemblage of northern buildings. The line of the farm buildings at Harthill Hall Farm, Alport, Derbyshire, for instance, is powerfully horizontal and it is the massive rectangle of the cowbyre and hayloft which most catches the eye. This building, which incorporates fragments of a 13th-century monastery in its rude masonry, is charged with a wholly unsophisticated air of grandeur which ennobles many northern structures of this kind. The dusky red sandstone ranges at Blencarn, and the gaunt tall cowhouse and hayloft at North Lees Hall Farm, Hathersage, with huge lintels and door jambs like those of a Saxon church, are among innumerable compelling images. Elizabethan and Jacobean farmers thought air and light harmful to the cattle: ventilation was provided only by slit apertures, two of which can still be seen at Hathersage, while at Blencarn they survive unaltered. Windows were inserted in the upper floor if grain was kept there, and the great first-floor storage rooms at both Hathersage and Alport are lit; at Hathersage the room is warmed by a wall fireplace. Chimneys can often be seen rising from granaries: there is one at Coln Rogers and another at Fenstead End, Suffolk. The grain was usually kept in chests (called 'kists' in the north) or in bins.

The ground-floor doors at Blencarn open into manure passages and drains. The cows are tethered noses towards their mangers and tails towards the manure passage. At Hathersage the arrangement was the same before the doors were blocked. The internal arrangement can be seen in the byre at Courthouse Farm, Hawkshead, Lancashire. Another plan is memorably embodied in the byre of Haddon Field Farm, Alport, Derbyshire, where the cows are stalled along instead of across the building, between shaped partitions, and in the shadow of a crushingly powerful king-post roof, a type of structure common in northern farm buildings of the 16th and 17th centuries. When the byre was built the stalls were yet more confined, for the roof then contained a loft.

At Cowmire Hall, Cartmel Fell, Lancashire, which bears a late 17th-century date, the hayloft and cowbyre conform to the design which emerged in Tudor times but they are articulated in a way which is peculiar to regions with a heavy rainfall. The joists of the hayloft floor project as for a jetty and support an inclined stone-slated roof, a welcome shelter for the labourer cleaning out the manure passages. The marked accent of this horizontal feature draws the eye to the abrupt and interesting contrast between the height, colour and texture of the walls of the hayloft and those of the byre below. The picturesque fabric of the upper storey, dry-stone walling tufted with bright yellow, long-haired bog moss, is intensified by the whitewash of the squat cowhouse to which, as at Blencarn, light is admitted through the tiniest openings, known locally as 'lap-oils'. At Brimmerhead, a stable with a hayloft above it shows the same projecting feature. One of the windows is original – for while early cowstalls were always low and dark, horses were given taller, better-lit quarters. The round opening at the top of the gable seems to indicate that the classical form of this nobly proportioned little building, which would not look out of place in the Tuscan hills, was intentional, but this is not so: such circular openings were traditional and were known as 'pitching eyes'. From them hay was flung to animals in the yard outside.

In the Lake District the projection often supported an open gallery in the 16th and 17th centuries, though such galleries were already becoming rare when De Quincey observed them during his visits to the Wordsworths between 1807 and 1809 and remarked that they were a peculiarity of the region. Only five examples were listed by Professor Barley in 1961, though his list did not include the gallery at Yew Tree Farm, Coniston, Lancashire. It rests on tremendous joists, open for most of its rugged length but filled with wattle-and-daub panels where it joins the farmhouse and roofed with huge mossy stone slates. Another unassuming little gallery juts from an

39 Gallery at Yew Tree Farm, Coniston, Lancashire.

42

40

46

Opposite
VIII Limestone (including two blocks of ironstone) at Stanion, Northamptonshire. Geraniums screen the inhabitants within.

40 *Above* Foldyard and midden at Blencarn, Cumberland.

41, 42 *Below and right* Cowbyres with haylofts at Harthill Hall Farm, Alport, Derbyshire, and Cowmire Hall, Cartmel Fell, Lancashire.

43, 44 *Opposite* Cowbyres at Haddon Field Farm, Alport, Derbyshire, and Courthouse Farm, Hawkshead, Lancashire.

outhouse at Hawkshead, approached by uneven rock-like steps which lead also into the hayloft alongside the gallery. Such roofed projections are thought to be spinning galleries, and may well be, for they usually face north where the light is good and at the time of their origin all the dalesmen's garments were spun and woven at home.

Dual-purpose farm buildings took other forms than the two-storeyed range. In northern pastoral country where little corn was grown the insignificant barn was often combined with a cattleshed under the same roof. And because the building generally stood in undulating, mountainous country it was ingeniously adapted to the terrain. A bank or slope suggested a building on two levels. Such a structure buttressed by lean-tos for pigs and poultry confronts a farmhouse at Lowthwaite in Cumberland from a high bank. A grass-grown ramp leads up to the door of the threshing barn, which faces a much smaller opening high up in the wall on the farmyard side and provides a draught for winnowing. The lower level of the building is entered directly from the farmyard so that the two or three cows it shelters can be easily exercised and watered.

Another dual-purpose building common in the north is the isolated field house, providing food and shelter for cattle and reducing labour in inclement weather and at harvest time. A typical field house affording occasional accommodation for cows at the lower level and with storage for hay at the upper end, fashioned of the pale magnesian limestone beneath it, stands near Hawkswick in Yorkshire. The lonely building is both a manifestation and an extension of the landscape, the quiet meadows going down to the Skirwith river and the immense solitary sweep of rock on the far side of the water, soon to become the precipice of Malham.

It may seem surprising to find large barns in regions such as the Cotswolds which derived so much wealth from sheep farming, but they testify to the practice of mixed farming which though varying in proportion was characteristic of traditional husbandry. Norden, travelling through Gloucestershire in 1620, admired 'the fertile corne grounde and lardge Fields greatly inriching the industrious Husbandman'. Such barns were already occasionally being used, as they would be later, for housing

47

45

45 *Right* An isolated field house built on two levels near Hawkswick, Yorkshire.

46 *Opposite, above* Stable and hayloft at Brimmerhead, Easedale, Westmorland. The rough masonry – slatestone, granite and random lumps of lava – is only lightly set with mortar.

47 *Opposite, below* A bank barn at St John's Vale, Lowthwaite, Cumberland. A building on two levels adapted to the sloping terrain and comprising a barn and animal shelter with lean-tos for pigs and poultry.

49 cattle. The barn of Old Hall Farm, Woodford, Cheshire, dated 1660, was built with a hayloft and cowhouse at one end. Subsidiary farm buildings were often attached to large barns. At Siddington in Gloucestershire, where the broad-aisled 16th-century building is so akin in shape and texture to the adjacent church; at Aldworth in Berkshire, with its enormous porch of ecclesiastic design pierced by cruciform openings and lit by a narrow glazed window beneath a sundial; in Gloucestershire, at Village Farm,

48 Winson, and at Ablington, where two barns, one of the early 18th century, the other a gigantic Elizabethan building, stand side by side – at all these places shelter sheds have been built under the extended roof of the barn, alongside the projecting porch.

These open-fronted shelters, where cattle could take refuge from the weather at their will, are often found in parts of the country where dairy cows were not housed for the winter in stalls. If they are not built against the barn they are often attached to the wall of the foldyard, and in the 17th century even these humble structures could achieve distinction, so exquisitely were they attuned to their setting. A remarkable pillared building near Coln St Aldwyns, Gloucestershire, deploys its weathered shafts and capitals of finest stone with the gesture of a grand classical colonnade. The farm stands on Akeman Street close to the site of a Roman villa, and it was from there, according to tradition, that the columns came.

48 Fine Cotswold barns at Ablington, Gloucestershire, with subsidiary farm buildings attached to them. In the porch is Michael À Bere, descendant of the original tenant.

Cart sheds as well as cow shelters were built with open fronts; and there are references to such sheds in the literature of the period. In his *Rural Economy of Yorkshire in 1641* Henry Best boasts of his seven carts kept in two sheds. It was not uncommon for the cart shed to occupy the open-fronted ground floor of a granary, as it does at Washford, Somerset, where the building is of red sandstone rubble and was once thatched.

Freestanding granaries used only for the storage of grain, found in corn-growing regions, are raised from the ground to keep out thieving rats. The shaped stones sometimes used for this purpose, called staddle stones, have now often become giant mushrooms in suburban gardens. The miniature proportions of a square granary at Arrington, Cambridgeshire, with a pyramidal roof topped by a rudimentary ball finial, seem to point to a low grain yield, though probably at the time when the building was erected the grain was kept for village consumption only.

FARMHOUSES AND COTTAGES

The distinction between farmhouses of the great centuries of vernacular building and what we now call cottages is far from clear. In the north the surviving 16th- or 17th-century 'cottage' was nearly always built as a farmstead and often still serves that purpose. The homes labourers built for themselves on the new enclosures were, according to contemporary accounts, the most wretched, unsubstantial hovels. Gough tells of a one-legged man who lived in a cave, though 'Bickley alias Hall' was not quite respectable: he was more often maintained by the parish than by his own work and was probably not married to the mother of his three children. 'He *says* shee is his wife', remarks Gough. Thomas Chidlow of Myddle lived in

49 *Above left* Barn of Old Hall Farm, Woodford, Cheshire, dated 1660, partly adapted as a cowbyre and hayloft with open timber front.

50 *Above* Open-fronted shelter of fine architectural character on Akeman Street, near Coln St Aldwyns, Gloucestershire.

'a poore pitifull hut, built up to an old oake'. Richard Carew, in his *Survey of Cornwall* written in 1580–90, describes cottages 'in times not past the remembrance of some yet living' built of rammed earth with 'low thatched roofs, few partitions, no planchings or glasse windows, and scarcely any chimnies other than a hole in the wall to let out the smoke'. The character of two cottages on the manor of Glupton in Oxfordshire can be imagined from the information given in an inventory that they were valued at £3 for the pair in 1631: each consisted of but one room. Any dwellings of this kind which may survive must be among those which were later improved; and there is evidence that alterations were occasionally made. Gough mentions several cottages which were enlarged by the addition of another bay or by the insertion of a chimney and an attic floor: Anne Chidley lived in 'a lyttle house in Newton that had noe chimney' but the next tenant, Richard Clarke, built a chimney. Daniel King, the Cheshire topographer, also writes of cottagers who 'builded chimnies and furnished other parts of their houses accordingly'.

Village streets usually show a little house here and there that looks as though it might have started life as a one- or two-roomed dwelling. A cottage at Dorchester in Oxfordshire may, like Anne Chidley's, have become two-floored with the later introduction of a chimney and a loft, for that is what is indicated by the partial withdrawal of the thatch from the picturesque roof to make room for tiles and a dormer window. But many cottages have been made by dividing former hall-house farms like those mentioned in the last chapter, and numbers of pairs of cottages have been contrived from the rectangular derivatives of the hall-house.

Pairs of cottages built from the latter half of the 17th century onwards were, however, frequently designed specially for rural labourers and their families. Two such little dwellings, thatched and of sandstone, shelter in an obscurity of myrtles below a rocky incline at Buckland-in-the-Moor,

51 The shape of this cottage at Dorchester, 23 Oxfordshire, may derive from the humble one-bay hall-house, or may be based on the plan resulting from the merging of hall and cross-wings into a rectangular design.

Devon: the chimneys are incorporated in the gable ends and the doors are symmetrically placed. The like of such cottages can be seen in most villages, always with the differences conferred by locality. Occasionally a row of cottages survives from the 17th century. The famous example in Gloucestershire at Arlington, Bibury, a single steep roof of stone tiles interrupted by irregular gables and dormers above oddly placed doors, was built to house weavers making cloth for fulling at Arlington Mill. A contrasting row carried out in clunch and thatch sweeps smoothly along the curve of the street at Melbourn, Cambridgeshire, while at Tattershall in 52 Lincolnshire one-storeyed cottages of brick stretch towards the church under a common roof, each little house containing two rooms. The ridges at the bases of the chimneys show that the roofs were once thatched.

All the delight, all the significance of these little houses lies in their diversity, in the informality of their haphazard compositions so often exaggerated by a huddle of lean-tos, outshots and projections, in the unsophisticated craftsmanship which has given each one of them its own singularity, above all in the way they are absorbed into the landscape, settling into it as naturally as a yellowhammer's nest into a hedgebank. To talk of anything like a deliberate plan seems absurdly out of place. Yet

53 At Westbury Farm,
Ashwell, Hertfordshire,
the jettied wings and hall
block are still distinct.
The higher roof level of
the hall block shows that
it was raised to give
headroom when an upper
floor was introduced.

traditional arrangements have shaped the cottages so far described and
when we turn to the dwellings we now call cottages, but which were
originally the homes of husbandmen, that tradition becomes more strongly
evident.

Confirmation of the sense that these houses were not built as cottages
comes from the thousands of inventories of the 16th and 17th centuries of
goods taken for probate, for many of them name the rooms in which the
objects were found and give a clear picture of the layout of the structure.
Again and again the records refer to very small houses consisting of but a
hall, sometimes called 'the house', a term still heard in the north, and a
parlour with a kitchen which may be an outshot at the opposite end. Robert
Smalley of Galby in Leicestershire, who died in 1559, and George Clinch of
Bletchingley in Surrey, who died in the first quarter of the 17th century,
though separated in time by more than fifty years, lived in identical houses
of this kind with a loft over the hall and parlour. They both owned several
cows, pigs and a team of horses, so they were more than labourers. Another
small farmhouse in the parish of Bletchingley, belonging to John Crackett
who was Robert Smalley's contemporary, showed the same plan but had
chambers instead of lofts above the parlour and kitchen. Similar farmsteads
are chronicled for Berkshire, Yorkshire, Sussex, Kent, Buckinghamshire,
Suffolk and Essex and it is probably true to say that where they still stand
they have become the cottages we know today.

V

The majority of larger farmhouses appear to have contained six to eight rooms. Thus William Laken of Elmsall in Yorkshire, who in 1563 was living in the farmhouse which a little later was rebuilt by Henry Best's grandfather, had three parlours, one of which was for his servants, and three chambers. Richard Wolfe of Roxwell, Essex, who owned a large farm and grew hops towards the end of the 17th century, had a hall, two parlours, a little closet, a kitchen, two butteries, a brewhouse, a milkhouse and a boulting house (where flour was 'bolted' or sifted to separate it from the bran); on the upper floor there were three chambers and a servants' chamber, and above that an attic where oats were stored. Henry Sharke of Writtle in Essex, who died in 1638, had a hall, parlour, great and little buttery, kitchen and milkhouse, and a servants' chamber and other chambers over parlour and hall. William Boosey, who was farming in the same parish nearly fifty years later, owned a house with exactly the same accommodation.

House design in this period was dominated by the trend, noticeable already in the later Middle Ages, towards the achievement of a compact two-storeyed form. The stages by which this came about can be observed and described, but the changes were attended by every conceivable variation that high-spirited craftsmen and owners could devise and the metamorphosis outlined here is necessarily a great simplification.

In numbers of early 16th-century houses, the hall block and cross-wings remain distinct although the house is two-storeyed throughout. The hall block, because it now has two floors, rises above the cross-wings and these are further differentiated by their jetties. The cross-wings of 17th-century houses are generally neither jettied nor projecting: they have become gables rising at either end of a flat façade, as at Abbey Farm, Hacheston,

54 At Abbey Farm, Hacheston, Suffolk, the cross-wings, brought entirely into line with the hall block, are marked only by their gables.

55 A thatched attempt to achieve a continuous roof line at Fuller's End, Elsenham, Essex.

56 At Office Farm, Methwold, Norfolk, even the gables have disappeared. The house has become completely rectangular and only the position of door and chimney recall the hall-house design.

Suffolk. The tradition of the cross-wings does however persist at the rear of Abbey Farm, where one wing advances slightly and a whole block comes forward from the other. This is a common feature: it was the 'backhouse' containing the dairy and perhaps the brewery. In the final stage of the emerging rectangular plan the gables disappear. In some instances the jetty may persist and continue all round the house, but more often the composition is a plain oblong. This form of farmhouse appears in many guises: it manifests itself in plastered half-timber at Methwold, Norfolk, in plastered clunch at Ashton Keynes, Wiltshire, in square-panelled black and white half-timber near Clifton-on-Teme, Worcestershire, grandly in brick and half-timber at Flemings Hall, Bedingfield, Suffolk, in stone and half-timber at Gardiners Farm, Aston Subedge, Gloucestershire, and in sandstone and thatch in the lonely, humble little farm of Higher Pudnes, near Buckland in Devon. These are but random instances of countless versions of the theme.

When old houses were altered to conform to the fashionable rectangular shape the results could be visually odd. The consequences of enthusiasm for the oblong shape in a farmhouse at Fuller's End, Essex, are entrancingly grotesque. The half-timbered house consists of the traditional hall, once one-storeyed but with a loft and dormer inserted later, and separately roofed cross-wings. Either at the time the hall was converted or later still the whole extent of the roof, cross-wings and all, was smothered in thatch in an attempt to unify the structure. Just as a square teacosy on a round pot fails to disguise the bulging rotund form beneath it, so the thatch at Fuller's End, while it presents the unbroken ridge of a rectangular house, leaves the hall-house design fully exposed below: the eaves line is wildly interrupted and the original roofs of the cross-wings can be glimpsed under the thick straw covering.

In these two-storeyed rectangular houses the former screens passage has become an entrance hall, often a through passage as at Newbourn Hall, Suffolk and at Pattenden in Kent, where the hall was ceiled and a chimney inserted in about 1530. In modest farmhouses there is often, however, no vestibule and the traditional screens passage is remembered only by the position of the door which opens straight into the principal room (sometimes, recalling the hall from which it derived, known as the 'fire-room'). A cottage at Great Leighs, Essex, built as a farmhouse at the end of the 16th century, still exhibits the characteristic arrangement. The door, placed according to custom near the kitchen end of the house, leads directly into the living room, and a small parlour opens from the upper end of this room.

There are four attic rooms at Great Leighs and it is apparent from an opening in the floor over the parlour that access to two of them was by a ladder from this room. There is no door between these two upper rooms and the remaining two; these last were entered by means of a ladder set against the outer wall of the kitchen. They were no doubt used for storage, as they were in a similar house at Pulborough, Sussex, where a 16th-century owner, Henry Miles, kept yarn, hemp and wool in the loft over the kitchen and part of the hall.

The present staircases at Great Leighs must have replaced the ladders some time after the end of the 17th century, for it was only then that stairs were constructed of boards for separate treads and risers. The wooden staircases which first replaced ladders consisted of solid blocks of oak and were of the newel design, like the winding stair in North Lees Hall Farm at Hathersage; or the quarter-newel design starting off as a straight flight, then turning up to the first floor, as at Crows Hall, Debenham; or of the

57
26

57 *Below left* Newbourn Hall, Suffolk: the entrance hall which evolved from the screens passage.

58 *Below* The steps of the staircase at Crows Hall, Debenham, Suffolk, are constructed of solid timbers and ascend in two short, straight flights. The turned balusters were a 17th-century addition.

59–61 Cheery Nook, Matterdale, Cumberland. *Above*, the long-house, the animal shelter of which was at the end nearest the camera. The inclined slates on the squat chimney prevent down-draughts. *Below*, the 'house-place' or living room, showing the traditional fitted cupboards against the cross-passage, and Mr and Mrs Abbott seated at the other end of the room by the kitchen range and glazed stoneware sink (see p. 197).

dog-legged type ascending in two straight flights, the second returning in the opposite direction to that of the first. Such staircases might be accommodated in a rounded or rectangular projection; more often they were placed in the hall, sometimes set against an internal chimneystack as at Office Farm, Methwold.

In the highland region a change was taking place in the plan of the long-house, bringing it closer to that of the two-storeyed farmhouse with or without a through passage. In the Lake District at Birk Howe the cows still share the farmer's roof but not his door. The door into the house is now separated from the cross passage by a little kitchen and there is no access to the house from the passage. Fellfoot Farm, grander in scale than most Lake District farmsteads and romantically sited below a frowning crag at the foot of Wrynose Pass, displays another modification of the long-house structure: the cowbyre and hayloft are separately roofed and are placed at the upper end of the farmhouse rather than at the service end, an arrangement which became increasingly common from the second half of the 17th century.

Sometimes, as at Cheery Nook Farm, Matterdale, the cross passage (or 'hallen' to give it the local name by which it now became known), divided from the cowhouse by a stone wall and entered by the broad, rugged porch characteristic of mountain cottages, is part of the living room but is separated from it by a screen of built-in cupboards – the 'heck' – with a door in the middle. This feature is instantly reminiscent of the medieval screen, though it seems only to have become customary in the Lake District

62 At Fellfoot Farm, Wrynose Pass, Westmorland, the house stands in line with its farm buildings but is not a true long-house because the structures are separately roofed and there is no communication between them.

29
62

59

60

89

in the early 17th century. The affinity with the screens passage is especially

p.1 striking if one stands in the passage of a farmhouse such as Underhowe, Grasmere, with the door between the cupboards open: it is at once obvious that they are a partition in a single apartment. In later houses where an actual wall divides passage and living room the traditional cupboards are still set against it, as at Wallthwaite Farm, Great Langdale. These cupboards of dark, highly polished oak, panelled and carved, usually bear the initials of the owner and the date. The cupboards at Matterdale are dated 1631 and those at Wallthwaite Farm 1711.

The development of farm buildings, farmhouses and cottages, even when like these Lakeland homes their wildness and kinship with the naked rock direct the thoughts to poetry rather than planning, depended on basic needs, and even ornamental features such as the fitted cupboards I have just
46 described or the roundel in the hayloft gable at Brimmerhead might be adopted in the first place for practical reasons. But in an age of such intense gusto, so ardently in love with the everyday business of living, it was not likely that the aspect of even such modest buildings as farmhouses should be wholly dictated by the incidents of utilitarian construction. A stronger urge too than the desire to conform to the latest fashion lay behind the lively appearance of so many farmhouses. The plain rectangle was an inadequate outlet for the sense of romance, the audacious fantasy, the passionate interest in the past which determined the climate of the period and influenced the taste of the yeoman farmer and the country craftsman as much as of the owners and builders of great mansions.

The tower which so captivated the imagination of Elizabethan magnates and their architects, embodying at the same time their glamorous view of the Middle Ages and their desire for self-advertisement, was not at that time necessary for defence, except in Border country, and it could not be put to essential use on the farm. Nevertheless it was occasionally incorporated in the farmhouse design. Something of the high romance of
63 the Bolsover keep informs the broad towers of North Lees Hall Farm at Hathersage, with their semicircular niched battlements and mullioned windows; neglect and the rudeness of the masonry quicken the romance and the make-believe fortress atmosphere. The rectangular hall block is itself like a tower with the actual tower containing a projecting staircase turret rising only a little above it. The date 1596 is carved in the stained and shabby plasterwork of a handsome, derelict room in the tower, where when I last saw it hens were roosting on a worm-eaten four-poster. At Boothby Graffoe, Lincolnshire, a tall rectangular house was set alongside a fragment of the curtain wall and the circular tower of Somerton Castle. The business of the farm, which is much in evidence here, the white-painted windows, the association of stone with a red brick buttress and warm red tiles, a door painted ginger grown and grained and a pretty Victorian railing weaken what must once have been the ostentatiously chivalric architecture of this conversion. But the tower still rises sharply from a densely overgrown moat and the building still commands the atmospheric view over mournful flats seen by King John of France when he was imprisoned in this very tower after his defeat at Poitiers.

The conspicuous angles and vertical thrust of gables and gablets and the

63 North Lees Hall, Hathersage, Derbyshire, an arresting late 16th-century version of the tower house carried out in rude carboniferous limestone. It was the home of the Eyres, and a descendant of this once powerful Catholic family was farming here in the 1950s.

strong chiaroscuro of boldly advancing wings and storeyed porches, all of which were present in the traditional hall-house, haunted the imagination of Tudor and Stuart builders. The old hall-house plan might still be preferred to newfangled designs: Manor Farm, at Lower Winchendon in Buckinghamshire, was built as late as 1620 with a one-storeyed hall and a cross-wing and a tall porch, though the roof line is continuous. Even when the house was two-storeyed throughout the hall-house plan with a central block and cross-wings might form the basis of an inspired composition and a delectably idiosyncratic interpretation of new motifs. So at Snitterton, Derbyshire, the exterior of Hall Farm takes the familiar form of a central block with cross-wings and an asymmetrically placed door. But the façade between the gables is crenellated, while the gables themselves are adorned with ball-topped finials and the door is surprisingly flanked by thin columns on high bases, a rural mason's eccentric version of the Ionic order, combined with a carved frieze of naturalistic flowers.

A spectacularly gabled variation on the hall-house design catches the eye
64 at Weobley, Herefordshire. Ley Farm is an expressive example of the small-
panelled timber style of the region and this encourages the effect of the
proliferating gables. From each gabled cross-wing a further two-storeyed
gabled projection starts forward. The tall, storeyed porch is surmounted by
a gable which jostles the central gable over the bay windows of the hall and
the room above it, while above them both yet another purely decorative
gable emerges from the slope of the roof.

The hall-house plan with a single cross-wing was much favoured. At
66 Broadoaks in the parish of Wimbish, Essex, the design is clothed in russet-
coloured brick, a romantic image, buttressed, yet with a classical roundel in
its high gable, bedizened with a display of tall, slim octagonal chimney
shafts with bulging caps of prickly spines in two rows: set in groups of two
and three on rectangular plinths and broached, moulded bases, they rise
from the junction of hall block and cross-wing and from the centre and rear
of the hall block itself. As one looks, the whole structure, because the gable
is not quite symmetrical, seems slightly to sway on its moated plot, an
impression strengthened by the tautly patterned fabric of the building, the
fine weave of the small bricks and the glinting criss-cross of the leaded
glazing of the large windows whose worn mullions and transoms are
moulded in pale terracotta, the Italian material introduced into England
some forty years before Broadoaks was built and still fashionable.

65 Hall and cross-wing make the same shape at Styal, Cheshire in the half-
timbered house of Oak Farm, but the mood and emphasis could not be
more disparate. Whereas the harmonious fabric of Broadoaks is all of a
piece, Oak Farm is stone-slated with brick chimneys above half-timbered
walls. Whereas Broadoaks tremblingly aspires, Oak Farm is earthbound:
the tall chimneys, diagonally set shafts on high plinths, shoot aloft
independently, giving no upward impetus to the building as a whole and
without power to draw the eye from the drama of the staring black timbers
coarsely patterning the white walls with a verve beside which the squares
64 and rectangles of Ley Farm seem to speak in monotones. But it is not just its
flamboyance which makes Oak Farm unforgettable, it is above all the
carpenter's free, bold allusion to tradition in the decorative use of mighty
crucks in the gable end.

The combination of hall and cross-wing was here and there yet more
overwhelmingly transfigured by the builder's eager, imaginative grasp of
67 possibilities. At Parsonage Farm, Burwell, Cambridgeshire, the cross-
wing, of towering height, brandishes twin gables on the façade of the house
and at the rear slopes precipitously down to within a few feet of the ground
in the form of an outshot backhouse. The 16th-century builder of Moat
Hall, at Parham in Suffolk (where an older house, the seat of the Uffords
and Willoughbys, had stood), concentrated all the important living rooms
– all the splendour of the house – in the cross-wing. Thus when the house
became a farm, after the sole heiress, Catherine Willoughby, married
Richard Bertie, of Berstead in Kent, the hall block became the backhouse
where the work of the farmhouse was done. The hall block is half-
timbered, the cross-wing of fashionable brick now faded, spectral and
poignantly beautiful in decay. Its lack of symmetry must always have been

64 Ley Farm, Weobley, Herefordshire, dated 1589, framed in small panels with a profusion of gables.

65 *Above* Oak Farm, Styal, Cheshire, a timber-framed hall-house with a single cross-wing.

66 *Left* At Broadoaks, Wimbish, Essex (*c.* 1560), the hall-house plan with a single cross-wing is carried out in brick.

67 Parsonage Farm, Burwell, Cambridgeshire. The single cross-wing is twin-gabled. The house and outbuildings are of local clunch and chalk lump.

68 At Houchins, Feering, near Coggeshall in Essex, the single cross-wing, three-storeyed and jettied, was added about 1600 to an earlier house and dominates the building. The attic storey was originally lit by small unglazed windows under the eaves.

entrancing. Two mouldering gabled bays with cusped arched lights now half blocked with wattle and daub, and a chimneystack adorned with arcading and, like the bays, with diaper work, project from the corroded walls into the dark moat, thick with weeds, that still encompasses the house.

The cross-wing is similarly exalted above the earlier hall at Houchins, and there takes the form of a huge, toppling house of three jettied storeys. The top floor was used for storage, probably of cloth produced in the area which was famed for its wool industry. (Houchins must have been the centre of arable as well as sheep farming, for the surrounding fields extend to almost 400 acres and an aisled barn of eleven bays is the most prominent of the farm buildings contemporary with the house.) There were two large rooms on both the first and ground floors, and the house was entered, as it still is, by a central door immediately in front of the chimney, which, set into a timber-framed bay, was a bold feature of the architectural design. The dragon beams of the jetties are supported by the swelling, polished carvings of sirens, not the fish-tailed beings of medieval lore but the bird-footed winged creatures of classical mythology. Exactly such fabulous images, according to the illustration in *Arches of Triumph* published in 1604, figured boldly in the spandrels of the arch erected to celebrate James I's entry into London earlier in the same year, and the builder of Houchins, perhaps Thomas Howchynge, who was baptized in 1569, might have seen both the book and the arch itself. The same image appears on either side of the porch of a cottage, once a farmstead, at Weobley. The siren was but one of countless motifs raised from the grave of the distant past by the magic of scholarship to become new sources of inspiration in every sphere and to merge with traditional forms in electrifying synthesis.

Where the flat-fronted style was adopted, gables frequently galvanized the sober rectangular façade into upward movement, departing from the position they had traditionally occupied at the extreme ends of the house. The space between the gables was often so reduced, as at Charendon Farm, Preston Bagot, Warwickshire, that only the placing of the door discloses the hall-house origin of the plan. In the Cotswolds the gables were usually moved still closer together and a little away from the ends of the house, as at Barrington Farm, Great Barrington, and at times they become no more than dormers, considerably lower than the roof ridge.

90

Endymion Porter's rambling rectangular house at Aston Subedge, a 69 rebuilding in stone of an earlier house, includes part of the old half-timbered manor, the panels now filled with stone. A tall ball-crowned gable marks the entrance and immediately beside it rises a twin gable giving a sudden unexpected flicker of movement to the façade, reinforcing the momentum of the tall chimneys and the picturesque irregularity of the long low farmhouse in its wooded hollow.

A widely popular design was the triple-gabled façade in which a third gable was set between the two derivations of the cross-wings. The gables on a farmhouse at Finstock, Oxfordshire, enliven the flat front with a quick, 70 sharp ascending and descending rhythm. Oval windows surmounted by dripstones look out from the ball-topped gables and are flanked by ball-topped finials; below them three square-headed mullioned, leaded windows with dripstone mouldings rise above the broader mullioned windows and the door of the ground floor. Already aspiring, the house is drawn yet more impetuously upwards by its tall, finely moulded chimneys. This improbable and felicitous assemblage of incongruous motifs is a typical product of the early 17th century and of limestone country, especially the Cotswolds.

The composition with contiguous gables assumes different forms and expresses other moods elsewhere. At Manor Farm, Toseland, Huntingdon- 71 shire, brick takes the place of the pale stone of Finstock and imparts fiery colour to a riveting image. The design is, for a modest house of 1600, obsessively and untraditionally symmetrical, with projecting bays beneath each of the three gables, a central porch and buttresses at either end of the house and between the bays. Only a small unpaired window on one side of

69 Farmhouse, granary and stable at Aston Subedge, Gloucestershire.

the porch indicates the persistence inside of a hall-house-based plan. A band of billet ornament in moulded brick defines the edges of the upstanding gables and leads the eye toward the preposterous outcrop of chimneys, brick columns with battlemented capitals outlined against the sky in flurries of two and three like gatherings of chess-set castles.

A vital feature of all the two-storeyed houses mentioned here was the chimney: the introduction of the chimney meant that the hall need no longer be open to the roof. The new chimneystacks might taper up at the
72 gable ends of a house, or at the front or back. In the second half of the 17th
70 century chimneys at the gable end were incorporated in the walls. But more
often the stack rose through the heart of the house, built between the hall
56 and the service end where there was no screens passage, as at Office Farm,
Methwold, or set against the screens passage in grander farmhouses such as
26,82 Pattenden at Goudhurst and Church Farm at Stebbing.

Where fireplaces had existed in medieval houses they had always been set against an outer wall, and the creative idea of building the stack in the centre of the house was quite as remarkable as the invention of the jetty. When it was added to a house already standing the structural problems, not to speak of the disarray in the lives of the inmates, must have been formidable. But the internal stack had practical advantages: it could service two back-to-back fireplaces on each floor and it gave additional strength to the whole structure. The traditional position of the open hearth may
18 perhaps have suggested the internal stack, and indeed at Tiptofts,
Wimbish, the chimney rises on the very spot where the fire burned – and with fantastic pictorial effect, for the hall has not been made into two floors and the great brick intruder fills the upper bay of the room with startling impact on its proportions: its height has become tower-like.

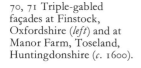

70, 71 Triple-gabled façades at Finstock, Oxfordshire (*left*) and at Manor Farm, Toseland, Huntingdonshire (*c.* 1600).

Chimneys vary in design according to the nature of their fabric and their site. Those of farmhouses on the limestone belt, even of the most unassuming character, are of stone, generally square and sometimes set diagonally on a square plinth, their height counterbalanced by one or two reticent horizontal mouldings. In the hills of north Devon and the mountains of the Lake District tall cylinders of irregular stone or of rubble plastered over facilitate the escape of smoke in a sheltered, overhung setting; downdraughts are controlled by two pieces of slate inclined against one another. Such chimneys are strange enough objects, but it was the new material, brick, which prompted the builder's most stupendous inventions and he used it widely, even occasionally where good stone was available. Chimneys were meant to draw the eye and to advertise the important fact that the house had fireplaces. Like the jetty, the chimney became a status symbol, and the number of shafts by no means always corresponded to the number of fireplaces.

To conceive of chimneys as aerial columns with bases, shafts and capitals of wild variety, clustered or single, was to do far more than proclaim a hearth: it was an invention of genius, as much a reflection of the high poetic excitement of the age as the richly polyphonic Elizabethan madrigal and just such another exotic hybrid. A number of these astounding compositions, those at Broadoaks and those at Toseland in particular, have already been pointed out, but their diversity and liveliness are endless. The chimneys at Flemings, Bedingfield, are in the form of four octagonal shafts set on high plinths with moulded bases and capitals and with a band of carved ornament, tiny panels filled with rosettes, round the tops. At Houchins a chimney of gargantuan proportions with a huge base and no less than twelve shafts sits darkly on the immensely tall cross-wing,

72 *Above left* A cylindrical Lakeland chimney at Esthwaite, Lancashire, on a building which was once the hall and has now become a stable and hayloft.

73 *Above* An ostentatious and ornate brick chimney at Newport, Essex, with four moulded brick shafts.

66,71

68

74 The ceiling and fireplace inserted into the former open hall of Pattenden Manor, Goudhurst, Kent, in the early 16th century. The magnificent moulding of the beams and lintel was executed with a simple chisel and gouge.

73 pressing it down. A group of four shafts with similar spiny, scalloped and corbelled tops soars with a magnificent flourish from a high, panelled plinth on the roof of a very modest house in the village street at Newport, Essex. But here the shafts are shorter and entirely overlaid with the most intricate designs superbly carried out in carved and moulded brick, a minute mesh of Saracenic character, a banded pattern of linked hexagons and another of loose, lacy openwork. The groups of lofty columns with oversailing capitals that shoot up so surprisingly from the calm white rectangle of a farm at Brent Pelham, Hertfordshire, are neither Gothic nor classic, and the reticulations, diapers, twists and spirals with which they are encrusted give a keener edge to the strangeness of their proportions. The shafts of the massive chimney sitting between hall block and cross-wing

82 at Church Farm, Stebbing, combine in a single ponderous square mass adorned with sharp, angular fluting like crisp pleats, and it rests on a square base with stepped gablets at each corner.

The fireplace whose presence the chimney published from the housetop might be of stone in a stone region but was more often of brick, crowned at the opening with a huge beam of oak, which in more important

74 farmhouses, such as Pattenden, might be carved or moulded. The back of the beam was canted to encourage a draught up the chimney. There was often a corner seat within the fireplace with a little niche near it where the occupant could place a glass or a cup. Iron plates protected the backs of hearths and in the districts of iron foundries – Sussex, Surrey and Kent – the fireback became the medium for robust relief work, figurative and heraldic, much like 17th-century tombstone carving in both form and feeling. The same bold treatment, the same unerring sense for strong, comely shape distinguishes all the other many appurtenances of the hearth which survive from the period: firedogs, an occasional long-handled fire shovel, tongs, roasting spits, chimney cranes, gridirons and pothangers, skillets, cauldrons, pipkins, pans and earthen pots.

Fireplaces in chambers became common in the 17th century. They were narrower than those in the 'hall' or kitchen and might be surmounted by a carving in wood or stone or by plasterwork.

Inventories reveal that the contents of larger farmhouses did not differ greatly except in quantity from those of the homes of husbandmen as humble as Robert Smalley (p. 84). Practically every house was furnished with at least one table and a few stools; and the tables were not just of the trestle type but of the more permanent or 'dormant' kind with legs. Alexander Reynoldson of Writtle, Essex, owned a 'drawing table' or table with leaves in 1671; and some farmers who died at about that date, as did William Garnon of Brant Broughton in Lincolnshire, occasionally possessed a round table. Chairs became commoner as the 17th century advanced; chests, hutches (used for clothes) and boxes were found in most homes. Pewter platters were replacing the wooden trenchers of the Middle Ages. Even George Clinch owned six pieces of pewter. Cooking pots and pans, spits, pothooks, often of elaborate design, and irons and gridirons, pestles and mortars, earthenware pots, and kneading troughs are named in most inventories. Beds, which often stood in the parlour, had low headboards and stout corner posts (like David Bird's bed in the brass in Boxford Church, Suffolk), or they might be four-posters with a canopy. A rich farmer of Roxwell, Henry Turnidge, whose inventory is included in Francis Steer's *Farm and Cottage Inventories of Mid Essex*, boasted a rare carved bedstead. Farmers seem to have slept most often on flock mattresses. Feather beds were a rare luxury, so it is all the pleasanter to know that John Crackett slept on a feather mattress with four pillows and two 'boulsters', a privilege indeed, for in his day pillows and bolsters were still often reserved for women in labour. Crackett's little 'hall' was hung with a painted cloth. Such cloths are commonly mentioned in inventories of the period: Robert Littlefield of Padworth, Berkshire, owned three, as did Thomas Wyhall of Boughton, Kent, in 1569. When hangings could not be afforded walls were still enlivened, as in the Middle Ages, with paintings done directly on the plaster. In an age no longer dominated by ecclesiastical influence, the designs might take the form of repeating patterns, either floral or geometric. The example in a farmhouse at Ashdon, Essex, shows 75 an arrangement of rectangular panels filled with arabesques and strapwork and with undulating briar tendrils climbing up the angles of the room; it was carried out in a range of colours popular at the time – dark green, dull rose and white (now much darkened and faded) – with that occasional deviation from absolute precision which gives such life and immediacy to a hand-painted decoration as opposed to a printed repeating design. The vehicle used for the pigment was glue, probably mixed with egg white.

In many inventories lists of the implements and tools of the farmer and his wife are longer and more detailed than those of household goods. When cloth and linen were spun at home, spinning wheels and sometimes looms, carding stocks and cards for combing out wool or flax were essential possessions. Thus in 1633 Richard Coliard of Thornage, near Holt in Norfolk, owned a spinning 'wheele & a pair of cardes – with a bushel of woole', and Thomas Waynforth of Roydon in the same county also left a spinning wheel and yarn in 1668; while John Addam of Copnall in

75 Painted decoration at Ashdon, Essex, completely covering the walls. The fireplace is of brick.

Staffordshire, who described himself as a yeoman, had two spinning wheels which he kept in the parlour in 1677. The numerous references in inventories to querns, coppers, vats, tubs of all sorts, barrels, hogsheads and malt shovels show that malt was made and beer brewed in many homesteads. Richard Mucklowe of Laphall in Shropshire owned a quern and a number of barrels; William Garnon had a 'brewing vessell' and six barrels; and Bartholomew Burch of Shadoxhurst in Kent, a relatively poor labourer whose home consisted of but hall and hall chamber with an attached dairy and 'drinke hous', owned three tubs and two barrels. The apparatus of the dairy or milkhouse also figures importantly in most inventories. Thomas Waynforth's dairy contained 'an old milke traye or salting traye & a cheese tubb, Eight Cheese fatts [vats], fower breds', a butter cooler and five other coolers, 'Eight old Bowles' and a 'Barrel Chirne'.

Agricultural implements, both hand tools – such as axes, billhooks, mattocks, sickles, spades, rakes, dung forks and pitchforks – and ploughs, harrows, rollers, wagons and carts, which varied according to the type of soil, were naturally prominent items in the list of any farmer's goods. The careful lists of farm animals ('seven Mares and Coltes', 'fower yeere Old Cowes' and 'fower weaneling Calves', '22 lambes yeare owld', 'one breeding mare and two coltes', 'four small horses', 'two old horses and their furniture', 'sixteen dry cows and one bull') show where the owner's chief interest lay. Now and then the names of the animals are recorded, and Swallow, Nut, Py and Marigold graze forever in the fields of Robert Colles, who farmed at South Kilworth in Leicestershire.

The close relationship between traditional farmsteads and cottages and their environment has become abundantly clear in the preceding pages: all the buildings so far described were constructed of materials found in the immediate locality. Something too has been seen of the imaginative development during the Tudor and Stuart periods both of the differences dictated by geology and of the range of possibilities inherent in each type of material. Thus the same basic design might take on the diverging aspects of brick and stone, as it does in the gabled farmhouses at Toseland and   71 Finstock, or emerge in such astonishingly contrasting forms as the brick   70 barn at Hales and the stone barn at Coln Rogers; and half-timber itself   34,28 might show striking variations. It is the craftsman's alert approach to his materials which is chiefly responsible for the vivid impact made by 16th- and 17th-century rural buildings, though other factors played a part in the establishment of local styles.

The trading relations of East Anglia with the Low Countries encouraged the predilection for brick in Norfolk and Suffolk and fostered the fashion in those counties for curved gables like those which, swelling and scrolling above the wings and lofty porch of Red House Farm, Knodishall, deter-   93 mine the whole expansive, stately mood of the house. The Netherlands too were the source of the pantiles which began to undulate on roofs in East Anglia, parts of Lincolnshire and the eastern side of the Vale of York towards the end of the 17th century. Their strong red colour, varied in Norfolk by a shining black which mirrors the blue of summer skies, invigorates many more farm buildings and cottages of the 18th and 19th centuries than of the time when Charles I granted a patent for the making of 'Flanders Tyles'; but those roofing a stable and granary, pigsty and cowshed at Aiskew, Yorkshire, may date from the end of the 17th century, judging from the internal roof structure and the rough character of the wall fabric – dark and light brown gritstone rubble mingled with thin brick, electrified by the sudden blood red of the granary and stable doors.

Maroon or ox red paint for the woodwork – and very often also for the heavy stone frames – of the doors and windows of cottages and farm buildings was traditional in the north, an instinctively felicitous choice in a   147 region of wetness and wildness. Where it persists it draws the eye to the stalwart character of the masonry, emphasizing rude and unconventional detail. The living-room window of a tiny one-storeyed long-house at Skirwith uniquely comprises three separate openings, two minute square-headed windows set immediately against a narrow pointed light. Together they make a lower-case h-shape in reverse, and this bizarre image is forced on the attention of any passer-by and rendered unforgettable by its deep red colour.

Thatch

Where timber and the unbaked earths were the chief available resources they continued to be employed as they had been from the earliest times, generally accompanied by that once ubiquitous and most primitive form of roof covering, thatch. Thatch was still widely found even in stone districts, but it was now used with more sophistication and with regional variations, while the unbaked earths and half-timber became specially associated with the areas to which they were largely relegated. The persistence of thatch for roofing and its common occurrence today, despite antagonistic regulations, are agreeably surprising. No other material so thoroughly sustains the sense of continuity, for thatching is at the same time one of the most ancient of the vernacular crafts and the one which most retains its traditional vigour.

Thatch must be frequently renewed: the life of the most durable variety of thatch, reed, rarely exceeds about eighty years; and whereas the village stonemason, bricklayer and carpenter have either ceased to exist or have been absorbed into commercial firms, the thatcher lives on as an individual craftsman. There are nevertheless fewer thatchers today than at any time and these cover areas far beyond the confines of their own districts, so inevitably some of the sharper regional distinctions must have been blurred or altogether lost. We know, for example, from a study of cottages by G. L. Morris published at the beginning of this century, that marked local differences still existed then between the ornamental disposition of the rods often fastened on top of the thatch at the ridge, eaves and verges as extra protection against wind, that the richest decoration was found in Norfolk and Suffolk, and that in Derbyshire the verges were coated with mortar even though the ridge and eaves might show a pattern of rods. At the present time, the rods generally make a criss-cross design known as 'dimenting' between parallels or are simply arranged in horizontal rows.

The thatcher's methods have been often and well described. Henry Best's account in his *Rural Economy of Yorkshire in 1641* is one of the most detailed and includes an account of the thatching of hayricks, the ridges of which were differently formed from those on houses, for loose straw was used held down by 'twyne hey bands'. C. F. Innocent's investigation of the craft is both thorough and of special interest for his recording of many old local terms still in use in 1916 and now obsolete. The forked instrument used to carry the thatching material up to the roof, generally known as the 'yelm-stick' today, was called the 'bow' in Cambridgeshire, the 'gillet' in Oxfordshire, and the 'groom' in Hertfordshire. Richard Jefferies described the apparatus used by the Wiltshire thatcher and Rider Haggard has preserved the details of the Norfolk thatcher's procedure in *A Farmer's Year*; Tom Hennell gives an artist's graphic description of the thatcher's preparation of his material in *Change on the Farm*, and a whole volume devoted to the craft, *Thatching and Thatched Buildings* by Michael Billett, was published in 1979. Even so, the subject of local and individual styles has never been – and probably can now never be – thoroughly explored.

The materials used in thatching are the straw of the cultivated grasses, wheat, oats and rye; reed, which yields the smoothest finish and most durable covering, and is seen at its best in Norfolk, Suffolk, south-east Cambridgeshire and the Fens; and sometimes, in moorland country where little corn is grown, heather or ling. The board on a master thatcher's cottage at Rockingham, Northamptonshire, announces that he is a specialist in 'Norfolk reed, Devon reed and long straw'. Devon reed, or Dorset reed as it is called in that county, is not reed but a superior kind of

wheat straw, which has not been threshed and has been specially prepared with a device known as a comber. The name by which it is usually known is 'wheat reed'. The term 'long straw' used by Mr Shouler at Rockingham is significant. Straw for thatching, unless it is grown for that purpose, is becoming increasingly difficult to obtain for two reasons: modern strains of wheat are too short in the stalk for thatching, and the combine harvester bruises and crushes the straw. Ideally – and this was the method described by Fitzherbert and followed for three centuries – the straw was grown long and then only the ears were reaped, leaving the tall straw standing to be mown later, or else the ears were cut off after harvest. Characteristic straw thatch can be seen at Bingham's Melcombe in Dorset, Monks Eleigh in Suffolk, and Chipping Campden in Gloucestershire. At Dunsford, Devon, pale, gleaming new thatch of ochre-coloured wheat reed is juxtaposed to sombre heather thatch, stiff as a brush, on roof and wall. Reed proper, smooth as a mole's back, covers the roof of a cottage at Linton, Cambridgeshire, and also that of the thatcher's cottage at Rockingham.

Innocent lists four thatching methods: the material can be sewn to the rafters; pinned to them by means of rods or ledgers (also called 'spars' or 'spicks') which are split wands of willow or hazel, pointed at both ends, or broaches, which are wands of hazel with a twist in the middle so that they resemble huge hairpins; worked into a foundation of turves; or merely held in place by means of a rope mesh, the ends of which are weighted with stones. This last primitive method does not survive in England; from Henry Best's account it seems to have been used only for haystacks even in his day. The second method, very often combined with the first, is the one most commonly followed.

76 *Left* Reed thatch with wheat straw ridge on the master thatcher's cottage, Rockingham, Northamptonshire.

77 *Above* Ornamental reed thatch with wheat straw ridge, Linton, Cambridgeshire. Note the pargework on the dormer gable.

79,78
80

77
76

78 *Left* Wheat straw roof, with a reed and straw dormer, at Monks Eleigh, Suffolk.

79 *Above* Thatched gables at Bingham's Melcombe, Dorset. The hipped gable has a decorative ridge and the suggestion of a little finial.

The straw is tied in bundles known as 'bottles' or 'yelms', which are carefully trimmed and wetted, combed downwards and held in position by rows of ledgers. In the case of wheat reed or reed proper the root ends of the stalks form the exposed surface of the thatch. The yelms are laid slightly diagonally, then combed upwards and attached to the underlying layer of bundles by means of broaches. The first layer of bundles is usually sewn to the rafters with a 12-inch steel needle and tarred rope. Thatchers, like tilers and slaters, work from the eaves upwards and generally from left to right, though the thatcher photographed at Sheepwash, Devon, is working from right to left. This craftsman is using wheat reed on a roof originally thatched with wheat straw. He is wearing traditional leather knee pads which enable him to lean against the rungs of his ladder for hours on end. His tools, apart from the yelm-stick already mentioned, are shears to trim the eaves and a 'patting board' to beat down the thatch. He pushed in the broaches with his hands, but other thatchers sometimes use a mallet. In East Anglia a 'legget' or 'leggatt', a tool consisting of a square, ridged board with a diagonal handle, is used to pat and smooth the thatch.

It seems more than likely that the distinctive ways in which thatch is used, as well as other idiosyncrasies of which traces can yet be seen, emerged during the centuries which are the subject of this chapter. Judging from medieval pictures of thatch it was originally without ornament at the ridge and eaves; in the Middle Ages the ridge was usually covered with clay or turves and the law required that thatched roofs in the vicinity of other buildings should be limewashed to lessen the danger of fire. Furthermore, although dormer windows had appeared before the end of the 15th century

VI

80 *Above* Cob, and thatch of heather and Devon reed, at Dunsford, Devon.

81 *Right* Chalk lump on a clunch base, and straw thatch, at Hadstock, Essex.

they only became common in small dwellings with the widespread introduction of an upper floor, and it was the thatcher's treatment of the dormer as much as his decoration of the ridge which expressed local tradition and his own individuality and skill.

The thatch may be carried straight across the top of the dormer like a gently billowing skirt. This form seems to occur frequently in south Cambridgeshire and north-east Essex, and sometimes on the eastern limestone belt and parts of the Cotswolds, with subtle variations. The dormers of the Rockingham master thatcher's cottage are straight-headed 76 but slope away from the window on either side with conspicuously trim angularity. In Hampshire thatch curves above dormers like thick eyebrows, and in Bedfordshire this curve becomes a sharply defined semicircle, which may be amusingly imitated by tiles when the original thatch has been replaced. A pointed gable habitually crowns the East Anglian dormer and its texture may contrast with that of the roof itself. Reed and straw combine in the dormer thatch of the wheat straw roof at Monks Eleigh. The dormer peeping from the thatch of a chalk lump 78 cottage at Little Sampford, Essex, is unexpectedly roofed with slate, and IV slate fills the spaces between the dormer sills and the eaves line.

The thatcher's treatment of gables varies as much as his approach to the dormer. He may regard the hipped gable as an exaggerated version of the dormer, as he does on one of the wings of a farmhouse at Bingham's Melcombe; or he may simply frame the gable with a neatly cut inverted V of thatch, as on the other wing at Bingham's Melcombe; or instead of treating the hipped gable as a single rounded shape, he may visualize the hip as a

Opposite
IX Moat Farm, Great
Tey, Essex: a
Georgianized farmhouse,
standing on an ancient
site. (See p. 149.)

separate entity, as at Elsenham, and draw up the thatch at either end of the ridge in a pert, pyramidal finial.

The most accomplished thatchers delight in a type of ridge ornament which is more ostentatious and more complicated than the limited rod decoration. The protective cap of thatch along the ridge, usually of wheat straw or perhaps of sedge, for Norfolk reed is too tough to be bent over the ridge, makes a pattern which is always a play upon the scallop, the V-shaped tongue and the half hexagon, and which is obviously related to the carved and moulded ornament of the Tudor and Stuart periods. The pattern may be repeated some way down the slope of the roof, as it is on the cottage at Linton. Here the beautiful precision of the ornamental reed thatch finely contrasts with a display of wattle design pargetting on a shining white dormer.

Formerly the thatcher would celebrate the completion of his work by setting a corn dolly on the ridge or gable. A thatcher at work at Buckland-in-the-Moor in the 1950s was making a Devonshire cross to put on the gable, and at that time a cock perched proudly on the ridge of a cottage at Ebrington, a village where the remarkable display of thatch above Cotswold stone walls perfectly demonstrates the suitability of this ancient and homely roofing material for every variety of rural dwelling.

Buildings made of earth

Buildings of earth are now found mostly in the West Country, in East Anglia and occasionally in the mild chalkland valleys and hills of Wiltshire, Berkshire, the South Downs, Hampshire and Buckinghamshire. The earth is known by varying local names: 'cob' in the south-west, especially in Dorset and Devon, 'witchit' or 'wichert' in Buckinghamshire, 'chalk lump' and 'clay lump' in East Anglia. Perhaps these names may have been coined in the period when the rural builder first became vividly conscious of regional diversities in the stuffs with which he was working, for the earliest use Innocent found of the word 'cob' or 'clob' was in a 17th-century Devonshire inventory.

The methods of preparing the earth were roughly the same in all districts and have been well described by witnesses. S. O. Addy gave an account in 1898 of the construction of a mud cottage at Mappleton in the East Riding of Yorkshire, and the architect Claude Messent watched the proceedings for the erection of a clay lump farm building in south Norfolk in 1926. The earth was dug near the site of the building, spread out in a layer about a foot thick, thoroughly watered, then mixed with straw and trodden by a horse or ox – though I was told by an elderly labourer who had himself worked on the restoration of a chalk lump cottage at Ashdon that the treading was traditionally done by the workmen in north-west Essex. The process was known as 'tempering'. Where chalk was at hand it was crunched up with the mixture; in Cornwall small pieces of broken slate, called 'shilf', were added, one load of shilf to two of clay; and in the heathy districts of Dorset and Devon sand and gravel strengthened the clay.

There were two ways of building the walls. In both cases the first step was to construct a plinth about 1½ or 2 feet high (though it was often much less). This might be made of rubble, as at Dunsford in Devon and Mullion

in Cornwall, or of pebbles, flint or brick, as at Duddenhoe End in Essex and Bryant's Puddle in Dorset. A cottage at Hadstock, Essex, built of chalk lump, is set on a plinth of clunch or chalk stone, the dazzlingly white, tractable limestone of Cambridgeshire and north-west Essex. The mixture might then be laid upon the plinth in courses with a dung fork, the thickness of the material, according to Addy, being about 5 to 7 inches. The walls at Selworthy, Somerset, where the whole village is of cob, are at least 2 feet thick and the walls of a cottage at Tacolneston, Norfolk, are about 18 inches thick. The courses diminished in height as the wall rose, the first course being about 2½ feet high. Each course was forked up when wet and pliant, thinly covered with straw, trampled down by the workmen and left to dry before the next course was added. The lintels of doors and window frames, if they were of wood rather than stone, were set in position as the work went along and sometimes cupboards would be fitted at the same time. Alternatively, the prepared mixture was put into wooden moulds and shaped into large blocks about 18 inches long, 6 inches deep and 9 inches wide for external walls, and smaller blocks about 12 inches long, 6 inches deep and 6 inches wide for internal walls. The blocks were turned out after a few days, then left for several months to dry thoroughly.

Whichever of the two methods was chosen the process was slow: it might take as long as two years to complete a two-storeyed building, so it is not surprising that the greater number of surviving earthen structures are very small farm buildings or cottages of one storey with an attic floor above. Nevertheless some rural craftsmen of the great age of vernacular building attempted designs of a more ambitious scale and character. Parsonage Farm, Burwell, the arresting shape of which has been remarked, is built of chalk lump with windows and door frames of clunch. The manor of Hayes Barton, the home of Sir Walter Raleigh at East Budleigh in Devon, translates into earth and thatch a form of hall-house design – the E-plan with a central porch and far advancing wings embracing a courtyard – usually reserved for great houses such as Barrington Court, Somerset; and a large farmhouse at Mundham, Norfolk, displays an exciting, sparsely fenestrated gabled façade with a tall staircase projection pressed against a low, long cross-wing and two colossal brick chimneystacks. The fireplaces inside this house are also of brick, some with moulded ornament, but in chalk country the chimneystacks and the fireplaces may be fashioned of clunch, as in the cottage at Duddenhoe End just cited and in a farmhouse at Elmdon, both in Essex.

The walls of earthen buildings naturally varied in colour according to regional distinctions in the character of the clay. Harrison observed that clay was either 'white, red or blue; and of these the first doth participate very much with the nature of our chalk, the second is called loam, but the third eftsoons changeth colour so soon as it is wrought, notwithstanding that it look blue when it is thrown out of the pit'. But usually the colour of the earth is concealed under a coating of plaster or roughcast and limewash. Roughcast, which consisted of coarse sand, slaked lime and shingle, gravel or other material, even cinders, was, as the name suggests, thrown on to the walls with a flat trowel. It may be seen on cottages at Bryant's Puddle, for instance, and at Melbourn in Cambridgeshire.

67

XIV

82 Close studding at Church Farm, Stebbing, Essex.

83 Square panels and bold patterns at Old Hall Farm, Woodford, Cheshire.

Timber-framing

A tentative outline of the construction of timber-framed walls was given in the earlier account of medieval farmsteads. The methods employed in developed timber building have been the focus of much recent expert investigation, so only the more salient features of regional styles will be discussed here. The timber frames manifesting these styles, which in the Middle Ages were no more than faintly adumbrated but which now burst forth with fantastical divergencies in the different areas with which this form of building was specifically associated, have been compared unfavourably by some authorities with the structurally more substantial products of the Middle Ages, yet these late examples of the carpenter's art, exploring as they do all the inherent decorative potentialities of the medium, make a most dramatic contribution to the visual delights of the countryside. We have seen the contrast between the narrowly spaced, ashen-hued stripes of East Anglian timber-work and the cruck framing, black-and-white square panelling and exuberant patterning of the West Midlands. A glance at Church Farm, Stebbing, the gable end of a cottage at Weobley, and Old Hall Farm at Woodford, with its lattices of cusped timbers, ornamental coving, cusped lozenges, stripes and bold zigzags, confirms the distinction. Close studding and square panels can both be seen in Kent and east Sussex, and romantic Castwizzel Manor, near Biddenden, is a particularly fine example of the former. Decorative panelling and close studding are combined at Sedlescombe Manor, Sussex, formerly a farm and now three cottages, but such ornament never in this area achieves the force and vivacity of a façade like that of Oak Farm at Styal. 65

The material of the wattle-and-daub filling of the panels varied according to the type of clay available, and intriguing regional names emphasized the differences. In Kent daubing was referred to as 'loaming'; in Cheshire wattle and daub went by the name of 'raddle and daub' or 'rad and dab'; in the West Country wattle work was known as 'freeth' or 'vreath', while in East Anglia the rods were called 'rizzes' or 'razors' and Essex churchwardens' accounts employ the terms 'splint' and 'stovett'. Innocent suggests that 'vreath' may be a variant of 'wreath'; and in a dictionary of 1602 'rathel' or 'raddle' is given as cognate with 'harthel' or 'hurdle'. In early timber-framed buildings, such as Pattenden, the filling was set back from the timber frame, but in a house of the date of Church 82 Farm, Stebbing, the panels are usually flush with the frame.

Laths replaced wattle in later timber structures, and when older framed farmhouses were enlarged and restored in the 16th and 17th centuries the panels might be filled with materials other than wattle and daub. Oak Farm 65 at Styal and Rose Cottage at Coalbrookdale, Shropshire (altered in 1642), both include panels filled with brick and stone rubble, all limewashed to preserve the black-and-white pattern favoured in the region. So tenaciously did West Midland craftsmen cling to this tradition that sometimes if a house were built entirely of brick they would adorn it with a painted semblance of timber panels. A brick addition to Old Hall Farm, Woodford, shows this extraordinary decoration. Brick replaced wattle and daub in the frame of the great Wheat Barn at Cressing Temple when it was rebuilt for the last time, and restorers used brick for many of the panels at Lower Brockhampton. Chalk lump can be seen between the timbers of the I hayloft at Parsonage Farm, Burwell.

Brick, because it was a novelty and fashionable at the time, was the alternative most preferred to wattle and daub. The most popular arrangement of the bricks between the timbers was the herringbone pattern: the narrow bricks of the 16th century zigzagging up and down the panels, improbably clasped by the contrasting timbers, can impart a most exotic air to a façade, especially if, as in the case of a cottage at Water Stratford, Buckinghamshire, the building is thatched and the bricks display VII irregularities in texture and colour. Here they range from dark plum red to palest terracotta. Sometimes the bricks are laid in the normal way, while at others diagonal courses between closely set timbers may be combined with horizontal courses in square and rectangular panels, as at Charendon Farm in Warwickshire.

The East Anglian custom of wholly encasing a timber-framed house in a 53–56 sheath of plaster no doubt developed as a means of defeating the draughts 67,68 which found their way through the timber frame as both the wood and the wattle shrank with age. Many medieval farmhouses and cottages were plastered in the 16th and 17th centuries. Timber-framed dwellings built in 23 the 17th century were generally encased in plaster from the outset because by then the timber used might well be inferior. There was a further, aesthetic, reason for the custom: smooth walls accorded better with growing classical tastes than the narrowly spaced stripes and insistent 82

84, 85 Late timber-framed cottages at Boughton, Kent, before and after 'restoration' – the removal of the coat of plaster and insertion of 'antique' windows and door.

84,85

verticality of East Anglian timber frames. Gleaming white or painted the traditional pink, buff, ochre or deep red, these plastered farmhouses and cottages remain as characteristic of the gentle East Anglian landscape as they were when Constable saw them as inseparable from his vision of Suffolk. The present fashion of stripping off the plaster sheath to expose the timbers can seldom be justified, even when it reveals medieval timbers that were originally exposed; but when the seemly covering is torn from rough work and poor timbers, and when an air of antiquity is falsely suggested by alterations to doors and windows, as for instance at Boughton in Kent, the result is aesthetically, practically and historically outrageous.

The astonishing distinction between timber-framed houses such as Oak Farm at Styal and Westbury Farm at Ashwell is heightened when the plaster is embellished with the ornament it so clearly invites. Although a gild of 'plaisterers' had been formed in London as early as 1501, the craft only reached its full development in the 17th century, with the emergence of external plaster ornament. Known as 'pargetting' or 'pargework', this decoration is a peculiarly English phenomenon associated particularly with Suffolk and Essex and the adjacent counties of Cambridgeshire and Hertfordshire. Sporadic instances do occur here and there in Norfolk and also in Herefordshire, where one of the gables of the Ley at Weobley displays a plaster sun head and a spray of thistles and oak leaves. The work may, like the well-known frieze on Bishop Bonner's Cottages at East Dereham, Norfolk, be raised in colour on a neutral ground, but the design is generally and most effectively conceived as white on white or buff on buff like the embroidery on the white or cream counterpanes that once graced cottage homes. The word 'pargetting' originally indicated any form of plaster sheath and in his *London Prices* of 1750 Batty Langley still uses it in this broad sense; it seems to have been restricted to external ornamental plasterwork only in the early years of the present century.

Traditional external plaster was composed of lime, sand, cow hair and cow dung, sometimes with the addition of chopped straw and stable manure. The resulting mixture was extremely tough and, unlike modern plaster which is mixed with cement and dries in a few minutes, fairly slow drying so that the pargetter had ample time to garnish the surface. The simplest adornment took the form of panels, perhaps suggested by the oak panelling which was the usual form of wall covering in the most important rooms of timber-framed houses from the first quarter of the 16th century. Usually the borders of these panels are recessed, an effect achieved by placing thin wooden templates on the surface of the last but one coat of plaster, then bringing up the plaster to the level of the templates before removing them. Occasionally roughcast might be used for this last coat, thus creating a contrast in texture such as can be seen on a cottage in Shilling Street, Lavenham. Small flints set in projecting panels give sudden unexpected prominence to a modest little dwelling in Saffron Walden. Less frequently, the panels themselves are recessed, leaving the borders in relief, a device which can be seen on a cottage at Ashwell.

Some of the panels at Ashwell exhibit huge scroll ornaments in deep relief and this is the most exotic form of pargework. Designs such as the ravishing honeysuckly frieze and panels of Tudor roses enriching a cottage at Sibton, Suffolk, and the flatter but much more intricate pattern of 161 arabesques, cartouches, rosettes and bell flowers that coils over great segments of the upper walls of a former farmhouse at Earls Colne, Essex, were executed by means of wooden or wax moulds. The giant sprays of leaves and flowers which cannot fail to catch the eye of anyone walking or driving along Nethergate Street in Clare, Suffolk, clambering all over a 86 cottage wall and gable, were modelled by hand with the aid of a trowel, a much smaller tool than the one used to apply the plaster sheath to the walls, the flowing lines having first been described in rope on the last but one coat of plaster. The craftsman would be holding the plaster in his left hand on a square trencher-like tool known as a 'hawke'.

Another less insistent but equally lively form of decoration, free and calligraphic, can be seen on the walls of a yeoman farmhouse, Hubbard's Hall at Bentley in Suffolk. For this the plasterer has used a pointed stick as if it were a burin to incise spontaneous representations of daisies in scallop-edged panels and small motifs of wavy lines, crosses and curving lozenge shapes. Sometimes a pretty pattern would be made by just pricking the plaster with a stick, and there is a delightful example of this on a cottage wall at Coggeshall in Essex; often a fan of pointed sticks, or a comb, would be used to create the most frequently occurring motifs – shell-shapes, zigzags and undulations. Frequently in north-west Essex a square wooden mould cut with three bars was pressed this way and that into the moist plaster to produce a pattern resembling wattling. Cottages everywhere in this district show this rudimentary design, while others display an all-over four-petalled flower pattern made by pressing a similar square mould into the plaster. At least one local craftsman still cuts moulds of this simple kind and uses them in the traditional way when the decorative plaster on an old cottage must be renewed. The hard, mechanical effect of such renewals is due to the nature of the quick-drying modern plaster.

86 Pargework at Clare, Suffolk.

Very occasionally at the end of the 17th century the plaster sheath of a house might be incised or moulded to simulate the appearance of masonry blocks: the walls of cottages at Steeple Bumpstead were treated in this way, although the pattern is almost obliterated by successive coats of limewash and the present leprous state of the plaster. But such imitation properly belongs to a later period when ever greater emphasis was put upon the stone façade.

Yet other methods were devised for protecting timber-framed walls, increasing at the same time the rich variety of their aspect. In Kent, east Sussex, Surrey, Essex, Suffolk and parts of Hertfordshire and Cambridgeshire clapboard made its appearance towards the end of the 17th century, the boards being pegged or, later, nailed to the studding. The tradition was ancient, for Innocent found oak weatherboarding of great age on a cruck house at Ewden, Yorkshire, and traces of former clapboarding in the fabric of medieval northern cottages, the walls of which had been rebuilt later in stone. This seems interestingly to show that like half-timber itself weatherboarding was only relegated to particular regions during the periods of rebuilding. In the earliest East Anglian and south-eastern examples, such as the barn and granary at Arrington, Cambridgeshire, the boards are irregular and follow the line of the tree's growth. They may be haphazardly spaced, as they are on the least restored section of the walls of the great barn at Wendens Ambo, Essex, and on those of a tumbledown cottage at Tenterden, Kent, where they jostle for

14

place with brick-nogged panels. In all these instances the boards are tarred. The sable walls of Essex and Suffolk barns, roofed with steep thatch or mossed tiles, and the frequent groups of black farm buildings clustered alongside a white plastered farmhouse, as at Abbess Roding, stand out against ripe cornfields or the green of spring with dramatic, almost abstract severity.

32

If it was not tarred the weatherboarding on farmhouses and cottages was traditionally painted white, as it is on two cottages at Nuthampstead, Hertfordshire, in one of which it is combined with a plaster sheath, a common occurrence. The boards here are made of elm, the wood generally used for this form of walling, and are laid with fair precision, regularly overlapping to cast thin lines of shadow and encourage a marked horizontal effect. This characteristic was to be deliberately developed as the horizontal mode became more dominant; and weatherboarding, as the following chapter of this book will disclose, is seen at its most sophisticated in buildings of the Georgian and Regency periods.

114

In the Weald of Kent, in Surrey and Sussex and now and then in the neighbouring counties of Berkshire and Hampshire, timber-framed farmhouses and cottages were weatherproofed by tile-hanging, the warm, russet-hued material deepening the congeniality and intimacy of a mellow countryside of orchards, tufted hills and hopfields. These wall tiles, not made prior to the 17th century, were flatter and thinner than those used on roofs. They were fastened to the laths with pins of hazel, willow or elder and bedded in lime and hair mortar. While the gable end, if it faced east or north, was often completely tile-hung, only the upper floor of the façades was generally protected, especially if it were jettied. The ground floor might be plastered, half-timbered, or encased in brick. The most harmonious effects are those created when roof and walls, crowned by a brick chimneystack of the same hue, are covered with tiles of a uniform, glowing texture. But just as the plasterer was excited by the marvellous decorative potentiality of his material so the tile-maker responded to the seductive possibilities of pattern. Walls were overlaid with fish scales, with alternating rows of beak shapes and semicircles, or, as at Capel, Surrey, with strangely flanged tiles creating a vigorously chiaroscuroed fret, which here consorts uncomfortably with a massive roof of sandstone slates quarried below the North Downs nearby. When sandstone presses upon clapboard the contrast is still more marked.

87

In the West Country the few timber-framed houses which were not rebuilt in stone were, from the 17th century onwards, hung with slates. No one looking at a Cornish roof and slate-enveloped wall would immediately connect this hard, tightly textured, brown-grey, sky-reflecting stone with mud and shale, but that is the composition of slate: mud and shale metamorphosed by enormous heat and unimaginable pressures more than three hundred million years ago. Craftsmen from the time of the Roman occupation onwards recognized the obvious usefulness of a rock so easily split, and the late E.M. Jope discovered that slates quarried in Cornwall and Devon were being transported to south and south-eastern England for roofing ecclesiastical buildings as early as 1187. The famous Delabole quarry near Camelford was opened during Elizabeth I's reign, and the

X,117

115

material may have come from there for the many slate-hung cottages and
farmhouses in and near St Columb Major. The slates on a house in that
village are attractively patterned, two rows of plain slates alternating with
two of half octagonal shape and a contrasting blue-grey colour and with
triangular and diamond-shaped panels interrupting the regular lines of
slates. That device is seen also on the upper tier of a three-storeyed row of
slate-hung timber-framed cottages at Dunster, Somerset. The overlapping
slates were generally attached to battens. The slater's tools, according to R.
Holme's *Academy of Armory and Blazon* published in 1688, were 'Hatchet,
Trowel, Hewing Knife, Pick to Hole, Pinning Iron to widen the Holes,
Hewing Block, Lathing Measure, and Stone *Do.*, and Pins, Stone nails or
Lath Nails and Laths or Latts'.

Thicker slates of a different colour, green-grey rather than brown-grey
or blue-grey, were quarried in Cumberland and are found not only on the
walls of Lake District farm buildings and farmhouses but also, though
rarely, on the walls. The upper part of the porch of Fellfoot Farm, for
instance, is timber-framed and slate-hung, the rows of plain slates varied by
a wooden panel bearing a carved criss-cross pattern, painted black.

116

Stone

The diversities in texture and style of the stone buildings which were
replacing earlier, flimsier structures on the farm and in the village during
the housing revolution of the 16th and 17th centuries have already found
their way into these pages. The contrasts between the oolitic limestone and
urbane aspect of the farm buildings at Ablington or Bibury in   48,31
Gloucestershire, the carboniferous limestone and primitive strength of the
cowbyre and hayloft at Alport in Derbyshire, and the sombre texture and   41
weight of the northern sandstone of the cowbyres and stables at Blencarn in   40
Cumberland, each in accord with its setting, strike the eye all the more
forcibly because of basic similarities in structure. A comparison between a
farmhouse such as that at Great Barrington and cottages at Kettlewell in   89,90
Yorkshire, where the rubble has been roughcast but where the dripstones
coarsely recall the Cotswold style, reveals them, both made of limestone
but differently constituted and of different origin, to be as distinct as the
encompassing landscapes, green and gently undulating on the one hand,
high treeless moor on the other. The reddish purple colour of the sandstone
at Blencarn is not common in the north, where this rock, usually known as
millstone grit, is of a forbidding grey, sometimes speckled, and found in   30
blocks of cyclopean proportions which are maintained when the stone is
dressed – as it is at Highlow Hall Farm, Abney, Derbyshire. Here the
hugely crenellated farmhouse is approached and dramatically opposed by a
heavy arched gateway, a local mason's personal interpretation of a classical
theme, incorporating short, eccentric columns in the upper stage, giant
balls, and a curving pediment sprouting scrolls and topped by a sphere. The
red Devonian sandstone of the south-west, of which the ground-floor walls
of the slate-hung cottages at Dunster are made, is of quite another
character, warm brown and rufous of hue and close in texture.

The greater number of traditional stone farmsteads are composed of
varieties of limestone and sandstone; but in parts of the north and the
south-west granite and ancient volcanic rock have been laboriously
fashioned into domestic shells. Awareness of the stubborn resistance of the
granite to the mason's will is the first sensation experienced in front of a
building such as the farmhouse of Penfound near the north coast of
Cornwall; the porch, in which a brave attempt has been made to shape and
mould the stone, stands out against the rough walls, adorned with a
painfully cut coat of arms in the faintest relief and the scarcely discernible
date 1642. The house seems as close to nature as the ruins of Chysauster.   3
This closeness is always felt with particular intensity when those rocks are
used which have come from titanic upheavings of the heavier, lower
materials of the earth. The whole village of Morvah, as it looked a quarter
of a century ago, might have risen by a natural process from its igneous
foundations, and in the same way the stable at Brimmerhead, of granite,   46
slatestone rubble and lava, seems to grow from the rock. All the wildness of
the Cumbrian fells lies concentrated in the walls of Cheery Nook at   59
Matterdale. Rough lumps of dark grey lava, brown tufa and dour slatestone rubble laid without mortar form the gable end, their barbaric aspect
only a little tamed on the façade by a modicum of mortar and a coat of
limewash.

88 Sarsen is the material both of the prehistoric monoliths and of a cottage at Avebury, Wiltshire.

With younger, more easily worked stones, the sense of order and of the human element is stronger than the overwhelming consciousness of nature. But the affinity with place remains, often making a memorable impression when the stone comes from one of the more uncommon formations. Buildings of that odd, toffee-coloured and toffee-textured XIII sandstone called carstone can never be seen without a sense of surprise as great as that inspired by the strange variegated cliffs of Old Hunstanton in Norfolk where the material is splendidly displayed in its natural state. It was not much used for entire walls before the 18th century, though it does make an earlier appearance as small random lumps on walls of mixed substances like the gable end of Bishop Bonner's Cottages, East Dereham.

88 Again the kinship of a cottage at Avebury, Wiltshire, with its setting is notably proclaimed by its fabric, for it is the same grey sandstone as that of the Bronze Age monoliths in the shadow of which it stands. Found as great boulders on the downs, the stones are called sarsens, from Saracen, because of their alien character.

The renowned limestone 'belt' ranges irregularly from the Purbeck Downs in Dorset, across Somerset, the Cotswolds and the Northampton-shire uplands into south Lincolnshire and up into east Yorkshire, where at Middleton-by-Pickering lively, shelly, rough-textured cottage walls support roofs of pantiles. Here the limestone is of a cool grey colour; in the Cotswolds it is of a honied and creamy rather than silvery pallor, though at XII Great Tew and Barford St Michael it becomes a rich ochre yellow. In Northamptonshire and Rutland the rock may again be impregnated with VIII iron, and the pale and the stained, nutty brown stone are sometimes set in alternate courses to produce horizontally striped walls. The limestone of Somerset and Dorset is of a delicate grey-gold. The stone farm buildings of this area, so many of them still untouched, are profoundly evocative of older farming traditions.

89 Carboniferous limestone at Kettlewell, Yorkshire, takes form in heavy roofing slates and coarse mouldings. Note the pigeon holes under the eaves.

90 Characteristic use of oolitic limestone in the Cotswolds: rubble walls, stone slates, dormer-gables, mullioned windows, drip mouldings and ashlared chimneys at Great Barrington, Gloucestershire.

It is in the Cotswolds above all that oolitic limestone (so-called because the most typical deposits look like masses of fish-roe) dominates the scene and it was here that skilled masons with a copious supply of fine, easily worked stone from countless small local quarries established and perfected a vernacular style in which traditional and classical motifs were fused in a unique synthesis. The style was retained throughout the 18th and part of the 19th centuries for farmhouse and cottage buildings, so that despite all the self-consciousness of such show villages as Broadway and Bourton-on-the-Water, the Cotswolds present the face of 17th-century rural England more clearly than any other part of the country. The components of the

70,90 style – the mullioned windows surmounted by square dripstones of Tudor style, the ball-topped finials, the oval or circular decorative panels, the prominence of gable and gablet, the elegant proportions of the square chimneystacks – have already been noticed. Stone porches, arched and protected by a hood mould, might distinguish the most unpretentious cottages; and the ground floor was usually flagged.

The infinite divergencies in the textures of stone walls are not only due to differences in the grain, colour and composition of the many varieties of stone: the stone itself can be treated in a number of ways, each of which brings out special qualities of the material. Most cottages and farm buildings are built of rubble – stone which has been left as found or only

59 slightly dressed. Some stones, like that of which the Matterdale farmstead is built, are too intractable to be shaped and they are used without order other than that the largest stones are placed near the base of the wall. Such irregular stones may be laid without mortar; in the long-houses of the north the distinction between the quarters of animals and men is often marked by the treatment of the masonry, dry-stone walling for the cowbyre and stone

29 bedded in mortar for the house, as at Little Langdale. A most interesting and vigorous texture was obtained when the mortar was used sparsely and set back, though the lively effects of this technique have nearly always been impaired by later infillings of mortar and even cement. Both textures, random rubble masonry as it was originally laid and as it looks with all its

45 sparkle dimmed after cementing, appear in the walls of the Hawkswick field house seen earlier.

Sometimes the rubble may be roughly squared, as it partly is in the wall

XII of a cottage at Great Tew, and sometimes it may be squared and dressed but not faced with smooth thinly cut stone as it is in the grandest buildings – though when the stone permits, this finish is used for the frames of doors and windows, wherever they are not constructed of wood, and for quoins.

38 The ashlared walls of the pigsty at Chipping Campden attest to its aristocratic origin, and a cottage near Meon Hill may owe the fine smooth surface of its walls to loftier beginnings. Toller Farm, Toller Fratrum, Dorset, shows a patchwork of ashlared masonry, squared and partly dressed stone and squared rubblestone. It is the living quality of walling

91 stones which have been dressed but not ashlared which makes a cottage in Broadway remain in the memory. The touch of the mason is warmly, strongly present in the façade of this little building – it quite literally embodies his procedures, the selection of blocks in the quarry, the careful examination of each one and the choice of a surface from which to square

91 Cottage at Broadway, Worcestershire.

the rest; the dressing of the rough stones with the chisels and punch whose marks they bear; and then the picking over of the differently sized stones to decide the exact place of each one in the close-fitting jigsaw of the wall.

The serene visual character of Cotswold farms and villages depends very much on the complete harmony of walls and roofs. The eye is never startled in this gracious region by the sudden contrast of half-timber and ponderous sandstone slates (as at Oak Farm, Styal), by the sight of even heavier stone slates above decorative tiles (as at Capel, Surrey), or by the unexpected change from big Purbeck stone slates and conspicuous mortar to tiles on a single roof (as at Toller Fratrum, Dorset). The limestone slates of the steeply pitched Cotswold roofs are of exquisite, not in the least mechanical regularity; and though they are in fact of tremendous weight, they could not look more unlike the thick, obviously massy slates of the low-pitched roofs of the Lake District and the north. The slates vary in size, diminishing as they approach the eaves. Like the thatcher, the mason worked from left to right and began at the eaves. It was probably when they were first widely used, in the 16th and 17th centuries, that the slates were given the apt and fanciful names which changed with the region. Randle Holme tells us the names of slates 'according to their Several Lengths' used in the north in 1688: 'Short Haghattee, Long Haghattee, Farwells, Chilts, Warnetts, Shorts, Shorts save one or Shorts so won, Short Backs, Long Backs, Batchlers, Wivetts, Short Twelves, Long Twelves, Jenny why Gettest thou, Rogue why Winkest thou'. In the Cotswolds the slates bore such names as 'cocks', 'cuttings', 'nobbities', 'becks', 'bachelors', 'nines' and 'hibbuts', 'elevens', 'sixteens', 'follows' and 'eaves'. In this area the ridges might be sawn out of the stone; but where the stone was less tractable, in the Lake District, the ridge slates were laid alternately on each side of the roof, notched and then locked together. Such slates were, from the time of Elizabeth I, appropriately known as 'wrestlers'.

65

87

70,90

Stone roof slates were originally bedded on hay, straw or bog moss and fastened to the rafters with oak pegs. Before mortar replaced the vegetable material it was the custom for a 'mosser' or 'moser', known also as the 'moss man', to make periodic inspections of stone-slated roofs: if the moss had decayed he would use a heavy square-ended trowel called the 'mossing iron' to poke new moss between as well as under the slates to keep out draughts and snow. In the Lake District the house leek, there called the aye-green, was also common on roofs and was grown above doors and windows as well. Thriving without soil and thought to have come from the Near East and to have magical healing powers, this plant was cherished as a generator of vitality and as a safeguard against thunder and lightning, just as the iron horseshoe, nailed above so many farmhouse, stable and cottage doors, was regarded as a sure protection against evil, a survival of the ancient veneration of the strange metal which in the far past had vanquished the race of stone- and bronze-weaponed peoples.

Brick

The tall, bedizened chimney-columns still announcing the presence of so many of the farmhouses and cottages which are the subject of this chapter are some of the more astounding of the inventions prompted by the revived use of brick. And brick, although much later, when commercially exploited, inimical to vernacular styles and materials, was at first as lively and as immediate a manifestation of place as stone or chalk lump. Bricks were made locally in simple kilns. As we have seen, they varied in colour with the nature of the available clay, from every shade of red to the pale yellow found in excessively limy districts like south Cambridgeshire. The undulating floor of Tiptofts, Wimbish, in another limy area, north-west

92 The hall floor of Tiptofts, Wimbish, Essex (see ill. 18).

Essex (one of the brick floors which, where stone flags were unobtainable, were beginning to replace ground floors of mud), is palest ochre suffused with delicate pink. This floor shows all the enchanting eccentricity, the slight imperfections in the bricks – creases and indentations due to inadequately controlled methods of firing – and the arbitrary system of laying them, rows of stretchers suddenly changing direction and as suddenly interrupted by rows of bricks set face upwards instead of on edge, which imparts such animation to early brickwork. The lack of uniformity in wall after wall of this period is a source of considerable visual pleasure.

No special method of laying or bonding the bricks was consistently adopted until at least the end of the 17th century. In Suffolk, at Flemings Hall, Bedingfield, headers alternate with rows of stretchers, in an arrangement known as English bond; at Red House Farm, Knodishall, a row of stretchers is succeeded by a row of headers, then by three rows of stretchers, and then a row of two stretchers alternating with one header is followed by one of two headers alternating with one stretcher; the walls of the barn at Hales are enlivened by bands of projecting headers, and here alternating rows of stretchers and headers consort with rows laid quite haphazardly.

93

34

A uniquely decorated brick façade compels attention at Wheatley, Nottinghamshire. The builder of a farmhouse there dated 1673 was carried away by the classical details he may have seen in some of the French and Netherlandish handbooks which had been circulating throughout the century, or may have observed on some of the great houses in his neighbourhood. The improbable, illogical façade wonderfully communicates his pleasure in rendering these motifs in brick and arranging them to suit his sprightly fancy. Extraordinarily tall pilasters – shapes in relief banded by projecting stretchers, their capitals an attempt at the Ionic order in rubbed and carved brick – flank the low arch of the porch and support nothing. Above them hovers a broad entablature of moulded and projecting bricks and from that, each set on a pair of brick roundels, two absurd obelisks rise in relief on either side of a lunette. The entablature is carried right across the façade and the lunette is repeated by a row of like shapes – semicircular pediments – partly made in wooden moulds, looping heavily along and finishing disconcertingly but deliberately with a half lunette at either end.

Flint

One of the most visually exciting building materials, flint, began to enrich the exteriors of cottages and farm buildings at about the same time as brick. Flint, like thatch, belongs to a tradition rooted in prehistory, for the flint knapping industry of Brandon in Suffolk, which only came to an end a year or two ago, was established by our Neolithic forebears. A mysterious and exceptionally hard silica, found in nodules of suggestive shapes, as though produced by stupendous pressure on molten matter, or in bands in the chalk districts of East Anglia, Sussex, Dorset and Wiltshire, flint gives local character to the medieval parish churches of Norfolk and Suffolk, but was not used for small domestic buildings in the Middle Ages because the corners and the angles of doors and window frames could not be managed without the support of another material, and the stone which was combined with flint for ecclesiastical work was not available for cottages and barns. But with the re-introduction of brick and the much wider use of stone for secular buildings farmsteads began to take shape in flint. The material was either gathered from the fields and used in its rough state or quarried and knapped, the process by which the craftsman shaped the flints for building, using different hammers, and squared them to different sizes, revealing the jet black or mixed coloured hearts of the stones.

Flint may occasionally be associated with bones in walls as late as the 19th century. Some flints indeed look like bone, and a horse bone takes its place almost unnoticed in a cottage wall at Cley-next-the-Sea, Norfolk. It perpetuates an ancient custom according to which bones were incorporated in the fabric of a house to ward off evil, for the virtue of a good horse was thought by this means to enter into the building and protect it.

By far the greater number of flint farmhouses and cottages found in the villages of Norfolk and Suffolk and parts of the southern counties were built in the 18th and 19th centuries, but some examples are of earlier date and are already informed with something of the originality and spirit which are particularly associated with this challenging and unusual material. The

village of Castle Acre, which lies in the district where the flint knapping
industry was centred, contains several flint cottages dating from Tudor and
Stuart times. The stones of some of these have been used in their rough
state, while those of others have been quartered (the first stage in the
knapping process). The walls are reinforced with brick and also with
fragments of masonry from the ruins of the great Priory at the end of the
village street. Blocks of ashlared stone play a still larger part in the walls of a
cottage near Hyde Abbey, Hampshire, where they form a rough chequer
pattern with flints intermingled with brick here and there. A 17th-century
farmhouse at Trunch exhibits walls such as everywhere delight the eye in
north-west Norfolk, made of small, close-set, rounded flint pebbles called
cobbles and forming a texture like plain knitting. The stones, coated with a
white patina of chalk, set off the brilliant red of the prominent brick
chimney clusters and the patterned arrangement of the quoins and gable
edges. The glinting, cobbled gable end of a row of one-storeyed cottages at
Lakenheath in Suffolk is spotted with brick headers and set with diamond
shapes in brick, one within the other. The walls of a cottage at Bingham's
Melcombe, where the small, roughly squared flints, laid in even courses, are
of a chalky brown colour, are banded by double rows of brick at intervals.
Much larger and wilder field flints join with brick to make a barn at East
Raynham, Norfolk, and to form the background for a charming piece of
decoration: ventilation is provided by a window filled with alternating
spaces and stretchers, the bold red bricks held together by white, pebble-
like dollops of mortar where they overlap.

It has not been possible here to point to more than a few of such
individual contrivances. They defy classification, but it is their like, so
richly abundant in every region, which, while the bulldozer is held at bay,
makes the exploration of local craftsmen's ways with their materials a
source of such perennial surprise and untrammelled delight.

4

A New Order

CHANGE IS TOO MYSTERIOUS, too subtle, to be measured by date. A slowly altering view of life, a shift of emphasis from the religious to the secular, had been manifest in countless ways during the 16th and 17th centuries, not the least of them the sharp decline in church building and the florescence of a domestic architecture which owed less and less to ecclesiastical influence and inclined more and more to the classical horizontal mode which was so perfectly attuned to the serene and confident philosophy of Locke and Shaftesbury, the new understanding of Nature's laws and the exhilarating sense of liberation from the darkness and barbarism of the Gothic past which this engendered. Even the humble farmhouse and cottage were affected by the prevailing habit of mind, and there is plenty of evidence, as the reader will have noticed, of a growing awareness of the changing outlook in the farming practices of the 17th century. The transformation of the English landscape and of methods of farming which went forward so energetically under the Hanoverians was but the continuation of a process set in motion by the scientific advances of the previous age.

When Daniel Defoe was riding through Britain at the beginning of the 18th century he saw great tracts of land, millions of acres, still farmed on the open field system, and desolate moors and heaths of vast extent even in such gentle counties as Surrey, Berkshire and Hampshire. He describes cottagers, yeoman farmers and craftsmen pursuing their traditional ways of living, working and cultivating the fields under the peculiarly favourable conditions created by enterprising middlemen who were finding new markets for farm produce.

But a number of reasons were conspiring to quicken the pace of the revolution already under way. The population of the country was mounting – it more than doubled between 1700 and the reign of George IV, from about $5\frac{1}{2}$ to over 11 million – and a larger proportion of it than ever before was concentrated in the towns. The traditional way of increasing the food supply by reclaiming new farmland from forest and fen, moor and mountain, was far from exhausted, as Defoe's account shows, but it was realized that inevitably the day would come when the ancient remedy could not be applied. It was wholly in key with the temper of the age, eager, experimental and inquiring, preoccupied with physical science and the phenomena of nature, that a solution should be sought in developing the new methods of tillage and breeding which the most enterprising farmers

Opposite
96 High House Farm, Bawdsey, Suffolk.

127

had already adopted, methods dictated by a scientific approach to agriculture. This approach was encouraged by a spate of publications on the subject, many of them written by practising farmers, such as Jethro Tull (inventor of the seed-drill, for more effective sowing), William Ellis, William Marshal (author of *The Landed Property of England* and of detailed, lively studies of rural economy in different counties and regions of England), and the prolific Arthur Young, agricultural reformer, traveller and journalist. Enthusiasm for farming became a cult embraced by great landowners and small squires alike. It was symptomatic of the vogue that George III wished to be known as 'Farmer George' and that he contributed to Young's periodical, *Annals of Agriculture*, under the name of Ralph Robinson.

The possibilities for growing new and better crops and for improved techniques could only be realized through enclosure and the creation of rationally planned, compact farmsteads under the firm control of the individual owner or manager. So a procedure which had been localized and sporadic became an all-embracing national policy carried forward by Acts of Parliament which multiplied from only 8 before 1714 to as many as 1,768 by the end of the century. More than 700 further Acts were passed after the General Enclosure Act of 1845 and even after than date there were more than a further hundred awards of the right to enclose.

The counties most severely affected by enclosure were parts of Lincolnshire and Rutland, Bedfordshire, Huntingdonshire, Northampton- shire and south Cambridgeshire, Oxfordshire, Warwickshire, parts of Berkshire, Gloucestershire and Derbyshire, and the East Riding of Yorkshire. In the pastoral hills of the far north and the south-west and in those regions such as Kent, Essex, Suffolk and Somerset where enclosure had begun early, the agrarian revolution made but a mild impact. But over a great area, especially in the Midlands, mazy landscapes of narrow strip cultivation, winding tracks and green lanes were turned into chequer- board patterns consisting of large, approximately square, hedged fields with straight, grass-verged roads running through them. The hedges had a ditch on one or other side of them; unlike the hedges of ancient enclosure, where many varieties of trees and shrubs flourished, they were always of hawthorn, interspersed occasionally with ash trees and elms and sometimes – in Cambridgeshire and the small area of Suffolk which had not previously been enclosed – with holly. In much of the limestone country, over part of 97 Yorkshire and conspicuously in Derbyshire, stone walls took the place of hedges, netting the land in a taut mesh of glittering rock fragments. In Northamptonshire thorn trees, now grown to giant size, spring here and there with magical effect from the stone walls.

This wholesale ordering of the countryside domesticated, tamed, it. It came near to realizing Addison's tentative suggestion that an entire estate, including the cornfields and meadows, might be made into a kind of garden; and while in the open country nature was subdued by enclosure, the formal gardens of earlier times, paradisian symmetrical plots walled against the dangerous chaos of wild nature, were thrown open to merge with the surrounding fields, and instead of formality the contrived irregularity of cave and precipice, lake and waterfall, trees and glades conjured up images of nature's more savage aspects without their physical hazard.

Professor Hoskins speaks of the Northamptonshire poet John Clare's poignant sense of loss when the woods, heaths and fields of his native Helpston were enclosed in about 1820, and of his rage against the 'improvers':

> Inclosure, thou'rt a curse upon the land
> And tasteless was the wretch who thy existence planned.

But only half a century later Richard Jefferies in Wiltshire wrote that nothing he had read of or seen equalled the beauty and delight of English fields and meadows, and he marvelled at the variety of birds rejoicing 'in the plenty of the hedgerows'. And the crowning touch in George Eliot's marvellous picture of the Warwickshire countryside at the beginning of *Felix Holt* (1866) is her description of the hedgerows:

> Perhaps they were white with May, or starred with pale pink dogroses; perhaps the urchins were already nutting among them, or gathering the plenteous crabs. It was worth the journey only to see the hedgerows, the liberal homes of unmarketable beauty – of the purple-blossomed, ruby-berried nightshade, of the wild convolvulus climbing and spreading in tendrilled strength till it made a great curtain of pale-green hearts and white trumpets, of the many-tubed honeysuckle which, in its most delicate fragrance, hid a charm more subtle and penetrating than beauty. Even if it were winter the hedgerows showed their coral, the scarlet haws, the deep-crimson hips, with lingering brown leaves to make a resting place for the jewels of the hoar-frost.

Before the recent destruction of many of these hedges the sight of the May landscape over a great part of England was the thrilling climax of all the visual pleasures of spring: the whole terrain, farm and cottage, church and village were embowered in a foam of blossom which everywhere filled the air with its heavy scent.

The results of enclosure for many cottagers have often been described. The rural labourer had been wont to supplement his wages by keeping livestock on the wastes; now these rights were largely lost, with a consequent accentuation of the problem of poverty. The fact that by the end of the 18th century more than £7 million were levied in taxes for Poor Rate, while taxations for other purposes amounted to only £1½ million, speaks for itself. The situation was made worse by the Law of Settlement which had been passed in 1662 to make each parish responsible for its own poor. It meant that a man who wished to qualify for relief had to remain in his own parish. When the numbers of paupers began to increase parishes made every effort to get rid of them; some landlords even allowed cottages to decay so that the inmates were forced to seek accommodation outside the parish. The parish they had left then became 'closed', a place where no Poor Rates were levied because there were no longer any poor. The needy were thus gradually driven into the 'open' parishes where Poor Rates were high. The confrontation lasted until long after the Poor Law Reform Act of 1834, which abolished 'outdoor relief' – the payment of subsidies from the parish rates to people who remained in their cottages – and made life in the workhouse deliberately harsher. After the rise in prices towards the end of the 18th century the lot of those living in open parishes might be utter destitution and starvation. A labourer, his wife and two children were found dead in a house on the village green of Datchworth in Hertfordshire in 1769, and in the same year four other labourers of that parish died of hunger.

The contrast between the records of such tragedies and the descriptions in the literature of the period of the more than ample fare served in some farmhouses – the delicious mutton, venison and veal, poultry and game, cream and cheese, ham and bacon, fruits and vegetables, all from his own farm, with which Smollett's Matthew Bramble, squire and farmer of Brambleton Hall, loaded his table; the 'fine Tench (taken out of my pond in the yard) stewed, a Rump of Beef boiled, and a Goose rosted, and a Pudding', which was one of the more modest of the dinners Parson Woodforde (1740–1803) describes in his *Diary of a Country Parson* – is symbolic of the gulf which had begun to develop between farmers and their workers, and which was to become unbridgeable. The old community life of the farmhouse was already disrupted: unmarried workers still lived in the house, though as J.C. Loudon observed in his *Encyclopaedia of Agriculture* (1825), 'sleeping rooms for unmarried farm servants, in most parts of Britain, are generally such as to merit extreme reprobation'. But maids and men no longer sat at table with the family: they ate apart at a scrubbed wooden table while the farmer and his family dined at a table spread with a snowy cloth. Successful farmers were putting on airs. William Cobbett, who rode and wrote about England a hundred years later than Defoe, indignantly criticized a farmhouse that boasted a parlour (which differed from the parlour of the 16th and 17th centuries in that it was used only for sitting), 'aye, and a *carpet* and *bell-pull* too'. And the poet Crabbe's Farmer Ellis had 'a superior room' graced by books and prints, and his wife was 'beyond our station clad' in fashionable dresses from the town.

Yet not all farmers prospered under the new system. Small farmers seldom owned the land they cultivated and when the landlord decided to amalgamate several farms, a frequent occurrence because large estates were more suited to the new agricultural methods, the tenants were squeezed out of existence. Cobbett gives graphic accounts of what was happening in the early years of the 19th century. 'The farmhouses have been growing fewer and fewer', he writes of Windsor Forest; in Wiltshire, 'only about 8 manor houses survive from an original 50 or more'; in the parish of Burghclere in Hampshire,

> one single farmer holds by lease, under Lord Carnarvon, as one farm, the lands that men now living can remember to have formed fourteen farms. In some instances, these small farmhouses and homesteads are completely gone; in others the house is gone, leaving the barn for use as a barn or as a cattle shed; in others the outbuildings are gone, and the house, with rotten thatch, broken windows, rotten door-sills, and all threatening to fall, remains as a dwelling of a half-starved and ragged family of labourers, the grandchildren, perhaps, of the decent family of small farmers that formerly lived happily in this very house.

97 The landscape of enclosure – Haworth Moor, Yorkshire.

For the practical farmer enclosure meant that in grazing country cattle and sheep could be moved from one field to another so that they were always feeding on freshly springing grass; and in corn country the more general use of root crops and clover improved the system of rotation: instead of a bare fallow following two corn crops, two corn crops were now separated by a crop of roots and a crop of clover. The new root crops, which were planted in exact rows by Jethro Tull's drill, enabled farmers to keep more animals and to nourish them during the winter. The annual slaughter of livestock was abolished, inferior stock could be weeded out and the breeder could encourage the most desirable traits in cattle, pigs and sheep. The winter fattening process was accelerated by the discovery during the 18th century of a new protein-rich food, oilcake, a by-product of the oil-seed crushing industry.

The adjective 'improved' resounds through the abundant livestock literature of the period and the names of breeders such as Robert Bakewell, John Ellman, Mr Fowler of Rollright and the Colling brothers became famous all over the country. The lively portraiture of prize cows, bulls, pigs and sheep – pictures like James Ward's *The Durham White Ox*, John Boultbee's *Portrait of a Ram of the New Leicestershire Kind* and Thomas Bewick's *Remarkable Kyloe Ox* – testifies to the breeder's success and records the gross forms of the 'improved' animals. But they were not gross in the eyes of those who bred or those who painted them: Bewick found the principles of beauty and utility united and exalted in 'the quality of the flesh and its propensity to fatness'. In his *History of Quadrupeds* (1789) he describes the transformation of the old longhorn cattle achieved by 'the late Mr Bakewell' with the help of cows of the 'Cauley breed' produced by Mr Webster in the Trent valley, and an engraving exhibits the short spindly legs, tiny head and fat loins and quarters of the remodelled beast. Juxtaposed engravings invite us to scorn the original black-faced muscular ram of north-west Yorkshire and the old long-legged, large-headed Teeswater breed of sheep, and wax enthusiastic over the bloated, improved ram and the monster of obesity, weighing 'sixty two pounds ten ounces per quarter avoirdupois' produced by Bakewell's method. That method was crowned with signal success in the case of the Holstein or Dutch breed of cattle: an ox fed by Mr Hall of Whitley, Northumberland, weighed 187 stones, 5 pounds. Together with a small-headed, similarly 'improved' cow it gazes complacently across Bewick's page to the artist's triumphant account of the beauty of its 'fattening quality' and its early fitness for the butcher.

The new farms created out of hitherto unused waste in this adventurous period were not all by any means made at the expense of cottagers and squatters. The celebrated examples of Holkham and the neighbouring country are cases in point. Arthur Young describes north Norfolk before enclosure as 'a rabbit and rye country', a landscape of 'boundless wilds and uncultivated wastes inhabited by scarce anything but sheep'. Enclosure and the fertilizing of the sandy topsoil with the underlying marl metamorphosed this barren prospect into an incomparable vista of rich cornfields punctuated by new farmhouses and cottages. Exmoor in Devon was a treeless unpeopled expanse, though cottagers in open villages on its fringes grazed their livestock upon it. They were each given a piece of land while 10,000 acres were bought from the Crown by John Knight, a manufacturer from the Midlands, who, after an heroic struggle going on for more than thirty years, enclosed it, introduced lime to increase the fertility of the soil and established seventeen thriving farms to which he and his son gave eloquent names – Honeymead, Cloven Rocks, Wintershead, Red Deer, Tom's Hill and Larkbarrow.

There had always been such solitary farmsteads in upland grazing 62 country: Fellfoot Farm at the foot of Wrynose Pass in Westmorland is an instance. Now, with the coming of enclosure on a nationwide scale, farmhouses in predominantly corn-growing regions were also built far from the village, isolated with their cluster of outbuildings in fields where no habitation had yet been seen, for farmers needed to be close to their hedged lands where new experiments were being tried out. Odstone Farm, near Ashbury in Berkshire, is such a case: the house, with attic windows recalling the farm servants who once slept in the dormitories they lit, stands prick-eared alongside the systematically arranged barns, granaries, stables, cowbyre, piggeries and carthouses. A greater emphasis on shelter reflects the larger number of beasts that were reared and retained by the improved methods.

Another farm, at West Burton in Lincolnshire, gives a clearer image of the concentration of the Georgian farmyard and its importance. It was in the yard that the manure upon which the new farming so greatly depended was accumulated, not haphazardly in the manner of previous centuries, but scientifically. The straw from the harvest went straight into the yard; the hay and the root crops fed the animals in the stock buildings and then, out of those buildings and into the yard came the manure which, trampled into the straw by the cattle, was made ready for the fields.

The little walled front garden of the farmhouse, with its gate opening immediately from the fields onto a path leading to the main entrance, which is never used, is a special and endearing feature of 18th- and 19th-century farmsteads of the enclosures. Here the farmer's wife could grow a few flowers away from all the business of the farm going on at the rear of the house. Not that she did not have her own domain there as well, for close to the back door lived the poultry and the pigs which, feeding as they mainly did on left-overs from the house and dairy, were her special responsibility. Pigs, which had still occasionally been permitted to forage in the woods in Stuart times, were now everywhere kept in sties 'as near as may be', as Young wrote, with little runs in front of them. And so they continued to be housed until the introduction of scientifically controlled, prefabricated, mechanized and windowless fattening houses of modern industrial farming in the late 1960s.

The other and major concern of the farmer's wife was the dairy, which at the West Burton farm occupied the projection at the back of the house. The propinquity on the farm of dairy, pigs and poultry is remarked by the Suffolk author of *The Farmer's Boy*, Robert Bloomfield, whose Giles, returning from the fields, finds

98 Farmstead at West Burton, Lincolnshire.

> The clatt'ring Dairy Maid immersed in steam
> Singing and scrubbing midst her milk and cream,

and cannot hear her speak

> For pigs and ducks and turkies throng the door
> And sitting hens, for instant war prepared.

So high was the value set on the farm dairy in the Georgian period that farmers were granted exemption from the Window Tax for this room, provided that it was labelled 'DAIRY' or 'CHEESE ROOM' and barred with wood or iron. Professor Barley mentions a farmhouse at East Coker in Somerset which in 1961 still had the word 'DAIRY' painted above one of the windows.

When new farmsteads were built out in the fields, old village farmhouses and sometimes the adjacent barns were often divided into two or more cottages, a process which has already been noticed. But not all farmers found it necessary to move from the village and many farmhouses can be seen confronting the street to this day with the remnants of their barns and outhouses clustered alongside or behind them – particularly, of course, in lands of earlier enclosure. Newton Farm, at Kewstoke in Somerset, built in 1710, went on operating as a farm right up until the last decade. In the north and in Devonshire farmsteads based on the traditional long-house design were still being built in villages at the end of the 18th century, and some northern villages, such as Milburn in Westmorland, consist wholly of little farms of long-house type built in the 18th and 19th centuries.

A small farm created on the east Sussex downs some three miles from Glynde by early 19th-century Parliamentary enclosure was actually planned to be managed from a farmhouse in the village, an arrangement which endured until 1970. Furlongs was a mixed farm combining corn-growing with cattle and sheep breeding. A pair of flint cottages set at the end of a long straight track originally housed a shepherd and a cowman, while open-fronted shelter sheds, a granary and a barn were ranged about three sides of a yard at the rear. Deserted now except during the lambing season, for the modern farmworker refuses to accept either their remoteness or their primitive inconvenience, these cottages stare with their blank windows from a tangle of brambles, nettles and knobbly apple trees to the far distant gate at the end of the chalky track.

Occasionally cottages which were built before enclosure can be seen thus stranded amid fields far from a road. Such cottages accentuate the complex and intimately co-ordinated harmonies of some of Constable's paintings of the Suffolk landscape, and a pair of ochre-coloured, half-timbered, steep-roofed little houses, one thatched, the other with its former thatch replaced by tiles, rise from a meadow of flowering grasses in the shadow of ash, elm and oak at Worlingworth Green. Their isolation is as much due to the Parliamentary commissioners as that of the Glynde cottages, for they mark the edge of a former common before it was enclosed.

Even if the Glynde farmer did not move from the village, his yard out in the fields corresponded closely to the description of the standardized plans which a report issued in 1814 by the Board of Agriculture (founded twenty

years earlier through the exertions of farming landowners) assumes to be those of all farmsteads 'where improvements have taken place': 'a main body or corn barn having a tangent wing at each end for stables, cow tyes, open sheds, etc., the yard opening to the milder points, the south or the south east'. And such numbers of farmsteads of the period do conform to this plan that the statement of the Board seems on the whole justified. The quadrangular yard was not new, but it was now regularized. A fine and compact example is Manor Farm at Thornton Steward, on the borders of north and east Yorkshire. There had been a farm on the site since the early Middle Ages, but at about the time of Trafalgar much of it was rebuilt to conform to up-to-date principles. The new three-sided foldyard is of local stone with open arcaded animal shelters, a barn, hayloft and fattening house; and while it is eminently practical it is nobly proportioned and reveals a new awareness of the visual possibilities of such utilitarian buildings. A farmstead near Holme in east Yorkshire, Aggthorpe Hall Farm, though a less complete interpretation of the standard plan, is informed with a pronounced sense of design. The range incorporating the stables, a granary and hayloft, brick-built and pantiled, at once catches the eye, for it is perfectly symmetrical, marked by a tower-like central bay suggestive of Palladian influence and articulated by restrained mouldings and decorative ovals, while the openings are based on the forms of lunettes and Venetian windows.

99

100,
101

135

Similar buildings appeared fairly frequently in the recently enclosed regions of east Yorkshire and Lincolnshire, and it was natural that they should house the stables: the horse had always enjoyed rather better quarters than other farm animals and now when horses were kept not only for fieldwork but for riding and fox hunting, the sport which more than any other fired the imagination and enthusiasm of every class of countryman, stables became an important architectural feature of the great country house and were often of distinguished design on the farm. The obstacles created by enclosure in the form of hedges and ditches seem to hâve encouraged rather than deterred the huntsmen, according to William Somerville in *The Chace* (1735):

> They strain to lead the field, top the barr'd gate,
> O'er the deep ditch exulting bound and brush
> The thorny-twining hedge.

Though the farmyard at Aggthorpe Hall Farm does not quite correspond to the quadrangle of the textbooks, it does include a magnificent barn filling the range opposite the stables. It follows the traditional plan of three bays with a central door opening onto the threshing floor, and the timber roof embodies the king-post design long favoured in Yorkshire; yet the interior is more suggestive of the spirit of ancient Rome than many a grand mansion built at that time to the precepts of Vitruvius: the proportions are of antique dignity and the classical affinity is enhanced by the plain arched openings giving onto a single aisle and by the colour and texture of the reddish brown, speckled brick.

Local farmers and builders were made aware of new elements in the design of farm buildings through plans and elevations which appeared in some of the books on the latest techniques of farming which have already been mentioned. Marshall gives a full account of the steading he built on his farm near Croydon, Surrey, in 1771, with lively references to the local carpenters who carried out the work, and offers it 'as a mirror in which others may see the advantages and disadvantages of their own farmeries'. Young reproduces plans for farms and farm buildings in his *Farmer's Guide in Hiring and Stocking Farms* (1770), pointing out the necessity for ample shelter for cows, carts and implements and for a layout concentrating the farmer's labours and facilitating the effective production of the all-important dung, but also stressing the importance of attention to 'symmetry and appearance'. C. Waistell, whose *Designs for Agricultural Buildings* appeared posthumously in 1827, at the end of the period of agrarian reform, has this to say about the style of farm buildings: 'Being intended solely for the purpose of utility, they should be simple in their forms and perfectly plain . . . to utility alone everything else in agriculture must be subordinate.' Yet Waistell's plans testify as eloquently as any other product of the age to its remarkable concern for aesthetics. His ranges are perfectly symmetrical. They are often fronted with blank or open arcading in the classical style, and the upper walls of his barns and granaries are sometimes adorned with ornamental roundels and ovals. In one design a barn planned to house the threshing machine (invented by the millwright Andrew Meikle in 1786) stands high between an arcaded haystore and

100
101

Opposite
100, 101 Aggthorpe Hall Farm, near Holme, Yorkshire: stables, granary and hayloft, and interior of the barn.

identical shed for the ox-driven gear propelling the machine; it has a central arched opening framed by pilasters, with blank arches on either side. The whole composition might be part of some great house, and the plan in which it is incorporated recalls that of the Roman villa-farm.

While the simplest elements of classical design in no way conflicted with the practical purposes of farm buildings, the trimmings of the Picturesque and Gothick taste might be outrageously inappropriate. Yet such was the influence of the taste of the day that even Marshall cautiously recommended a decorative, polygonal farmyard; and Loudon, an experienced farmer as well as a sensitive artist, the author of the remodelling of Great Tew, Oxfordshire, and of its enchanting setting, suggested extravagant Italian and Gothick styles for some of the farm buildings shown in his massive *Encyclopaedia of Cottage, Farm and Villa Architecture* (1833). Other writers – for the most part architects with no connection with farming addressing themselves to aristocratic and wealthy patrons – give greater rein to fancy and conceive of the farm as a picturesque incident in a landscaped estate. In his *Fermes Ornées or Rural Improvements* of 1800, John Plaw, for instance, looks upon farm buildings as 'calculated for landscape and picturesque effects' rather than as food-producing units. He describes a farmhouse as an object to be seen from a gentleman's mansion and presents one design for 'A farmyard having the Appearance of a Monastery', an idea which the courtyard layout of the Georgian farm might quite readily suggest, though Plaw views it as a cluster of towers and turrets which, 'embosomed with stately trees, give an air of antiquity, consequence and grandeur, which would form a leading feature on an estate of considerable extent'. In his book of plans for 'Cottage Farms' (1805) Joseph Gandy mentions the traditional half-timbered building in tones of horror, as exhibiting 'all the deformities of the timbers': he includes drawings for farm buildings in a comparatively sober classical style, but they are nonetheless decorative rather than convenient. Among them is a huge circular dovecote, surmounted by a cupola and weathervane, a pleasing object but one which was unlikely to take shape on any of the new working farmsteads since pigeons were no longer indispensable for the addition of variety to the winter diet. W. Barber designed an octagonal farmyard in the Grecian manner, and Robert Lugar drew up plans for a farmhouse and farm buildings in the 'Old English Style', a picturesque version of traditional thatch and 'brick, stone or lath and plaster, as most convenient for the situation'.

Although Arthur Young saw a great ambitiously and ornamentally designed semi-circular piggery in Sussex, and at least one great landowner rejoiced in a Dairy 'in the Chinese Taste', fantasies like those of Plaw and Lugar had little impact on farm buildings. Their considerable effect on the farmhouse itself and on the cottage will be considered in the next chapter. Judging from Lugar's remarks, his picturesque plans might have been carried out by local craftsmen using local materials. But many of the designs illustrated in Loudon's *Encyclopaedia* demanded the skills of professional surveyors and engineers. This was significant for times to come, but for the moment local workmen with their traditional skills were still able to erect farm buildings that met the new requirements and to

XII

102 *Above* Granary over a cartshed, and from right to left cowhouse, stable and open-fronted shelter at Painsthorpe, Yorkshire. The materials are brick, limestone and pantiles.

103 *Below left* Barn with a hay storage loft, Little Barrington, Oxfordshire.

104 *Below right* Granary, hayloft and cowbyre at Gnaton, Devon.

translate textbook designs into their own idiom. Village craftsmen, for example, built the model fattening house for oxen which Young saw at Retford, Nottinghamshire, in 1771; and local builders in the hop-growing areas of the southern counties constructed and equipped the oast houses which were becoming more and more numerous and which changed their shape during this period from the rectangular design of Flemish origin to the circular. Flues from enclosed iron stoves rose all round the inner walls to the conical roof, discharging smoke and fumes through a chimney furnished with a pivoting cowl (at first made of wood, later of metal) painted white, shining against the sky above the pippin red of the tiled roof and brick cylinder.

It is interesting that the textbook writers either specify local materials for the realization of their designs or make no reference to the subject, taking the use of traditional resources for granted. In most districts, even when the layout of a new farm might be of the standardized pattern, the buildings themselves were scarcely distinguishable from those of the 16th and 17th centuries. Cobbett does not record any particularly modern buildings, and indeed many of the farms he saw had remained quite untouched by the improved system of farming: old-fashioned implements were still being used, threshing with the flail was the custom, and seed was sown broadcast in the biblical way. In the Cotswolds and along a great part of the limestone belt the vernacular style which had crystallized during the 17th century was preserved with only the most superficial changes, and a late 18th-century barn at Little Barrington in Gloucestershire hardly differs from those of the previous two hundred years except in the poorer quality of the roof timbers. A granite and slatestone group at Gnaton in Devon, where cowbyre and hayloft are aligned with the farmhouse although separately roofed, maintains all the traditions of the region, and shows the influence of contemporary taste only in the simple formality of the design, the ordered openings and low-pitched roof. It is the huge expansion of unbroken wall space and its wonderful texture which, unselfconsciously exploited by the village stonemason, gives such distinction to the buildings. The multi-sized pieces of granite and splinters of slatestone, softened and delicately stained by the weather, varying in tone from silver grey to moss brown, look as though held in a mesh and make a background like a deep etching for the red Devon cows in the yard and the swallows pitching up and down in their season. An 18th-century barn at Wimpole, Cambridgeshire, built of timber on a brick base with a thatched roof, discloses its date by the use of iron nuts and bolts in the carpentry, but it remains a traditional barn and is seen at once as an attenuated, aisleless version of the medieval masterpiece at Great Coxwell.

The fashion for brick, which is such a conspicuous mark of the period, is as evident in farm buildings as in farmhouses and cottages, and it is brick structures on the farm – such as those at Aggthorpe Hall – which most often display innovations in style. But again, though perhaps more neatly and conveniently ordered than they might have been a hundred years earlier, there are many groups of 18th- and early 19th-century brick-built farm buildings in which a 17th-century farmer would encounter nothing unfamiliar. Local limestone and brick are combined in such a group at

Painsthorpe, Yorkshire. The granary above the cart shed contains sufficient space for the storage of two harvests, an innovation suggested by Young, and the cowhouse adjoining it is provided with chain ties, divisions between the animals and up-to-date sloping standings; but it is as ill lit and low as the one at Hawkshead.

One new building did make its appearance on the 18th-century farmstead and might have seemed strange to a farmer of an earlier period. The threshing machine, which took the form of a drum fitted with pegs and revolving within a concave casing, was powered by steam as early as 1804 on a Norfolk farm visited by Young. This was exceptional: where it was used the threshing machine was generally horse-driven and on some farms, especially in the north, where it was known as the 'gin gang', a small circular, polygonal or occasionally rectangular building was sometimes set next to the barn door like an ecclesiastical side chapel or chapter house, to shelter the horse and the driving gear. The gin gang might be open, the king-post roof resting on stone pillars, as at Blencarn in Cumberland, or the intervals between the piers might be boarded, as in the brick and pantile example at Howden in Yorkshire. Another structure which was mentioned for the first time in the 18th century – by a Swedish traveller, Pehr Kalm, who saw an example in Hertfordshire in 1748 – was a thatched timber skeleton built out in the open fields to give protection to carts and implements. Such structures were probably traditional, for an exactly similar ephemeral shelter was constructed in Essex at Clay Wall Farm, Steeple Bumpstead, some thirty years ago with the most primitive type of flat roof formed of rough saplings laid like joists across the timber frame and heaped with straw. Another such structure at Bloys Farm in the same parish was used as storage for hay and itself looked just like a haystack. It served much the same purpose as the Dutch barn, and may have inspired that Victorian innovation; though unlike the prefabricated metallic open barn it took its place naturally in the landscape.

*　　*　　*

The urge towards symmetry and order which underlay 18th-century farmstead plans animated the design of farmhouse and cottage as strongly and in general more effectively, for the appearance of the vernacular house suffered a change as vital as that which turned the hall-house with cross-wings into a rectangular block. The façade at Toseland is an early instance of the desire to achieve a rational, balanced disposition of doors and windows, and Ufford's Hall at Fressingfield, built in the late 17th century with a central entrance and tall panelled chimneys at either end, is another. But the gabled individualism of these houses could not now be tolerated by any farmer or landowner who knew anything of fashion. The domestic front, whatever happened behind, must now be designed in the terms of a classical order, the proportions of the floors ideally conforming to those of an antique column. Through the medium of books and prints far exceeding in number those concerned with farm buildings, specifically addressed, very often, to masons, joiners, carpenters and bricklayers and published at prices within the reach of most craftsmen and farmers, this strange notion,

Opposite
XII A Picturesque porch at Great Tew, Oxfordshire, added by J.C. Loudon in the early 19th century to a 17th-century cottage of warm Cotswold stone.

105,
107

106

71

which could only have been so eagerly accepted because it corresponded to a deeply felt attitude of mind, penetrated the most remote rural areas.

Among the few books owned by Arthur Partridge, tenant farmer of Shelley Hall in west Suffolk, at the time of his death in 1789 was William Halfpenny's *Twelve Beautiful Designs for Farmhouses*. Halfpenny, who himself started out as a carpenter, was one of a stream of authors of pattern books which followed on Moxon's pioneer *Mechanick Exercise* published in 1682. Halfpenny's most popular production was *Magnum in Parvo: or The Marrow of Architecture*, a practical handbook on the classical orders which appeared in 1725; while his *Art of Sound Building* informed the local builder how to set out brick arches, niches, columns and pilasters in the Doric, Ionic, Tuscan and Corinthian styles. Isaac Ware's *Compleat Body of Architecture* (1756), dealing thoroughly with the use of the orders, with proportion and ornament and with materials, sites and foundations, must have meant uphill work for the craftsman reader of the mid-18th-century village, yet it was studied to such effect that a doorcase with an open
114 pediment and rounded fanlight shown by Ware materializes again and again, with slight variations, on farmhouse façades all over the country. Francis Price's *British Carpenter* went into four editions and then there were Batty Langley's many titles, the most widely read architectural textbooks of the time, the best known of which were probably *The City and Country Builder's and Workman's Treasury of Design* (1740) and *The Builder's Jewel* (1741). With the aid of these and many similar publications master carpenters, bricklayers and masons were inspired to produce the multitude of enchanting small symmetrical houses and cottages which enrich English country towns and English villages and grace the fields of enclosure.

Despite the dissemination over all parts of the country of pattern-book designs farmhouses and cottages were still being built in the vernacular styles. New cottages of stone and thatch in the Northamptonshire village of
108 Ashby St Ledgers sustain the tradition already established there in every detail except that they are uniform and are furnished with the simple form of the sash window which, moving sideways and thus dispensing with weights, was ideally suited to low cottage walls. In the north, as at
109 Whashton, in the North Riding of Yorkshire, one-storeyed dwellings continued to be erected according to old local usage.

Even when the orders were fully adopted by country craftsmen vernacular building had not come to an end: the new vision, at least before the spread of standardized, mass-produced materials, was absorbed into the vernacular. There is rarely anything stereotyped or academic about a farmhouse or cottage in the Georgian style. A feature taken from a pattern book invariably turns out to be more than an imitation of the model. The interpretations of the doorcase just mentioned, for instance, each bear the impress of the carpenter's individuality in the rendering of proportions, pilasters, door-head and panelling. And as long as bricks were not mechanically produced and were fashioned of local clays, their popularity constituted no more than a minor threat to the close relationship between house and soil, and extended rather than diminished the scope of the country builder. Brick and white-painted wood are the materials most
readily associated with the period; and the ways in which local craftsmen

105, 107 *Top and above* Gin gangs, housing the horse-driven gear to power a threshing machine in the barn, at Howden, Yorkshire, and Blencarn, Cumberland.

106 *Left* Roughly constructed open thatched shelter, Clay Wall Farm, Steeple Bumpstead, Essex.

108 Ashby St Ledgers,
Northamptonshire.

with the traditions of medieval carpentry and of those wonderful Tudor chimneystacks behind them translated the vocabulary of classical architecture into brick and wood are a source of delight in all the country towns and villages of south and south-east England. There was no form of classical ornament – modillions under the eaves, capitals, complicated mouldings, decorated keystones and swags of fruit – which was beyond the skill of brickworker and carpenter. The choicest refinements are generally found in houses built for the wealthier landowners and for the increased number of professional men and gentry with little connection with the land who were now living in the country; but countless smaller farmhouses either newly built or refronted in brick from the early 18th century on-wards abound in ingenious and rustic adaptions of textbook examples which reconcile a formal design and classical embellishments with their setting.

Sometimes a farmhouse design corresponds so closely to the pattern-book prototype that the effect in the landscape can be startling. The formidably plain expanse of the academically correct quoinless façade of the second half of the 18th century appears with hardly any distinguishing details at both Foulden in Norfolk and Bawdsey in Suffolk. The very name High House comments on the unexpectedness in remote farming country of a tall building of urban aspect rising through three floors: High House Farm, Bawdsey, is indeed a remarkable sight in the flat lonely fields, beside a lonelier shore, of the strip of east Suffolk between Orford Ness and the mouth of the Deben. The Foulden farm is just anchored to its foundations by the vermilion colour of its local brick and its shining pantiled roof. The wall of flint cobbles separating High House Farm from the road establishes its region. Here the touch of the local carpenter gives life to the doorhead,

96

where a small white-painted pediment sits whimsically on top of the
fanlight within the enclosing broken pediment of the doorcase; and the
sober grey-brown bricks of the front and the paler, silvery grey bricks of
the window heads were locally made. These window heads, so quiet and
unobtrusive, bear triumphant witness to the brickmaker's art, for the finely
jointed, wedge-shaped bricks have been most delicately cut and gauged to
resemble pleating.

The window heads of two-storeyed Red House Farm, Withersdale
Street, also in east Suffolk, display similar careful jointing and pleat effects
and may perhaps be the work of the same craftsman. This house, like that at
Bawdsey, consists of a new fashionable block set across the gable end of an
older farmhouse. Here the local bricks are of a clear light red with a
stronger colour for the big parapet which is dotted with vitrified headers
and half conceals the roof of pantiles. The doorway is an elongated version
of the design followed at Bawdsey; screen walls on either side of the façade,
each adorned with a pineapple and pierced by an arched opening, create an
illusion of country-house wings, while the Palladian ideal is further
brought to the notice of the passing villager by simple ball-topped piers.

At Bretforton in Worcestershire and at Much Wenlock in Shropshire,
the abrupt height of brick-fronted additions to earlier buildings and the
eccentricities of the designs attract the eye to farmhouses standing a little
distance from the road behind hayfields. At Much Wenlock a band of pallid

109 One-storeyed stone
and pantiled cottages,
Whashton, Yorkshire.

110 An older farmhouse refronted at Bretforton, Worcestershire.

111 A former hall-house transformed at Little Common, Hooe, Sussex.

stone divides the dark brick façade exactly in two, so that the upper half with its exceptionally tall side chimneys looks like a separate house which could be lifted from the ground floor and put down elsewhere. The triple windows of the ground and first floors at Bretforton and the central, arched window of the first floor are of grotesque aspect. Emphatic blocks of local masonry ray out against the brickwork, aping in stone Adam's device of fanfilling over the Venetian window but omitting the order framing the light.

For all the subtleties and oddities of handling which link them to their environment – and closer study would doubtless reveal many more localized details – the relationship between houses such as these and the traditional farmhouses and cottages of earlier centuries is distant. But when the building materials are wholly those of old tradition, a symmetrical façade and a pilastered, pedimented porch readily become part of the vernacular and of the landscape; and sometimes, when the adjustment of the old-fashioned to the modish is only partial (as it so often is in the case of houses built just before or just after 1700), the actual process of the absorption of the new by the old can be watched.

A unique transformation of the traditional into the Georgian idiom 111 occurs at Hooe in Sussex, where the front of a vernacular farmhouse was brought into line and furnished with a central, pilastered and panelled porch and a balanced arrangement of sash windows. Yet it remains un-classical: the roof of the former hall block still inclines steeply, the eaves line is not continuous, and the former cross-wings are marked by a rise in the height of the modish parapet. White-painted woodwork conspicuously outlines the whole composition, and a complete covering of the timber frame above the brick base with russet tiles accentuates the individuality of this encounter and fusion of the old and the new.

112 At Slough Farm, Acton, Suffolk, a cross-wing has been left in position and fashionable alteration has been concentrated on the former hall block. It has been extended at the front to form a new two-storeyed house with a balanced façade. At the rear the roof still slopes at its original steep angle

and with the jutting cross-wing covers the kitchen, dairy and former brewhouse. The profile is one which is met with again and again in both farmhouse and cottage. This was one way in which the rural builder could adjust the foursquare plan of the pattern books to the traditional farmhouse: the outshot was made as wide as the main rooms and consisted of two service rooms, while in front were the hall and parlour. Even when the farmhouse conforms outwardly to the foursquare plan and looks as though it might be the very replica of Barton Cottage as described by Jane Austen within, it may well have come by this shape in the course of the natural development of the vernacular plan: the sloping extension at the rear may have been raised to the height of the front in answer to the continual and general desire for more and improved accommodation. This is indeed what seems to have happened at Moat Farm, Great Tey, Essex, which stands on a long inhabited site, for the large external chimneystack serves only the front half of the house.

The characteristic 'double-pile' (two-rooms deep) plan of the Georgian house does occur rather more frequently that I seem to have suggested, though it is usually found in much larger and grander farmhouses than humble Great Tey, and the instances are often Victorian. Professor Barley saw examples of the Hanoverian period in Nottinghamshire, and the houses at Odstone and West Burton described earlier incorporate the plan.

Moat Farm, timber-framed and washed pale ochre, and Slough Farm, which differs from the traditional Office Farm at Methwold only in the height and symmetrical arrangement of its front wall, could not be anywhere but in East Anglia. At Stoke-by-Clare a more imposing but equally eloquent example of the Georgian style in Suffolk dress blandly regards the fields of which it is the focus. With walls of small, glistening flints, both rough and knapped, with yellow brick quoins and window heads, a parapet of variegated yellow brick, brick stringcourses and vertical rows of alternating single headers and stretchers marking the bays and flanking the windows, Flint House quaintly suggests the elements of Palladian articulation in two dimensions.

112 A new symmetrical front added to an old timber-framed and flint farmhouse at Acton, Suffolk. The projections on either side of the chimneystack contain a bread oven and a side oven.

113 The Georgian style in local flint dress at Stoke-by-Clare, Suffolk.

IX

98

112
56

113

Timber-framed, clapboarded cottages have already been encountered. In Essex, east Hertfordshire and Kent, where the half-timbered style had flourished with exceptional vigour, timber frames were still popular even though often now of imported deal. They assumed the current rectangular shape with studs closely set to carry an outer covering of weatherboarding, plaster or tiles. The translation of the Georgian style into any of these mediums enhances the intimate, homely character of the traditional idiom and invests both farmhouse and cottage with a toy-like charm. But when symmetry is manifest in an overdress completely of wood the resulting doll's house is always irresistible, whether it be faded and neglected with bow windows on either side of a correctly proportioned and elaborate door emerging from a thicket of bay and berberis, brambles and convolvulus, as

114 at Goudhurst; whether the carpenter has exaggerated the element of make-believe by curiously grooving the weatherboarding to simulate stone, as on a farm façade at Tenterden; or whether it stands precariously, its single lateral chimney only just balanced by an outshot on the opposite side, as at Cranbrook, or sits firmly and trimly at the end of a garden path, its white paint and horizontal lines set off by a blaze of flowers and the glowing red of

115 chimneystacks and roof tiles, as at Sissinghurst.

The classical influence in cottages such as these last two is no more than skin deep. The builders of many a humble cottage and many a modest farmhouse came no nearer to pattern-book examples of the Georgian style than the creation of an impression of symmetry, combined with a rustic version of the sash window and the merest attempt at a classical doorcase.

IX The carpenter at Great Tey was content with just the suggestion of a simple pediment. At Poynton Green in Shropshire, the square panels of the traditional black-and-white house of the district take a reluctantly

rectangular, balanced shape with a central porch on spiralling supports
116 more suited to a four-poster bed than a door. A stone cottage at Arncliffe
and a stone farmhouse near Thackholme, both in Yorkshire, a slate-stone
mill house at Lerryn, Cornwall, for all that it rises through three floors, and
the farms and cottages on the green at Ravensworth, again in Yorkshire, all
speak the language of their region far more distinctly than the vocabulary
of Palladianism.

Where the long-house was indigenous the farmer's quarters might now
exhibit an orderly disposition of door and windows in an otherwise
scarcely changed exterior, as at Milburn in Westmorland, or in Cornwall at
a farm near the Fowey River and in a farmstead of slate-hung cob at
117 Warbstow, where the shippen later became part of the house.

Not only is the rendering of the classical ideal delightfully eccentric and
sketchy on the façades of innumerable farmhouses and cottages but very
116 often the door is not precisely in the middle. At Arncliffe and Poynton
Green, in some of the cottages at Ravensworth and in a refronted former
farmhouse at Cranbrook, the entrance only approximates to the central
position. The door of a cottage at Manningtree is directly in line with the
chimney, which remained in its traditional position when the façade was
Georgianized, and just inside the door is a small lobby set against the jamb
of the fireplace, an arrangement frequently found in plans deriving from
the hall-house and of course controlling the position of the door. At
Cranbrook and Arncliffe, where the chimneys are at the gable ends, placed
thus to leave ample room for the staircase, as was normal in houses of two
or more storeys built after the beginning of the 18th century, the door has
been pushed considerably to one side to give greater length to the parlour,
and this disposition also harks back to the hall-house plan. At Cranbrook
the parlour opens from a passage (now called the hall) which preserves the
position of the old screens passage, while at Arncliffe the front door leads
directly into a corner of the kitchen. At Poynton Green the plan, though
not quite symmetrical, is of the foursquare type with four rooms on each of
the two floors, the front two on the ground floor consisting of the living
room to the right and the little-used parlour to the left, the kitchen and
former dairy at the rear with the staircase between them.

Our knowledge of the appearance of farmhouses and cottages from
about 1700 onwards is augmented by pictures and prints and also by the
reports of the many travellers encouraged by the improvements of roads
and waterways. Between the accession of Queen Anne and 1750 more than
four hundred Road Acts were passed and during the second half of the 18th
century more than sixteen hundred were passed. Travellers less well known
than Marshall, Young and Cobbett, among them Charles Vancouver who
wrote of Hampshire farms, William Stevenson who journeyed through
Dorset, William James and Charles Malcolm who wrote memoirs of a tour
in Sussex, Alexander Dennis who gives an illuminating account of rural life
in Devonshire, John Bailey who recorded what he saw in Durham, and
William Hutchinson who kept a diary of his experiences in the north,
confirm the evidence provided by surviving farmhouses and cottages that
traditional materials were everywhere being used despite the widespread
infiltration of brick and the substitution in some areas of tiles for thatch.

Opposite
116 Local tradition –
stone slates, walls of
rough mountain stone,
the house distinguished
from its outbuildings by a
coat of whitewash – is
stronger in this little
farmstead at Arncliffe,
Yorkshire, than Georgian
influence.

117 A converted long-
house of cob, slate-hung,
at Warbstow, Cornwall.
The upper window on the
left was once the opening
into a hayloft.

Such writers sometimes give glimpses of internal structure too, which add background detail to the information provided by probate inventories. John Bailey saw single-storeyed cottages in Durham which exactly resembled those at Whashton mentioned earlier; they generally consisted of but one room measuring about 15 by 16 feet in which the cottager and his family lived, while another smaller room housed a cow, tools and coal. New stone cottages in Northamptonshire are praised by William Marshall for their large living rooms and two bedrooms. Earth and brick floors were common in the Midlands and over much of the south-east; stone-flagged floors were encountered in the north, the south-west and the Cotswolds. Dennis saw floors of cobblestones in Devon kitchens and dairies as well as floors of plaster which were made from lime, coal ashes, loamy clay and horse dung. Pehr Kalm speaks of upper floors in the farmhouses of Essex and Hertfordshire constructed of imported deal. Farmhouse parlours in many districts were boarded with oak or elm. Walls in larger farmhouses, like The Grange, Yattendon, might be panelled, or wainscotted, but in general they were limewashed. Wall-paintings and wall-cloths were no longer fashionable, and although colour-printed wallpapers were available from the mid 18th century only the richest farmers hung them in their parlours. But Crabbe's Farmer Ellis, it will be remembered, furnished his walls with prints, and framed paintings sometimes appeared in the homes of well-to-do farmers. Theophilus Lingard of Writtle, who died in 1744, had two pictures in his parlour and twenty prints in frames on the stairs. Gilpin saw prints on cottage walls in 1777 and observed that some cottagers had pasted 'ballads on the wall with good effect'.

The fashionable dalliance with the Rococo in great houses and town mansions, a well-controlled reaction against the severe regularity of the orders, had little influence on farmhouse- interiors, though the extraordinary instance of its introduction into the modest farmhouse at Belton, Suffolk, known as Browston Hall must not be overlooked. A wholly unpretentious exterior conceals a riot of scrolly and free figurative plasterwork. A huge eagle hovers uncertainly above the staircase and in the parlour a sun face beams from the midst of symbolic representations of the Four Ages of Woman, strong featured heads in medallions, and above a unique, shallow relief of wonderful spontaneity shows a shepherdess and her swain, lovers trysting, and a man and woman standing on a promontory in a high wind gazing across a river to a little mill, while at the top of the picture a pennon waves from a towered house.

Several travellers noticed stores of coal in both farmhouse and cottage. Thomas Pennant remarked in 1782 that because of the development of canals and the deepening of navigable rivers 'places which rarely knew the use of coal are plentifully supplied with that essential article'. The effects of Theophilus Lingard almost forty years earlier already included 'coal racks, a pair of iron cheeks, fender, shovel, tongs and poker'. The new fuel supplemented the traditional farmhouse and cottage faggots, logs, furze and turf; and where coal was used dog grates (with dogs, firebacks and bars all united), and occasionally the elegant basket of polished steel, replaced the open fireplace with its firedogs; and later on the dog grates gave way to fixed cast-iron grates which filled the whole of the recess and assumed a

variety of forms. The famous Carron Foundry, with extensive warehouses in London as well as in Scotland, opened in 1759 and was soon followed by foundries in Glasgow, Birmingham and Manchester; and standardized grates, stoves, fenders and ironmongery of all kinds slowly found their way into country homes from the last quarter of the 18th century onwards. A local craftsman would occasionally create his own version of one of the fashionable grates: the best bedroom at Harthill Hall Farm, Alport, is furnished with a pleasingly crude imitation of the double ogee hob grate with cheeks made of roughly hewn stone.

But in a great many unassuming farmhouses and most cottages, as inventory lists of fireside implements and accessories show, the fire was still laid on the open hearth, and firedogs, firebacks, chimney cranes, iron pots, skillets and pipkins were as prominent as ever they were. Some hearths were furnished with floors of iron plates raised on brickwork at each side to leave an open space under the hottest part of the fire, which could be used for baking and for keeping food hot. Such an arrangement was still in daily use in the kitchen of Frog's Hall, a farm near Biddenden, Kent, in 1953. Dr Pococke in his *Travels through England* (1750) says that in the West Country bread was baked under an earthenware pot placed on top of the iron plate.

118 Rococo plasterwork of the parlour ceiling in Browston Hall, Belton, Suffolk.

156

119

The parlour fireplace of the grander farmhouse might be a Palladian composition with an opening framed in a classical order and with the cornice exaggerated to form a mantelshelf. It might well be the work of the village carpenter or mason working with the aid of a pattern book, but by the end of the reign of George III it was more often than not ordered from London or from the county town. The two-storeyed compositions seen in the houses of landowners, professional men and gentry living in the country – the 'continuous chimneypieces' such as those at Langleys at Great Waltham or Peckover House at Wisbech – seldom grace the tenant farmhouse. The chimneypiece most generally found in farmhouse parlours had side pilasters with consoles under the cornice like the one in the present drawing room at Newbourn Hall, Suffolk. Varied by individual details and enrichments, it remained popular throughout the 18th century and for most of the 19th. The rustic cottage version, which persisted until well into the present century, was a tall, plain rectangular opening with a mantelshelf supported by stout consoles or brackets. The chimneypiece of Mrs

153 Holman's cottage at Crewkerne represents a design which had been repeated with little diversity in cottage after cottage all over the country for almost two centuries. Just below the mantelshelf there usually hung, on a rod, a valence to increase the draught. Theophilus Lingard owned such a rod and valence, and valences are shown in 18th-century paintings of cottage interiors – in Morland's *Cottage Fireside*, for instance. The valence was still commonly seen in cottage homes of the mid-20th century, and Mrs

120 Tye's living room at Little Barrington displays a freshly laundered one of faded pale blue rep.

We have already come across some of the books of Arthur Partridge, a Suffolk farmer. Just as the fine libraries of the great country houses and the modest libraries of country gentlemen like Jane Austen's Mr Bennet testified to the remarkable literary civilization of Hanoverian England, so the books owned by many tenant farmers bear witness to a vigorous interest in reading. In addition to Halfpenny's volume of farmhouse designs, Partridge owned Foxe's *Book of Martyrs*, Gerard's *Herbal* of 1579, the *Spectacle de la Nature*, *The Guardian* in two volumes, several historical works, and the '*Dictionarium Rusticum and Urbanicum*', a farming and household encyclopaedia published in 1704. An Essex farmer of Great Wigborough who died at the end of the 18th century left historical, topographical and technical books together with an English dictionary, the Bible and *Tristram Shandy*.

Judging from inventories very little of the fine and lighter mahogany furniture we associate with the Georgian period found its way into the farmhouse and cottage. But the remarkable number of pieces, especially chairs of the late 18th and early 19th centuries, which have survived show with what zest and humour and originality and with what piquant touches of personality the village cabinetmaker interpreted the achievements of the great furniture designers, again from pattern books, in elm, beech and oak. His chairs prance, stamp or stand sturdily and heavily inert with hearts or flowers cut out of their splats; their backs may turn into ribbon fretting (catching the spirit but never the letter of Chippendale), or they may be adorned with twisted plaiting emulating in wood the straw plaiting of the

119 *Below* The hearth in the living room at Frog's Hall, Biddenden, Kent.

120 *Right* Mrs Tye in her living room, Little Barrington, Oxfordshire.

corn dolly maker. Ladder-back and spindle-back chairs were the country craftsman's particular invention, and of these there were endless individual varieties. Theophilus Lingard owned six such chairs, as well as a 'cane couch and squab'. The chair seats were of the same rustic rushes which were still the principal source of light in farmhouse and cottage, as they had been in Tudor times. Traditional iron rushlight holders occur as frequently in 18th-century inventories as tea kettles and teapots. Tea, brought to England by the East India Company, was drunk in large quantities by all classes, and even John Piper, a pauper of Bottisham, Cambridgeshire, whose goods were listed when he asked for poor relief in 1782, owned two teapots and a tea kettle.

Theophilus Lingard also included amongst his possessions a piece of furniture which is not mentioned in inventories of earlier than 18th-century date – the farmhouse dresser. It stood in his pantry where it was resplendent with fifty-five pieces of 'Delph and earthenware', sixteen pewter plates and two small dishes. The dresser in its early form was a long narrow table with drawers upon which food was 'dressed' for the pot, and had only recently developed into a feature fitted with drawers and cupboards below and with shelves above it displaying plates and dishes.

5

Rustic Homes for Rural Labourers

THE ORIGINAL LIVING QUARTERS of the little long-house at Warbstow 117
visited in the last chapter are lit not by sash windows but by casements with
pointed lights in the Gothic style. Venetian windows with ogee-shaped
central lights and a straight-headed porch on spiralling posts invest an
ochre-coloured, timber-framed farmhouse near Portchester, Hampshire,
with exotic charm and piquancy. A porch at Bibury, Gloucestershire, of 125
grey limestone mottled with black-spotted raw siena coloured lichen, set
on Ionic columns with a scrolling ogee pediment adorned with delicately
carved paterae and with the name 'IVY COTTAGE' in rustic lettering, brings a
breath of the enchanted palaces of Thomas and William Daniell's *Oriental
Scenery* to this Cotswold village. At Wylye, Wiltshire, a jaunty little stone 123
front sports upper bull's eyes ingeniously made from cart wheels and
pointed openings like the tops of lancets on either side of a Gothic door
shaded by a pert canopy. Not even an ugly cement rendering can destroy
the alert, cheerful air imparted to the long plain façade of a pebble and
pantiled cottage at Knapton, Norfolk, by five identical small pointed 124
windows widely and symmetrically disposed above and on either side of a
pointed door with Gothic panels. Huge cusped and pointed windows
overwhelm the diminutive front of Chapel Cottage at West Bradley,
Somerset, and, with the crocketted panel carved with a Paschal Lamb over
the door, parody the medieval domestic style, conspicuous in this area,
favoured by Abbot Selwood. At Court Farm, Damerham, in Hampshire, 122
actual 14th-century stone-mullioned windows look irrationally from a
balanced, pedimented façade.

These and countless other spirited, unselfconscious rural echoes of
Horace Walpole's Strawberry Hill Gothic, perhaps in some instances
sparked off by a pattern book (for several of the writers who instructed
country craftsmen in the art of Palladian design included in their manuals
examples in the Gothic style), constitute no more of a threat to the
vernacular tradition than the wholly classical composition. Village builders
responded with energy and wit to the fashionable demand for a mimic
revival of the style which had first nourished their traditional skills. Their
approach to both Gothic trappings and medieval fragments was as
spontaneous, untrammelled and confident as that of the Yorkshire farmer
who built a severely classical house at the end of the ruined arcade of
Coverham Abbey, which happened to stand on his land, and set Purbeck
marble effigies of cross-legged knights in alarming, upright positions in the
farmyard wall. Earlier in these pages it was suggested that the symmetrical
square or rectangular farmhouse might be seen as a natural development of

Opposite
121 Milton Abbas,
Dorset, a planned
Picturesque village of
local cob and thatch set in
a contrived landscape (see
p. 170).

122 *Above left* Court Farm, Damerham, Hampshire. 123 *Above right* Wylye, Wiltshire.
124 *Below* Knapton, Norfolk. 125 *Opposite* Bibury, Gloucestershire.

the hall-house plan, and so long as local materials were used ties with the past and with place were strong enough to withstand the addition of a few mock Gothic ornaments. The hint of artificiality they bring with them is all the more attractive because it speaks the language of *Northanger Abbey*, the authentic language still of 18th-century sanity and moderation.

The real danger to vernacular tradition as well as to classical form rose from the absorption of the taste for the Gothic into the cult of the Picturesque. The cottage at Chippenham in Wiltshire, once rural, called Bagatelle, exhales a suspicion of what this might mean. The rough dark limestone of its walls, laid with the minimum of mortar, the pallor of the deliberately rudimentary stone porch and large-scale Gothic details magnify the effect of its Lilliputian size. Almost as fantastic a play upon the traditional image of the cottage and outshot as the folly Convent-in-the-Wood at Stourhead, it is as consciously rustic, a cottage conforming to an unreal dream of rural life.

Just such a stage-like view of rusticity, though generally more inflated than this, determines the appearance of all those circular, square, rectangular or polygonal, extravagantly thatched miniature cottages and occasional farmhouses, some with ostentatiously rustic porches, others with flamboyant bargeboards or with wide eaves held up by slender columns, which embellish park scenery and roadsides in every part of England. Neat, irresistibly pretty compositions such as the rectory 126 farmhouse at Winterborne Came in Dorset, with its tall thatched roof and pannier-shaped thatched verandahs; the beguiling little lodge at Wantisden, Suffolk, a single low storey topped by tea-cosy thatch gathered into a tall central chimney and with a pointed door in the middle of its tiny 127 front; a minute thatched and plastered hexagon at Finchingfield in Essex, with black-painted hoodmoulds above the porch door and Gothic lattices, prototype of the pottery cottages made a little later in Staffordshire; the

128 Lodge, Stratton Park, Hampshire.

lodge at Mendham, Suffolk, with three dwarf bays divided by fragments of columns from Mendham Priory and with a big finial sprouting from its central gable – they are all enchanting, but about them, however faintly, clings that air of reverie and escapism present also in much of the literature of the period, which was eventually utterly to pervade and destroy the vernacular tradition.

The dwellings I have just mentioned are carried out in local materials – Winterborne Came in Dorset cob and thatch, the Wantisden and Mendham lodges in flint, the Finchingfield hexagon in plaster over a timber frame – but they are not so much the village craftsman's version of a fashionable novelty as the correct realization of a drawing or plan by a professional designer, like those published in W.F. Pocock's *Architectural Designs for Rustic Cottages, Picturesque Dwellings, etc.* (1807) or in Charles Middleton's *Picturesque and Architectural Views for Cottages, Farmhouses, Villas, etc.* (1802). A lodge at Hainton, Lincolnshire, built of brick with a roof of the Welsh slates which the new canals were bringing to many inland counties by the end of the 18th century, exactly corresponds to a model cottage shown in Loudon's *Encyclopaedia*, of which he says: 'Though no marked features of any style appear in this elevation, yet it must be acknowledged to exhibit something more than the mere expression of purpose; because it would be equally, and to all appearance, as much a human dwelling, without the columns as with them.' There could hardly be a conception more removed from that which animated the cottages and farmhouses briefly described at the beginning of this chapter. The lodge unites classical and Tudor elements with remotely oriental overtones. The very way in which the slates are laid is as much an affront to local tradition as their origin, for instead of being arranged in diminishing courses they are all the same size, the exact number having been calculated and ordered through an agent from the distant Welsh quarries.

129 The Tattingstone
Wonder – cottages
masquerading as a church,
at Tattingstone, Suffolk,
1760 – seen from the rear.

The cast-iron casements at Winterborne Came, delightfully decorative
though they are, represent a similar alien intrusion in the rural craftsman's domain, for they were mass-produced. Their counterparts and
innumerable variations on the theme can be seen everywhere in buildings
of widely different 19th-century dates, for instance in rows of cottages at
Horsham, Sussex; Hawley, Hampshire; Calmsden, Gloucestershire (in the
windows of otherwise typical Cotswold cottages); and in the Victorian
brick lodge at Stratton Park, Hampshire, where the startling whiteness of
the window filigree is matched by that of vigorously looping and
undulating bargeboards and prominent finials, while roughcast quoins
stripe every projection including those of a shallow, hugely castellated bay
window. Arresting, aggressive even, this outlandishly patterned, fancy-
dress cottage bears high-spirited witness to the opposition between the
Picturesque and the traditional and has as little connection with its setting
as the lodge at Hainton. As the Rev. Samuel Jackson Pratt exclaimed in his
Cottage Pictures, as early as 1790,

128

> Farmhouse and farm too are in deep disgrace
> 'Tis now the lodge, the cottage and the place!
> Or if a farm, ferme ornée is the phrase
> And if a cottage, of these modern days
> Expect no more to see the straw built shed
> But a fantastic villa in its stead.

But Picturesque architecture could go to greater lengths than this. The
furniture of the landscape garden, the sham ruins and the follies, moved out
into the surrounding countryside to form part of pictorial compositions

which extended far beyond the domain of the big house. Tenants of Squire White at Tattingstone, Suffolk, were housed in three cottages disguised as a 129 church tower and nave; a Gloucestershire cottager at Cerney Wick was given a round tower pierced by Gothic lights; a cottage covered with bark was considered suitable for a forester; the new toll cottages, usually round or polygonal, sometimes took the form of toy castles, like the fat little fortress, white with a black outline, which once transfigured the main road near Hungerford in Berkshire; and it was thought appropriate that the door of the village smithy should be framed in a giant horseshoe, as it is at Tinwell, Leicestershire (though the smithy has now become the post office).

The most practical men were not immune from the prevailing craze for ruins and for the sublime and fearful aspects of Nature. Arthur Young, that passionate advocate of agricultural reform, so eager when touring Britain to point out the merits of enclosure and the benefits of the latest methods of fertilizing the land and breeding livestock, describes Duncombe Park in Yorkshire and the ruins of nearby Rievaulx Abbey in terms worthy of that apostle of the Picturesque, Dr Gilpin. He cares nothing for the style or detail or even the history of the ruins but with a shiver of delight extols 'the broken, rugged and terrible' aspects of the remains 'half seen from a distance, for thus the imagination has a free space to range in, and sketches ruins in idea far beyond the boldest stroke of reality'. It was a Surrey farmer who, according to an *Essay on Design in Gardening* by George Mason, had

130 Cinder Hall, Little Walden, Essex.

131 Detail of the sham ruin masking the front of The Jungle, Eagle, Lincolnshire.

132 Random carstone at Wells, Norfolk.

first thought of making his domain part of an 'Elysian scene'. In about 1768 Philip Southcote enclosed his farmstead at Chertsey and the surrounding meadows and cornfields with a belt of trees in which he established a menagerie and built a Gothic temple. Fifty years later, when enthusiasm for the Picturesque had become frenzy, another farmer, Samuel Russell Collett, who also had a menagerie and for this reason called his farm The Jungle, turned his Georgian house at Eagle, Lincolnshire, into the 131 semblance of a fantastic, rugged Gothic ruin merging into the landscape and achieving just that vague, indeterminate character which Young admired. The true front of the farmhouse is entirely masked by a castle disguise with a square tower at one end, a semi-circular turret at the other and a bastion-like projection in the middle. But it is a castle in the process of dissolution: its outlines are blurred by the gnarled confusion of the masonry, the roughness of purple-red bricks and huge clinkers laid this way and that in wild disorder, and by the clutching arborescence of ancient ivy, scarcely distinguishable from the curving oak boughs from which the openings, crudely and uncertainly Gothic, are fashioned. Another 130 farmhouse, one front of which masquerades as a corbel-turreted castellated tower house, exhibits the same predilection for rough unconventional materials. It confronts the road near Little Walden, Essex, its flint and brick façade electrifying the landscape with a dazzling display of fleur-de-lys and pendant lozenge and ball shapes, mock machicolations and quoins, all carried out in black clinker on a silvery flint ground, and a clinker frieze decorated with squares and diamonds outlined in pebbles. The Jungle and Cinder Hall belong to the world of folly and fairy tale, and 132 so does a tiny cottage at Wells-next-the-Sea in Norfolk: its carstone fabric is in mad disarray and the absence of a balancing window on the ground floor of a near symmetrical façade gives singular edge to the voice of unreason.

Conceits such as these sprang from an attitude very different from that which gave rise to Slough Farm at Acton or High House at Bawdsey. '*Je sens donc je suis*' had taken the place of '*Cogito ergo sum*'; and the cultivated sensibility for Picturesque effects was allied to a new and fashionable interest in rustic life and in the cottager as well as the cottage. The cottager's humble dwelling was the inspiration for the rural retreats from the hurry of town life which, as the architect Edmund Bartell observed in 1804, made 'pleasing objects in the landscape'. Like his cottage the cottager himself represented that earlier, simpler form of existence in which it was believed true happiness lay. A series of treatises, poems, novels and plays exalted the natural over the civilized man, the primitive over the sophisticated, the rustic over the urban. Cowper celebrated the health and wholesomeness which dwelt among the poor; Wordsworth preferred the homely truths of children and rustics to the utterances of philosophers; Thomas Day and Mrs Inchbald found virtue in the cottage, vice in the palace; Nathaniel Kent, author of one of the earliest pattern books to include plans for farm labourers' cottages (*Hints to Gentlemen of Landed Property*, 1775), thought that 'cottagers are indisputably the most beneficient race of people we have'.

Views such as these, disastrously mistaken though they have proved to be, were sometimes, of course, associated with dismay at the actual conditions in which many cottagers were living. John Wood the Younger of Bath recoiled with horror at some of the sights he encountered in Somerset in 1792 – 'shattered, dirty, inconvenient, miserable hovels, scarcely affording a shelter fit for the beasts of the forest'; and Thomas Davis, the steward at Longleat in Wiltshire, in a pamphlet about the housing of farm labourers addressed to 'the Landholders of this Kingdom' and published in 1795, protests that 'Humanity shudders at the idea of the industrious labourer with a wife and five or six children being obliged to live or rather exist, in a wretched, damp, gloomy room of 10 or 12 ft. square, and without a floor; but common decency must revolt at considering that over this wretched apartment there is only one chamber to hold all the miserable beds of the miserable family.'

But if benevolence prompted the building of some of the many new cottages dating from the period of agrarian revolution onwards, there were other motives quite apart from the widely enjoyed pleasure of indulging in the Picturesque for emotional and aesthetic reasons. The landlords of enclosed fields, particularly when several farmsteads had been amalgamated, were unable to get labour without providing cottages for the married men. The desired 'closed' parish, where no Poor Rates could be levied forcing landowners to support the local poor, could sometimes be created by building a new village with exactly the required number of cottages. In the 'open' villages parish officials were putting up cottages of the cheapest local material, like those seen at Whashton, while squatters continued to live in ephemeral huts they had built themselves or to occupy makeshift homes in derelict buildings. H. P. Wyndham, one of the stream of late 18th-century topographical writers, saw a number of families living wretchedly in the stables of a house at Seagrove on the Isle of Wight which had never been completed. The cottagers in the 'closed' village might live

133 Model cottages in the village of Houghton, Norfolk, 1729.

rent-free but they were entirely in the hands of the landlord. 'They've allus got to do just what they be told, or out they goes, neck and crop, bag and baggage' – as, a century later, Flora Thompson heard the labourers of Lark Rise, an open hamlet in Oxfordshire, say disparagingly of those who lived in estate cottages.

133   The very idea of the planned village is a negation of traditional development. One of the first to be built, Houghton, designed for Sir Robert Walpole's tenants in 1729 perhaps by his agent and built by the men employed in the estate yard, has as little connection with the typical Norfolk village as the ubiquitous group of modern council houses. Rows of austere paired cottages line the road leading up to Houghton Hall. At its gates stand two farmhouses, one with a raised, pedimented central bay, and a row of one-storeyed almshouses. All the buildings are of whitewashed brick, tenuously linked to their setting only by their pantiled roofs. The pairs of cottages, which are not always identical but which together make up a square plan, bear no relation to traditional paired cottages; and except that, because of their early date, they have no Picturesque trappings, they prefigure the suburban semi-detached convention. But with their large gardens and well-proportioned, if small, rooms, they provided cottagers with homes which beside such miserable hovels as those seen by Wood and Thomas Davis must have seemed utopian. They were a good deal better even than some of the romantic cottages built later as rustic landscape ornaments: one of the lodges at Audley End in Essex, of brick with pretty flint panels, a Gothic porch and a fine, ornate Tudor chimney, consisted of but two minute ground-floor rooms, one of which contained the stair, and one upper room – and it was the home of a family of six.

Yet though the accommodation might sometimes be excellent the 18th-century planned village, designed by a well-known architect for a landlord with aesthetic interests but not much feeling for the vernacular, was not always congenial to the cottagers and could diverge more widely from the evolutionary path of rural building than Houghton. A traveller passing through Lowther, Westmorland, in 1802 described it as half empty and neglected, and it was as desolate more than a hundred and fifty years later. Designed for Lord Lonsdale perhaps by James Adam, it is based on 18th-century urban concepts and was to have taken the form of Greek crosses opening from either end of a circus. The village was never completed: today a crescent of one-storeyed dwellings flanked by two-storeyed houses, and one side of one of the Greek crosses made up of one- and two-storeyed cottages, stand bleakly in open, remote country. Not even the use of local stone for walls and roof can bring them into harmony with the older farm buildings and cottages of the region. Harewood in Yorkshire, planned as a terraced street leading up to the park gates of Harewood House by John Carr of York for Edwin Lascelles at about the same time as Lowther village, presents a similarly urban, alien face to its surroundings, a beautiful ridge of country above the Wharfe.

Ripley, also in Yorkshire, begun in 1827 but completed only in 1854, affords as great a contrast to the truly vernacular theme. The texture of the terraced cottages is rougher than at Harewood. Some of them are gabled, and the windows are filled with Gothic lights and surmounted by Tudor dripmoulds, introducing a light touch of fantasy to the strictly ordered layout which is confirmed by the mock medieval cross in the middle of the little square to which the terraced street leads. It is a toy theatre image despite the robust character of the cottages, and a toy theatre town rather than a village. Then suddenly with the intrusion into the street in 1854 of the extraordinarily inappropriate town hall gentle dalliance with Gothic trimmings explodes into heavy Picturesque caprice. With its ornate stepped gables and finial-chimney, its battlemented turret and buttressed bay and huge mock Perpendicular windows, the town hall dominates the village and imbues it with that unreal atmosphere so often engendered by the Picturesque attitude.

The planned village offered such obvious opportunities to the amateur of the rustic and the Picturesque that it is surprising to find one such village at least which is not an architectural exercise and where rusticity is not emphasized, the Picturesque is not consciously sought and tradition is upheld. Blanchland, Northumberland, built on the site of an abbey in the mid-18th century by the trustees of the Crewe estate, about whom little is known, follows the ancient pattern of many villages in the eastern coastal counties above the Thames, for it consists of an open space with the cottages built in terraces about its perimeter – just as the Anglo-Saxon settlers built their dwellings close together about such a space as the best means of defence in a region vulnerable to attack. The professional architect had nothing to do with Blanchland. The cottages, of roughly hewn big blocks of sandstone from the Fells, were built by village masons. They are not identical, and fragments of the monastery fabric appear in some of the walls, or in the structure of a door or a window; now and then the remains are more than fragments, and a mysterious stone recess or a curious passage may give a Gothic air to a little interior, though never with a hint of sophisticated contrivance. Seen from afar the village, lying in a wooded fold of the high moors, sinks into the natural landscape, wholly at one with it. Audley End village too, a row of plastered timber-framed dormered cottages with an irregular roof line, proclaims the idiom of its region, Essex, with no more than a suspicion of conscious striving after Picturesque effects.

121   The case of Milton Abbas in Dorset is different. The cottages – perhaps designed by the great Sir William Chambers, who remodelled the Abbey – take the same semi-detached form as those at Houghton, though they are much smaller: each contains only four rooms. The pairs are set like the Houghton cottages in straight rows in a disciplined rhythm not found in traditional villages, though the cob and thatch of which they are fashioned does relate them to the soil. But what distinguishes this village from Houghton or Blanchland, Ripley or Lowther is that it has been imagined and planned as part of an artificially created landscape composition. Milton Abbas was so sited by Capability Brown for Joseph Damer, later Earl of Dorchester, that together with the perfectly placed lake and the carefully planted valley and enveloping hills it made a living picture. The cottagers, like the inhabitants of other planned villages, Nuneham Courtenay in Oxfordshire, for instance, and Wimpole in Cambridgeshire, had been moved from their original homes in the interests both of Picturesque layout and the creation of a closed village.

At Great Tew, as I have already mentioned, Loudon successfully fused the old and the new, traditional and planned rusticity in a design which perfectly realizes Sir Uvedale Price's formula for the Picturesque village: it is characterized by variety in outline and texture, the cottages are scattered about little irregular greens on an uneven terrain, the colour of the Cotswold stone is just 'of that rich, mellow, harmonious kind so much

XII enjoyed by painters', climbing plants twine about porches and flourish in warm angles and crannies, and the whole composition is brought into deep luxuriant harmony by tree planting. It is the forest of giant evergreens and great chestnuts crowding the sloping site, plunging the village into verdant shade, which more than the delicately Picturesque details – the two-storeyed porch with a Gothic arch and curvilinear bargeboards added to a 17th-century cottage, the hooded, latticed casements, the sinuous eaves line of steep thatch – gives substance to the sense that Great Tew is a lost domain into which one has stumbled by chance, hardly of the same world as nearby Nether Worton or Sandford St Martin. Loudon's village, like his *Encyclopaedia*, when considered in relation to his other manifold interests and activities, is as revealing of the power of contemporary taste as Arthur Young's transports over Picturesque scenery. At the time, 1809, Loudon was managing the estate of Great Tew Park and setting up an experimental farm on the most advanced scientific lines. If when entering Loudon's village we are aware of contrivance, we are not conscious of a single jarring note: the planner's aesthetic intervention heightens the charm of the Cotswold vernacular and the danger to tradition inherent in the Picturesque is held in check.

The threat declares itself openly in the group of estate cottages known as Blaise Hamlet, near Bristol, which John Nash designed only a year later for the Quaker banker John Harford of Blaise Castle House. Nine cottages disposed at random about a shaven lawn and an off-centre sundial on a tall stone shaft evoke a stage image of the village and the green, a concentrated display of rough contrasting textures, unbridled irregularity and extravagant rusticity. The cottages are constructed of local rubble, but the traditional method of laying the stones with the biggest at the bottom has been abandoned in favour of the rugged and the anomalous. Tall red brick chimneys, clustered or single, round, rectangular and star-shaped, start from the tiles, heavy stone slates or bulging thatch of the roofs; gross finials ornament the gables, one of which takes the form of a weatherboarded dovecote while a plastered cove sweeps forward from another. The miniature scale of both the green and the hamlet, the delightful vegetation – hollyhocks and old cabbage roses smothering latticed casements, wisteria and clematis and honeysuckle trailing over crazy stonework – and the profound tranquillity of the place, despite the fact that it is now encompassed on three sides by suburban development, all conspire to engender a sense of timeless well being. Yet viewed in the context of vernacular tradition these cottages and their setting come no nearer to it than the sentimental, nebulous Christmas card cottage.

134 Cottage in the Picturesque Blaise Hamlet, near Bristol, Somerset, designed by John Nash in 1810.

A like Picturesque and hazy conception of traditional cottage architecture gave rise to the village of Old Warden in Bedfordshire, built from about 1830 onwards for Lord Ongley. Shadowed like Great Tew by dark evergreen trees, terraces of thatched cottages display caricatures of the Bedfordshire thatcher's semi-circular dormers, while the walls are roughcast and here and there overlaid with struts simulating the appearance of half-timber, and the doors are framed in trellis porches. Trellis work, though one of the most unfailingly pleasurable of Picturesque inventions, conveys no feeling of place. Like the ornamental bargeboard it did however offer wonderful scope for the skill and imagination of the village carpenter; the infinite variety of design, the grace and zest with which Gothic and classical motifs in every kind of combination have been translated into airy fretwork, delight the eye in almost every region, whether the trellis redeems a plain façade or enhances the attractions of a 'cottage ornée'.

The elephantine heaviness which, in a climate of growing uncertainty, soon overtook the theme formulated at Blaise is seen in a peculiarly grotesque form in a group of estate cottages at Sudbourne, Suffolk. The alarming rapidity of industrial growth and its social consequences emphasized the differences between urban and rural life. At the same time, the increase in the number of landlords who derived their income from commercial enterprises rather than farming, and the incipient threat contained in the Reform Bill of 1832 to the social system with which English agriculture had always been associated, created an atmosphere of deep unease which was reflected in a monstrous intensification of Picturesque affectation – particularly, as might be expected, in the design of estate cottages. Every roof at Sudbourne is enveloped in the thickest thatch, embellished with every ornamental device in the thatcher's repertoire and often sweeping to within a few feet of the ground. Steep gables supported by coarse brackets jut forward over every door and ground-floor window, thrusting dormers break every roof line. Massive bargeboards, lofty chimneys of diverse shape, rough tree trunks, interlacing twigs and bogus half-timber all manifest a vulgar fancy-dress view of rusticity while announcing the death of the true vernacular.

At Sudbourne, bloated and obscured though they are, the basic components are recognizable as derivatives of English rural architecture. But the habit of assembling elements suggestive of various regional characteristics had already expanded to embrace themes from distant lands. Loudon's *Encyclopaedia* showed eclectic designs and he had included details of porches and campaniles in the Italian manner, and the architect J. Thomson, author of *Retreats* (1827), recommended a Grecian cottage, a Corinthian villa and an eccentric 'Irregular House' which boasted an Italianate tower, a colonnade and a rotunda as suitable additions to village architecture. P.F. Robinson, who had made drawings for farmyards and cowbyres in the Swiss and Italian styles, designed a whole village in the Picturesque mode for which the 'scenic drawing' showed fanciful half-timber alongside Norman arcading, Cotswold and Tuscan details and a Moorish verandah; and he also drew up plans for cottages which were Grecian, Swiss, Palladian, Elizabethan and Tuscan in character.

Ingredients such as these went into the extraordinary mixture which became the Derbyshire village of Edensor when it was removed from its original unacceptable site in full view of Chatsworth in 1839 and rebuilt on the edge of the park in a setting of beeches and hills laid out by the great gardener Joseph Paxton (who was later to design the Crystal Palace). The cottages masquerading as pretentious villas were planned by John Robertson, an architect from Derby. Local stone can do little here to reconcile these houses with the landscape. North Italian, Romanesque, Gothic and Tudor motifs mingle in a single building; rustic porches are furnished with obelisks, spiralling chimneys and scrolled bargeboards consort with ball-topped piers, a castellated entrance lodge looks towards a Lombardic tower and a Swiss chalet adorned with a Georgian pediment. Yet the fantasy is lifeless, all the early Picturesque enthusiasm and gaiety have evaporated: this is escapism in earnest, a pedantic association of themes from every architectural source which never becomes a vital whole.

Fortunately the international eclecticism of Edensor had no more than a minor influence on later farm and cottage building: the village was essentially a precursor of urban villa development. But estate cottages continued to be built in the Picturesque manner until the artificially prolonged life of the system with which they were associated came to an end in the present century. The forms they took generally originated in

135 Homes for cottagers disguised as a massive villa displaying unrelated stylistic motifs, in the planned village of Edensor, Derbyshire, begun in 1839.

native styles, however feeble, distorted and confused the treatment. They might assume the comparatively sober shapes of cottages such as those in the village of Ridgmont on the Duke of Bedford's land or those built by Baron Dimsdale at Anstey in Hertfordshire, brick cottages grouped in twos or threes, gabled and with Gothic porches and Tudor chimneys. In a favourite mid-Victorian design, exemplified by some of the Audley End estate pairs of cottages, the bricks were red with ornaments of yellow brick, and bargeboarded gables dominated every elevation, those on the end walls decorated with rusticated Palladian niches. Later on, as at Elveden in Suffolk, the estate cottage might become almost indistinguishable from the final suburban manifestation of the Picturesque with sham half-timber in the front gable and rugged roughcast concealing the brick of the bay window. Alternatively, in the face of the break up of regional styles, the Picturesque impulse inspired nostalgic, self-conscious, vain attempts to reproduce them without exaggeration. The upper storeys of a group of estate cottages at Radwinter, Essex, designed by Eden Nesfield in 1877, are plastered and decorated with scattered pargework motifs of vaguely Baroque flavour which entirely fail to recapture the spirit of 17th-century pargetting, while a single-storeyed lodge at Moyns Park, timber-framed, plastered, neatly adorned with pargework bunches of grapes in panels about the window heads and with a pargework cock on the front of the two-storeyed porch, fails as signally to evoke the local vernacular. Looking at it, it is Warwickshire rather than Essex which first comes to mind.

The character of many estate cottages was a direct reflection of changes in society, of the ambiguous and unreal position of the country gentleman who acted the part of a feudal lord but whose estates were supported less and less by agricultural rents and more and more by investment and the proceeds of industry. But at the same time, owing to the accidents of history, numbers of cottages and farm buildings in areas untouched by industry went on testifying to the traditional skills of rural carpenters, bricklayers and masons. Those last survivals of the vernacular will appear in the course of the next chapter.

6
The Last of a Tradition

FOR THE BUILDINGS and way of life with which this book is concerned the most significant single event in the farming history of Queen Victoria's reign was the collapse of British agriculture in the 1870s. For this disaster slowed down the progress of industrialized farming, prolonged the life of the traditional homestead and halted the decay of the old village community until well into the present century. Of course the whole social fabric of rural life, depending as it did on inherited practices, was doomed from the moment the machines appeared on the scene and from the moment new communications by rail, road and canal were opened up. The break between old and new was an unavoidable consequence of changing attitudes to human endeavour and human labour; the race for material gain ineluctably destroyed the quality and harmony of ancient village self-sufficiency, individualism and pride in work.

In the decade preceding the collapse, the period known as the Golden Age, the advanced farm already foreshadowed the mechanized factory of today and when J. Wilson wrote his *British Farming* in 1862 he could refer to the farmstead as the farmer's manufactory with full confidence in the acceptability of the term. Enthusiasm for the poetry of the vernacular must not however be allowed to eclipse the glory of the farmer's achievement during those years of high prosperity. The population of the country had risen to more than twenty million by the 1860s, and all those mouths were fed without help or competition from overseas. Earlier methods of raising food for an expanding market were no longer relevant: reclamation could only go forward in the most limited way and enclosure was coming to an end. Between 1865 and 1875 the destruction of the remaining commons by enclosure was halted by the protest not of villagers but of the more articulate urban population, whose appreciation of rusticity, nurtured by the cult of the Picturesque, was heightened by the new and alarming conditions in the cities in which so huge a proportion of the English people were now living. The necessary increases in food production could only come from the more intensive cultivation of existing farmland and more intensive breeding of livestock. So the ideal Victorian farm was an industrialized version of its predecessors.

The almost obsessive interest in agriculture of the period was reflected in a mass of technical literature, particularly in articles published in the *Journal* of the Royal Agricultural Society, which had been founded in 1838 and

Opposite
XIV Brick- and stone-paved path leading directly to the door of a cottage at Welcombe, north Devon – the only part of the cottage garden where flowers are grown.

incorporated by Royal Charter in 1840 with the Queen as its patron. This literature discloses the same tendencies as the most up-to-date buildings of the time, for whereas earlier writings on husbandry are marked by a strong sense of regional diversity, in 19th-century publications discussion of local problems and local performances is submerged by the weight of information dealing with national agriculture. The farmer everywhere relied more and more on manufactured sources for feeding cattle, for fertilizers and for machinery and power. The work of the German chemist Liebig had revealed the intimate relation between the composition of the soil and the nutrition of plants and so had encouraged a keener and more widespread awareness of the connection between agriculture and science which resulted in the establishment of the experimental station at Rothamsted as early as 1843. The traditional farmer found himself relying on urban specialists: on the chemist who supplied substitutes for dung; on the many scientists in different fields who tested and defined the effects of food upon animals, verified the results of manuring on different soils and explained the scientific basis for the rotation of crops; and on the engineer who designed mass-produced implements in varieties never before seen – harrows suited to diverse operations, ploughs for every type of land which needed no sharpening, grubbers, cultivators and clod crushers and sheaf-delivering reapers like those shown in the revised edition of 1870 of Henry Stephens' *Book of the Farm*. One of the most profitable improvements on the farm was the development and installation of cylindrical drain pipes, mass-made by a machine patented by Thomas Scragg in 1845. Good drainage secured an earlier seedtime and an earlier harvest and increased the number of days on which it was possible to work the land. But the new system was not superior to the ancient East Anglian practice. There trenches of about 2 feet in depth were dug and then at the bottom of each of these another smaller channel was cut with a special wedge-shaped drainage tool. Boughs of thorn, heather or alder were tightly packed in this lower channel and the soil above them replaced. Water on the surface of the land percolated through the bush and found its way to the outlet of the drain in the side of the field ditch. Rider Haggard reported that this method was still used in Suffolk in 1902.

The threshing machine, an 18th-century invention which had been the focus of rural agitation and distress during the black period between the end of the Napoleonic wars and the accession of Queen Victoria, a time of poor harvests and dwindling rents, was now allied to a 19th-century power unit, the steam engine. The steam-driven triumph of urban industry seemed about to be repeated to the accompaniment of smoking chimneys in the harvest fields. One Yorkshire manufacturer turned spare-time farmer, a characteristic phenomenon of the age, described by Sir James Caird (who made an agricultural tour of the country in 1850–51), did realize this vision and with the aid of steam transformed his barn into a factory for grinding corn, crushing oil cake, pulping roots and converting all the farm produce into food for man and beast. Richard Jefferies too, in *Hodge and his Masters* (1880), draws a portrait from life of a progressive Wiltshire farmer whose outlook and methods thoroughly anticipate those of the typical farmer of the 1980s. For him farming was 'emphatically "business" the same as iron,

Opposite
136 Village pump,
Pembridge, Herefordshire
(see p. 195).

coal or cotton'. The beat of the engines never seemed to cease on his land; all the hedges had been grubbed up and the whole of his arable had been thrown into one vast field and levelled with the theodolite. The land had been drained at enormous cost and was irrigated by a centrifugal pump. Tons of artificial manure were brought by canal to the farm. Chaff cutters, root pulpers and winnowing machines were all driven by steam and a light railway transported men and materials from one part of the farm to another. Just as on the late 20th century farm, the accounts and administrative work were dealt with in a specially built office equipped with the apparatus of the most modern business techniques.

But very few farmers could afford such machine-aided efficiency; and as Richard Jefferies' 'Man of Progress' remarked, it was not easy to introduce scientific farming into England in the face of tradition and custom. In any case that man came to grief in the years of the depression – as did a farmer at Littlebury, Essex, and others who had invested extensively in the new machines. Sales catalogues of the last quarter of the 19th century show that mechanization on farms was largely confined to various drilling and reaping machines, turnip cutters, oil cake mills, bean crushers and root pulpers. And although some farmers might dream of self-moving ploughs, the chief use they found for steam power was in the form of a mobile engine by means of which corn was threshed in the fields instead of in the barn. The sight of corn being threshed in the harvest field was still common for some years after the Second World War.

But the steam engine did not revolutionize farmstead planning even if the ways in which it was used by a few of the wealthiest and most mechanically minded farmers did change the functions of the barn. It was a long time before the machine was generally accepted. In southern England the flail was almost universally used for threshing, partly to ensure that labourers should be supplied with winter work. In the north the horse-driven gin gang continued in use at least until the 1930s. Mr Ridley of Chollerton readily recalled in conversation in 1953 the gin gangs in operation in his corner of Northumberland some twenty years earlier and spoke of the amazing agility and docility of the horses. Horses were indeed much more widely used than steam to drive machines right up to the early decades of the present century, and the Suffolk Punch was recognized as the finest draught horse. This splendid creature, called Punch because his smooth legs are rather short and his body is barrel shaped, like those of Mr Punch, was – in common with other Shire horses such as the 'Large Black Old English Cart Horse' and the Cleveland Bay – descended from animals originally bred to bear the weight of armoured men on the battlefield. Enclosure and the consequent replacement of the ox by the horse were favourable to the heavy breeds and the second half of the 18th century was a formative period. But the full development of the draught horse, especially the Suffolk Punch, belongs to the Victorian era when Thomas Crisp of Butley Abbey perfected the chestnut coach horse bred by his ancestor and namesake at Ufford towards the end of the previous century.

At the time of the depression, despite some scientific innovations, nothing had yet disturbed the intimacy of the relationship between the farmer and the animals on whom he was dependent for his livelihood.

When Victorian farms were sold up, as they were in great numbers at that time, the animals were usually listed by name. In 1884 the working horses on Justice's Farm, at Finchingfield in Essex, were Gilbert, Ball, Charlie, Captain, Prince, Boxer and Depper; Mr Buller's stables at nearby Newport housed Polley, Smiler, Short, Moco, Boxer, William and Peg. Cows were not then merely 'livestock', but were still, as they always had been, individual creatures who answered to their names, typical of which and tending to recur on widely separated farms were Cherry, Snowflake, Cowslip and Judy, Tulip, Rose, Brindle, Polly and Spotty. Bulls were often called Rufus and Orion.

Just as farming methods based on traditional wisdom handed down from generation to generation and on the farmer's personal experience, observation and detailed knowledge of the subtle differences between field and field were beginning to be supplanted, theoretically if only occasionally in fact, by the precepts of agricultural science, expert soil analysis and the application of text-book rules, so the buildings demanded by this more exacting farming were also beginning to be supplied by specialists from the city and the village craftsman's skill was becoming irrelevant. Although in his *Farm Homesteads of England* (1863) J. Denton conceded that 'local materials should not hastily be set aside', he hastened to point out that imported timber, standardized bricks and Welsh slates transported by rail were cheaper than those materials; and many newly invented substances were appearing on the farm.

Concrete was used as the foundation for all good farm buildings, and concrete blocks were being made as early as 1860. An article in the *Journal of the Royal Agricultural Society* in 1874 actually proposed concrete as a suitable building material for cottages as well as farm buildings. The first concrete farm building was a fattening shed with a tiled roof erected in about 1870 at Faringdon in Berkshire by Robert Campbell. A farmstead on the Cambridgeshire-Essex borders near Duxford, a rectangular yard with livestock buildings and cartsheds of traditional plan, was constructed almost entirely of concrete about twenty years later and still stands as sullenly and uncooperatively in the landscape as when it made its first appearance. Factory-made asphalt was used for flooring; creosote had been applied to timber as a preservative by 1840; and corrugated iron sheeting, appreciated for its cheapness and lightness, appeared on roofs and was also used for walls. Sometimes a cottage even might be fashioned of this material, and although totally alien to any landscape, the pictorial effect, unlike that of concrete, could be amusing and folly-like. The little house on a smallholding at Bawdsey, Suffolk, one of many created to help rural XI labourers during the depression, artlessly assumes the traditional design of a central block with cross-wings, the corrugated iron walls painted viridian, the corrugated iron roof and lean-to porch vermilion, the incredible colours and wavy surfaces vibrating to the harmonies of the shingle beach and the marshes between which it stands.

Prefabricated parts, mostly of cast iron, came from the factory to modernize barn, stable and byre. The 1884 catalogue of the hardware merchants Pfeil, Stedall & Sons of Bloomsbury, London, shows illustrations of cast-iron stall divisions, mangers and pig troughs, bases for stall posts, cow ties, ventilation sashes for stables, rails and rollers for sliding doors, farmyard gates, stable gutters of ornamental design and portable farmyard boilers. The farmer was already able to buy the commonest and simplest structure on the farm, the Dutch barn, ready made and consisting of steel members and corrugated iron sheeting. All he had to do was to prepare the concrete foundation and a gang of workmen sent by the manufacturer would then erect the industrially produced barn. Henry Stephens noted that such barns were very plentiful and they were to be seen on farms in every part of the country earlier in the present century.

The basic farm buildings changed little in principle during Victoria's reign, though published plans included prophetic designs heralding the conditions of the modern factory farm. Farmyard fowls were by and large still allowed to scrap round the kitchen door and roost in the barn and hay loft; but in an article written in 1866 J. A. Clarke describes a building like a vast greenhouse, more than 300 feet long, for the production of eggs and table poultry by mechanically precise means.

Clarke's article was published in the *Journal of the Royal Agricultural Society* and the impression made by leafing through this periodical is that the industrial and scientific approach to farming had left little room for traditional methods and that by the end of the last century the farmer was already the urbanized and unrecognizable John Bull he has since become. Yet though the expansion of agriculture was one of the most notable manifestations of the age, when Caird went on his tour of the country he observed that the majority of farmers had adapted existing vernacular buildings to more productive methods, that most of them set as much store by intuition and experience as by the new scientific and mechanical procedures, and that a desk in the parlour and one or two documents stuffed behind the clock on the kitchen mantelshelf were the average farmer's nearest approach to an office.

It is clear from the testimony of writers such as George Borrow, Thomas Hardy and Flora Thompson that although the village was no longer a self-contained community, though the recently introduced village shop was stocked with goods from the cities and from overseas, and although the age of the local craftsman was passing, the immemorial customs of rural life had not come to an end. The calamity which from about 1875 onwards followed on the repeal of the Corn Laws, a sequence of unkind seasons and the importation (by means of new steamers and new railway systems) of frozen meat from Australia, New Zealand and South America and above all of cheap grain from the limitless cornfields of America, halted the progress of industrialized farming. 'Prolonged depression', writes Lord Ernle, 'checked costly improvements. Drainage was practically discontinued. Both owners and occupiers were engaged in the task of making both ends meet on vanishing incomes. Land deteriorated in condition; less labour was employed; less stock was kept; bills for cake and fertilizers were reduced.'

The sufferings occasioned by these conditions have been often and eloquently portrayed. They were as acute in counties like Essex where mixed farming was still practised, where many flocks of sheep still grazed in the pastures and where weaving was still carried on in some of the cottages, as in Suffolk which had become predominantly arable. Many farmers,

137 Prefabricated Dutch barn, Shipton Hill, Dorset.

unable to stock their farms, abandoned them; and the plight of the agricultural labourer, especially in the open villages where there was no resident squire to regulate migration and where tradesmen from the expanding towns were buying up derelict cottages and letting them to farmhands just as they stood, was often appalling. Contemporary descriptions show scene after scene of misery – a father, mother and six children crowded together in one bedroom at Burwell, Cambridgeshire in 1874; a labourer at Barrow, Suffolk, whose bedroom was so tiny, only 7 feet 6 inches by 6 feet 9 inches, that he could not shift his poor bed away from the rain dripping through a hole in the roof. Richard Heath, author of *The English Peasantry* (1874), had been into a cottage at Rotherfield in Sussex where ten hungry children and their mother huddled in two bedrooms, one of which contained nothing but a makeshift bed on the floor.

Oppression and near starvation led to union activity and the organization under Joseph Arch of the Warwickshire Agricultural Labourers' Union. Unrest, emigration and a drift to the towns threatened the continuity of rural life: as Jefferies remarked, there was 'a general feeling in the villages and agricultural districts that the landed estates around them are no longer stable and enduring. A feeling of uncertainty is abroad, and no-one is surprised to hear that some place, or person, is going.' The rumblings of catastrophic upheaval mutter in the background of the whole agricultural scene. Yet the time when farming ceased to be a way of life and became one industry among many still lay in the future.

Because the increase in food production came chiefly from the more intensive exploitation of existing steadings, only a small number of new farmhouses were built during the Victorian period, some to serve land won from the last wildernesses, others to replace village homesteads by farmhouses in the enclosed fields. As for cottages, landowners continued to build homes for the men working on their farms. The new farmhouses and cottages usually displayed some symptoms of a disintegrating tradition: it was only in areas remote from large towns and not easily reached by the new forms of transport that they remained the unselfconscious creations of local craftsmen. A farmhouse designed by Eden Nesfield near Crewe Green, Cheshire perfectly exemplifies a late phase of the Picturesque style at its most indeterminate, for it combines tile-hanging in the style of Kent or Sussex with half-timber work reminiscent of East Anglia. Another farmhouse in the same district, Leighton Hall Farm, many-gabled and with tall chimneys adorned with classical niches, is constructed of locally made bricks of mottled brown and pink colour though the roof is of Welsh slate and the elevations and general eclectic aspect are almost identical with those of a farmhouse near Trumpington in distant Cambridgeshire.

The interiors of these farmhouses included more rooms than either the traditional or the Georgian farmhouse: in addition to a large kitchen and a dairy with a scalding room leading from it there were store rooms, a pump room, a parlour, a dining room and the modish 'morning room'. This is just the kind of farmhouse which Jefferies visited in Wiltshire in the 1870s. He describes it as more of a large villa-like mansion than a farm. The parlour was filled with rosewood and ormolu, ottomans and 'occasional' tables and furnished with 'semi-ecclesiastical' grate fittings. Glass glittered everywhere: there were mirrors over the mantelpieces and mirrors let into panels and prisms of glass dangled from the candlesticks. The dining room was resplendent with an array of electroplate and round the table stood a set of straight-backed oak chairs of medieval flavour.

138 Leighton Hall Farm, near Crewe, Cheshire: the stable range with hayloft and accommodation for a groom above.

None of the more dramatic innovations recommended in the technical journals are encountered in the Leighton Hall farm buildings except that the open yards are rather larger than those of earlier steadings, the barn is small and the cowhouse and stable are floored with concrete and well drained. They are of brick and in the style of the previous century with haylofts pierced by roundels and with ventilation holes making geometric patterns in the fabric. The doors are all painted a traditional deep blood red.

Another Cheshire farmhouse, at Stretton, realizes a prim, compressed design from C. A. Audsley's *Cottage, Lodge and Villa Architecture* in which the plans and elevations show earnest, somewhat forbidding Victorian versions of the Picturesque Gothic, Elizabethan, Italian and 'Old Scotch' styles. The façade, behind the cast-iron gate and whitewashed concrete piers of a suburban villa, is of Tudor derivation and the sharply pointed, narrow gables and tall chimneys primly condense and parody the image of Manor Farm, Toseland. Nonetheless its plum-coloured tiles and dark bricks, sandstone lintels and sandstone gable outlines all belong to the region.

Brook Farm, at King's Pyon in Herefordshire, offers a greater affront to local tradition: not only does the classical temple portico show no evidence of the rural craftsman's personal interpretation of the pattern-book design, but the whole brick façade has been limewashed to imitate stucco, that substitute material of which John Nash was the master and which, essentially theatrical and *trompe l'œil*, was a prime destroyer of the vernacular. Blank sash windows of commercially produced sheet glass stare across standardized cast-iron railings topped by gilded ornaments such as were still being advertised by O'Brien, Thomas and Company of London at the end of the 19th century. Fortunately a sense of place and of reality is restored by a pretty dovecote, brick nogged and of late, probably 18th-century date, but still expressive of the black-and-white tradition of Herefordshire.

139 Brook Farm, King's Pyon, Herefordshire.

71

139

A few instances of 19th-century cottages in closed villages and on the farms of great estates have already been seen. Some landlords converted farmhouses, which had been left empty by the amalgamation of two or more farms, into cottages for labourers, as they had done earlier. The Earl of Stradbroke, for example, turned an old farmhouse at Sotherton in Suffolk into three dwellings, each consisting of a sizeable living room, washhouse, good pantry and two bedrooms, and either a second pantry, a cellar or an attic. A considerable number of new estate cottages built during the second half of the Victorian period had three bedrooms. The forms they took were generally Picturesque and disruptive of local tradition. Cottages built for farmhands in the 1870s at Sudbury, Derbyshire – for Lord Vernon to the design of an architect from Derby – could scarcely be more unlike the traditional cottage of that region. Paired and taking the form of a cluster of steeply gabled projections, from the middle of which rises a tight, rectangular mass of ornate chimneys, their light brick walls are richly patterned with deep red headers, bands, and arch and gable shapes. Narrow lancets light the smaller of the three bedrooms, while the main windows are of Tudor form. Side porches like those of a church, with ogee entrances and precipitous roofs, lead solemnly into a high-ceilinged living room with a capacious scullery and pantry behind it and a fuel store and pigsty close to the back door.

Pallid machine-pressed bricks were used for a terrace of six cottages at Southwell, Nottinghamshire. The pantiles of the roofs were probably made in the county, but Welsh slate protects the latticed porches and the heavily bargeboarded and half-timbered attic dormers. Another row of six dwellings at Warter, Yorkshire, reveals even less of its geographical situation. Of whitewashed brick, thickly thatched and with counterfeit half-timber in the dormer gables and above the doors of the thatched and latticed porches, the home counties might well have given them birth. The accommodation provided by such cottages was, however, much better than that of the cramped and insanitary hovels of the open villages. The front doors at Southwell opened directly into the parlour, but there was a passage leading to the stairs at Warter. On the ground floor there were two rooms, a scullery and an ample larder. The attics at Southwell seem never to have been used as bedrooms, however large the family, but for storage.

140

140 *Below* Cottage row, Warter, Yorkshire.

141 *Below right* Rat-trap bond brickwork at Henlow, Bedfordshire.

Some new cottages, just as unrelated to their settings, were erected in open villages, generally for urban landlords. In the Cheviots near Kirknewton a row of six such dwellings unite in one brick frontage, the eaves of the slate roofs broken by six dormers, a feature as unlikely in this region as the materials, to house the workers on a farm – a fragment of back-street city housing misjoined to that majestic and desolate landscape of huge rounded russet hills and stone walls. And the commonest form taken by the speculative builder's cottage was of urban origin, two-storeyed, four-roomed, of brick and paired or part of a terrace, like those at Henlow, Bedfordshire, where in some of the little dwellings, to save cost, the bricks are laid on edge in the style known as 'rat-trap bond'.

While mass-produced and standardized materials were finding their way into most country districts, Welsh slate even making a dramatic appearance on the gable end of a timber-framed cottage at Ivinghoe, Buckinghamshire,

142 Farm labourers' cottages near Kirknewton, Northumberland.

141

in the form of fishscale cladding of mechanical uniformity, the vernacular tradition was still very much alive in the more inaccessible areas. Villages described by Hardy were nearly as self-sufficient as they had been two centuries earlier: the prominent figures in the community, apart from the squire and the farmers with their carters, shepherd and labourers, were still the blacksmith, the mason, the thatcher, the miller and the baker. William Crossing, the author of *A Hundred Years on Dartmoor*, written at the end of the last century, had recently seen labourers living under the same roof as their cattle on food produced on their own patches of rough land – barley bread, potatoes, leeks, onions and bacon. Their cottages were of granite crudely thatched.

In parts of East Anglia local craftsmen continued to show fresh vigorous invention in the use of flints. In Norfolk, many later farm buildings are simply and straightforwardly constructed of tweedy-textured flint roofed with pantiles. Similar flints, alternately chalk-coated and displaying their gleaming hearts, are held on the walls of a cottage at Hingham in a light red network of brick diamonds and hexagons; the builder of a cottage at East Raynham chose the biggest and most irregular flints he could find for a tiny symmetrical front with twin pert miniature bay windows, and its dynamic rugosity surpasses the liveliest of earlier achievements in this medium. A row of labourers' cottages at Saffron Walden in Essex, constructed of equally rough but smaller stones, glitters with the same bursting vitality, only just restrained here by bold bands of red brick. Kidney cobbles were never made into walls of more pleasingly homespun character than those of two small cottages at Uggeshall, Suffolk.

143 *Below* Flint galleted with clinkers at Stoke Ferry, Norfolk.

144 *Below right* Flint and brick at East Raynham, Norfolk.

145 *Above* Clunch and brick at Burnham Overy, Norfolk.

146 *Right* Kidney cobbles, pantiles and clematis, Uggeshall, Suffolk.

Again in Norfolk, dusky red local brick and alternating chalky white flints speckle the glinting façade of a very modest farmhouse at Great Massingham, while a pair of cottages at Stoke Ferry of near suburban form 143 is transfigured by the adventurous treatment of the walls: they are fashioned of irregular flints interspersed here and there with red brick and galletted with tiny black clinkers. At Burnham Overy a ground floor of 145 strong red brick is unexpectedly topped by a first floor of staring white clunch. That strange material peculiar to Norfolk, carstone, which had XIII already made a tentative appearance in local buildings, came into its own at 132 the very time when vernacular styles and crafts were in jeopardy. Small thin slabs of the sandy yellow and dark brown substance were used dry and with quoins and window frames of pale ochre brick to make a forceful impact at Blackborough End in two joined cottages of otherwise undistinguished and untraditional design.

Farther afield, cottages of the same plan as those at Henlow, a much 141 pared down and degenerate version of the Georgian terrace house, might, as at Bonsall in Derbyshire, be both rooted and animated by the use of local stone. Two pygmy cottages built at Green How, Yorkshire, in 1854, later made into one, given the grand name of Groom House and inhabited by a shepherd, top a bleak hill, a trenchant emanation of it with their walls of dark sandstone and heavy stone slates.

New farmhouses in the north might occasionally take the form of a freestanding rectangle lit by sash windows of unrelieved sheet glass, but more often the style of the native long-house was retained and the materials

147 The long-house tradition persists in this farmhouse at Dufton, Westmorland, but there is no communication between house and farm buildings. The group is known as a 'laithe house' ('laithe' means a combined barn and byre) because it adjoins a barn and byre.

were those of ancient usage. A wonderfully harmonious example, the farmstead stretched against the high fells at Dufton, Westmorland, was described at the beginning of this book in relation to the primeval custom which it continues (p. 16). And when at Newlands Hall Farm, Frosterley, Co. Durham, a new house was built in the late 19th century it continued the line of the earlier long-house (see the frontispiece, p. 2).

Life inside more distant farmhouses such as this sometimes continued with very little change into the present century. At Hodge Hill Farm, Cartmel Fell, Lancashire, the home in the early 1950s of a lady farmer as forceful as Hardy's Bathsheba Everdene, if a good deal older, the furniture in the cavernous living room or house-place included, apart from fine examples of the screen-cupboards of the region, a long oak table with a bench on one side of it, a waxed chest with a carved back that turned it into a settle, an eight-day clock ticking loudly in a tall case and a big dresser on which pewter plates shone amid a mixed collection of mugs and beer jugs. Bread was still baked in the oven beside the generous hearth, and this small farm was one of the very few where at that time butter and cheese were still made in the dairy. The scene was little different from the interior of Hall Farm so vividly evoked a hundred years earlier by George Eliot in *Adam Bede*, with its bright cool dairy and its shining house-place with scrubbed floor, high mantelshelf set with brass candlesticks, brilliantly polished clock case and its oak table, usually turned up like a screen. And that room would have looked much the same a century earlier still. Mrs Gaskell's description of the parlour and house-place at Hope Farm in *Cousin Phillis* breathes a most comforting sense of continuity and tradition, and unforgettably conjures up the atmosphere of a remote country interior, not only of the time at which she was writing (1863), but such as could still be experienced by anyone old enough to appreciate it almost a hundred years later:

> The parlour was a large room with two casemented windows on the other side of the broad flagged passage leading from the rector-door to the wide staircase, with its shallow, polished oaken steps, on which no carpet was ever laid. The parlour floor was covered in the middle by a home-made carpetting of needlework and list. One or two quaint family pictures of the Holman family hung round the walls; the fire-grate and irons were much ornamented with brass; and on a table against the wall between the windows, a great beau-pot of flowers was placed upon the folio volumes of Matthew Henry's Bible. . . . The large house-place, living-room, dining-room, whichever you might like to call it, was twice as comfortable and cheerful. There was a rug in front of the great large fire-place, and an oven by the grate, and a crook with the kettle hanging from it, over the bright wood-fire; everything that ought to be black and polished in that room was black and polished; and the flags, and window-curtains and such things as were to be white and clean, were just spotless in their purity. Opposite to the fire-place, extending the whole length of the room, was an oaken shovel-board, with the right incline for a skilful player to send the weights into the prescribed place. There were baskets of white work about, and a small shelf of books hung against the wall, books used for reading, and not for propping up a beau-pot of flowers.

The prosperous mid-Victorian years of high farming naturally brought changes to some farmhouse interiors, especially if the farm lay within reach of a sizeable town, and there were numbers of rooms which were not unlike those which so outraged Jefferies. Because after a short period of affluence, when they had accumulated more possessions than had ever been seen in modest rural dwellings, numbers of farmers were forced to sell up during the depression to discharge their debts, auctioneers have sometimes preserved minutely detailed catalogues of the contents of farmhouses and farm buildings. Remarkably complete records for north-west Essex exist for the whole of Victoria's reign and they reflect most of the fashionable additions to the home.

Old farmhouses were altered and enlarged to create the rooms which were considered essential in newly built homesteads such as the one near Crewe. Gifford's Farm, Little Sampford, where the house was of modest size, consisted in 1845 of the 'keeping room' (or living room), the parlour, a pantry, washhouse and dairy on the ground floor, a 'little chamber', servant's chamber, 'middle room', bedroom and linen cupboard on the first floor, and above that an attic and a man servant's room. The word 'chamber' was used less and less frequently during the second half of the century and the term 'bedroom' became general. Sometimes the bedrooms in larger houses might be given such pretentious names as the Red Room, the Blue Room or the Grey Room. The parlour kept its name, though in sale catalogues of the 1880s it is called the 'Drawing Room' and on one occasion it becomes the 'Front Room', a term later associated with the best room in little town houses. At the end of the 19th century the breakfast room, the dining room, the drawing room and the morning room were found in many farmhouses; the 'keeping room' had become the 'sitting room'. There might also be a 'gun room'.

During the years of prosperity farmers and their wives filled these rooms with new furniture and fashionable ornaments, though older tables and Windsor and ladderback chairs seem to have been kept and at New House Farm, Wimbish there was still an oak hutch of 17th-century date in 1884. The keeping room at Hole Farm, Little Sampford, when the contents and farming stock were sold on 20 November 1844, was furnished with a large oval dining table, a small deal table, a flap table of the kind which appeared in the early 18th century, an eight-day clock, five elbow chairs and six 'flat-seat' chairs, and a 'beaufet' (a new name for the sideboard, a backless version of the dresser), together with a set of fire irons and a fender, a baking pan, a dripping pan and a cleaver, a brass ladle, a round copper boiler and a chimney crane and hooks. There were two meat safes in the pantry and a few tubs, but carpenter's tools were also kept there; indeed it seems to have served as a lumber room, for it contained a fire screen, a cob iron, a brass boiler, a cupboard and 'sundries'. In the parlour stood another dining table and an oval table and fourteen chairs, among which six were mahogany with fashionable horsehair seats. There was in addition a painted 'beaufet' with nine wine and beer glasses standing on it as well as a tea tray and tea service. Various ornaments and a pair of brass candlesticks garnished the mantelshelf and six paintings adorned the walls. The three bedrooms, still called 'chambers', all contained wooden bedsteads, two of which were four-posters. In one of them was a 'wardrobe' – a word which was beginning to replace the 'hanging-press' or 'press-cupboard' of earlier inventories.

When we turn to the kitchen, dairy and farmyard, where the work of Hole Farm was done, the equipment differs little from that of earlier centuries. It is true that the iron boiler in the kitchen would formerly have been of copper or brass and the table might not have been of deal, but the familiar cob irons, gridiron, roaster, hob iron, peel and oven fork, skillet and stand, copper and brass pots, pot hangers, brewing copper and kneading trough were all present among the bowls, pitchers, bottles and cream pots. In the dairy stood a barrel churn, a milk stand and milk pail, four milk pans, a pair of butter scales, two cream pots, several pork pots, a pork tub and a quantity of pork. Down in the cellar were stored five hogshead (54-gallon) casks, six half-hogshead casks, an 18-gallon cask, ale stalls (to save bending low over tubs and casks), a 'runnel' (funnel of wood) and a tap 'ooze' (hose), five wort tubs and a jet, a mash tub and four one-gallon stone bottles. The tap was used to draw off the wort (the liquid which had percolated through the mash of malt in the first stage of beer-making) from the mash tub, so that the hops could be boiled in it. The large number of implements at Hole Farm included nothing more up to date than an iron breast plough for three horses and four iron harrows. A wooden plough was still in use. Among the livestock were two carthorses, Short and Prince, as well as a pony, a herd of shorthorn cows and yard fowls.

A bankrupt tenant farmer of Hobs Aerie, Arkesden, whose possessions were all sold on 28 February 1887, had lived more grandly in a house with more rooms. On the ground floor were the kitchen, a store room, the brewhouse and dairy, the 'right hand room', the housemaid's closet, the breakfast room, dining room, drawing room and hall, while upstairs there were two main bedrooms, one with a dressing room adjoining it, a back bedroom and a servant's room. The brewhouse contained all the traditional utensils and gadgets, including the 'underback' (the broad, low tub into which the wort was put when drawn off from the mash tub before being transferred to the copper) and a set of steelyards, a form of scale in which a counterpoise was moved along a graduated beam. One new piece of equipment was kept in the brewhouse, Bradford's Patent Washing Machine.

The Arkesden house was crammed with objects, among which some were mass-produced and of recent origin. In the kitchen, where the floor was covered with 'coco' matting, there was a paraffin stove together with four oil lamps; against the wall stood a new article of furniture known as the 'Davenport', a form of writing table. A new green and white dinner service in 74 pieces and a 'Chinese' tea set in 29 pieces were kept in the store room. There was a great deal of mahogany and horsehair furniture in the principal rooms draped with antimacassars and including one of those horsehair couches with a roll at one end, not quite high enough to permit sitting up in comfort, but which nevertheless made all thought of going to sleep on it out of the question. There was an 'old oak table' in the breakfast room and the dining-room chairs had leather seats. In this room there was also a tripod table, and paired vases and ornaments adorned the mantelshelf. Brussels carpets and Brussels rugs enriched the floors. Among the pictures were two watercolour landscapes, a set of 'Fox-Hunting' prints, a framed engraving, an oil painting and a map of Essex. In the breakfast room there were ninety-four bound volumes of popular periodicals. An umbrella stand and a stuffed magpie and stuffed gull under glass domes were conspicuous objects in the hall, where the boards were covered with 'floor cloth and coco mats'. On the upstairs landing was a large flower stand displaying potted plants.

While in the living rooms the curtains were of 'moreen', a new heavy material of mixed wool and cotton, in the bedrooms they were of muslin or green damask. The bedsteads, except for one of mahogany in the back bedroom (so it was little esteemed), were no longer of wood but of fashionable cast iron. Marble-topped washstands figured prominently, furnished with sets of green and white jugs, basins and soap dishes. The dressing room contained not only a washstand with a 'japanned' toilet set (black-stained, in imitation of lacquer) and a mahogany towel rail, but a bath standing on a piece of felt carpet and a mahogany night commode. The servant's room was provided with a painted washstand and another, corner, washstand, a japanned French bed with a flock mattress, a 'Queen Ann' glass and a toilet table with a framed mahogany mirror. A crib and bedding for it were kept in this room together with five bushels of potatoes and, most unexpectedly, a double-barrelled 12-bore breech loader.

The Siggs family of New House Farm, Wimbish, had furnished their house in similar style. Here the davenport was more suitably installed in the drawing room, where there was also a walnut loo table and where a glass in a fine gilt frame hung above the fireplace. The carpets, as they seem to have been in many farmhouses of that time, were either Brussels or

Kidderminster, and one of them had a flowered border. The hall was decorated with stuffed squirrels and stuffed jays in cases and with antique pistols; it was lit by large bronze candlesticks, a wall barometer hung near the door, and beside it stood an eight-day clock in a wainscot case. Mahogany and horsehair furnished the dining room together with a dwarf armchair and an easy chair, both covered in oiled American cloth. On a rosewood writing table inlaid with brass stood a rosewood workbox and a case of stuffed hummingbirds. On the walls hung seven coloured prints of hunting scenes in maple frames and two needlework pictures. The upstairs landing was furnished, as at Arkesden, with a flower stand and also with a stool, three shells and a doll's bedstead. There were four bedrooms with either mahogany or cast-iron beds. In the 'second bedroom' there was another stuffed bird, a kingfisher, under a glass dome, an engraving of Lord Nelson in a gilt frame hung on the wall, and two bronzed plaster figures and three 'figured' chimney ornaments graced the mantelpiece. There were two dressing glasses in mahogany frames in this room and two chests of drawers, as well as a dressing table and a painted washstand and two mahogany bonnet stands. In the same room also stood a white foot bath, a tin water can and a hip bath. Besides dinner, dessert and tea services, some of which were 'green and white' like those at Arkesden, and a quantity of glass, the Siggses possessed some Spode and Lowestoft bowls, basins, cups, plates and a teapot. The kitchen, brewhouse and dairy remained traditional, displaying copper warming pans, gridirons, roasting jacks, copper pots, brass preserving pans, wort and mash tubs, runnel and jet, cheese presses and moulds, skimmers and strainers, churn and keeler (cooler), though there was one novelty – Ransome's Patent Mangle, which was of cast iron with wooden rollers.

The tenant of Freeman's Farm in the same parish, who only a year earlier, in 1883, had to sell all his implements, stock and household goods 'under a Distress for Rent', furnished the interior of his 17th-century timber-framed house in much the same way again – although it was considerably smaller with only a 'sitting room', kitchen and dairy on the ground floor and three bedrooms and a lumber room above. He had an American clock in a mahogany frame on the kitchen wall and the same room was furnished with four old Windsor chairs and a painted dresser. An old trestle table of the type listed in early inventories as a 'planke table' stood in the dairy. In the sitting room, as well as the usual mahogany-framed horsehair chairs, a mahogany loo table and a gate-legged table there was a piece of furniture which was rapidly becoming a status symbol, the upright piano – here a 'six and a half cottage piano' by 'T. Smith'.

Another piece of furniture which was occasionally seen now in the farmhouse was the mahogany or rosewood 'cheffonier' (akin to the sideboard); and the tiered mahogany 'what-not' (a set of small shelves for the display of knick-knacks) and the ottoman were popular household gods. Besides oil paintings and prints the farmhouse pictures now included oleographs. Oil lamps are listed in most sale catalogues but many rooms were candle-lit. Hangings were often of the machine-printed chintz and cretonne which had replaced the hand-blocked cottons of the 18th century. In some farmhouses there was no sign of a book other than the Family

Bible, though the Reynoldses of Gifford's Farm, Little Sampford, had a shelf in the keeping room on which were two Bibles, 'sundry books' and six volumes of *Doddridge's Family Expositor*. Mr Osborn of Quendon owned Whitfield's sermons and twelve other books; and Captain R. Bird Thompson, who was farming at Little Walden Hall until 1885, when he had to sell up and leave the neighbourhood, owned a collection of books which were characteristic of the taste of the period. They were *Dwight's Theology* in five volumes, Horseley's *Book of Psalms* and *Biblical Fragments*, *Macknight on the Epistles* and Butterworth's *Concordance*, the works of Cowper and Cowley, *The British Essayist* in six volumes, Bingley's *Animal Biography*, Pinnock's *Guide to Knowledge* and ten years of *The Field*. Captain Bird Thompson also owned a magic lantern and twelve slides and an egg cabinet fitted with drawers and an 'excellent collection of birds' eggs'.

With all their fashionable furnishings and furniture, much of which, if we are to judge from survivals, was made by country joiners as inventive as their predecessors, it seems that old traditions were still upheld on these Essex farms. Conditions remained almost static from the time when the contents were listed until after the Second World War, when, from the 1950s onwards, the industrialized farm visualized by the Victorians did not only rapidly become fact but took forms beyond the dreams of even Jefferies' progressive Cecil. It was not very common before this period of intensive factory farming had got under way to come across an interior like that of Hodge Hill Farm where no piece of furniture was of later date than 1800, but it was extremely common to find farm kitchens much like those of Hole Farm and New House Farm – though both the dairy and brew-house were seldom used and though 'convenience' foods and sliced bread were often enough put on the farmhouse table. In the fields the implements which had been introduced in the 19th century were still widely used. A two-horse mowing machine of wood and iron such as was produced by the Yorkshire firm of A.C. Bamlett, Ltd, was at work in the fields of Little Langdale, Westmorland, just as it had been a hundred years earlier, soon after this type of machine was singled out by the Yorkshire Agricultural Society for its steady motion and absence of friction.

The outshot back kitchen at Hillside Farm, Hapton, Norfolk, seen a few 148 years after the end of the Second World War, with its big bread oven, copper, oil lamps still in use, pot boiling on an open fire and coco matting on the uneven flagged and tiled floor, showed few signs of change though electricity had been installed a month or two earlier and Lucy the servant was using an electric iron. In a similar kitchen at Pembridge, Herefordshire, 150 a kitchen range filled the fireplace opening and á stone copper against the wall at right angles to the range (with a zinc bucket and an oil cooking stove standing on it) conveniently adjoined the sink. Such sinks, of stone, shallow and with a gentle slope, sometimes called 'slop-stones', had been a normal feature of manor houses since the 16th century but had only been common in small farmhouses from about 1750. The one at Pembridge was connected by a lead pipe to a runlet outside, but there was no tap in the house. Water had to be fetched, as it still was in many rural districts, from a 136 communal pump. At Frog's Hall, Biddenden, the kitchen hearth of which 119 has already appeared in these pages, the farmhouse had its own pump set

148 *Above left* The kitchen, Hillside Farm, Hapton, Norfolk.

149 *Above* The pantry, Harthill Hall Farm, Alport, Derbyshire. The partly timber-framed wall separates it from the dairy.

150 *Left* Cottage kitchen, Pembridge, Herefordshire.

beside a splendid example of the traditional sink, constructed of the same brick as the floor. Next to the sink stood a cast-iron and wooden mangle just like the one used at New House Farm, Wimbish, some seventy years earlier. At Mr and Mrs Abbott's in Matterdale, Cumberland, the sink had 61 been fitted into a corner of the house-place (as it continued to be called in the north): it was still shallow but was of dark brown glazed earthenware of Victorian manufacture, surrounded by pretty Victorian transfer-printed tiles. Water had only been brought to the little farmstead two years before the time of our visit.

Pantries had for the most part not then been modernized and refrigerators were never seen on small farms. The pantry at Harthill Hall 149 Farm, at Alport in Derbyshire, lit by a deeply embrasured window, with one stone and several wooden shelves set against the cool, whitewashed walls to hold finely glazed earthen pots and bowls of local workmanship and a number of standardized pudding basins, is typical of many except for the meagre store of provisions it contains. Mr Twyford was an elderly bachelor farmer and lived alone in the old house that was formerly the home of the aristocratic Derbyshire Cockayne family.

The cottage interiors of the older generation of farmworkers in the 1950s had remained extraordinarily like those so movingly because so faithfully described by Flora Thompson in the opening chapters of *Lark Rise*. They combined a sense of old tradition with collections of objects which might include both earlier and Victorian pieces of furniture and ornaments, but little of 20th-century date except family photographs – of which there were generally a great number – and photographs of the Royal Family.

Mr Moseley, a bachelor cottager of Lightmoor, Shropshire, cooked on 154 an open fire before which stood a bright steel trivet, steel tongs, poker and shovel and handsome steel firedogs joined by bars, all of 18th-century date. But the cast-iron kitchen range was an almost universal feature of unaltered cottages, generally with a central open fire with an oven on one side of it and perhaps a small boiler on the other. The original wide fireplace of old cottages was usually filled in, as could be seen in a cottage at Nunney, Somerset; but at old Mrs Bowditch's in Crewkerne the 'kitchener' was set right at the back of the original opening, still leaving an inglenook. In front of the central grate there was often a profusely decorated cast-iron three-sided movable object jutting out almost to the fender. There was one in Mrs Holman's cottage at Crewkerne and another in young Mrs Bowditch's. They were intended to prevent hot coals and clinkers from falling onto the hearth and were late versions of the rarely seen cover-fire or curfew, made of brass, which was used from medieval times for covering or extinguishing fires at night.

The mantelshelf, usually with a mirror over it, was adorned with candlesticks of pewter or brass, decorated tins and tea caddies, flashy vases, an occasional lustre mug or plate and in some cottages Staffordshire figures, those most free and vigorous products of popular art, modelled from illustrations and engravings by unlettered country potters with a simple sense of humour specially for the farmhouse and cottage mantelpiece. Amongst the ornaments on a battered chest of drawers in Mrs Holman's living room at Crewkerne were three fine Staffordshire figures – a large

Overleaf, left
151 Household gods in the living room of Mrs Holman's cottage at Crewkerne, Somerset.

Overleaf, right
152 *Above* Mrs Bowditch, senior, by her fireplace at Crewkerne, Somerset.

153 *Below left* Mantelpiece and cast-iron kitchen range (made locally) in Mrs Holman's living room at Crewkerne, Somerset.

154 *Below right* Interior at Lightmoor, Shropshire. The cottage was built in the early 18th century for an ironstone miner.

155 Interior with sideboard and table carpet in Mrs Tye's cottage at Little Barrington, Oxfordshire, the same room as that seen in Ill. 120.

156 Bedroom in Harthill Hall Farm, Alport, Derbyshire, showing a crude stone version of the double ogee hob grate, cottage chair of local joiner's design, washstand, and cast-iron bedstead with half tester. Note, in the window embrasure, the thickness of the wall.

spaniel and a pair of Highlanders – and an interesting portrait of Sir Francis Drake standing on a pedestal, of the type made at Liverpool in the early 19th century, together with two teapots, never used, each set in a fluted glass trifle dish, and a jug and basin. The last and the teapots with their sunken lids were typical of the Japanese imports which appeared in small country town shops in the early years of this century. The teapots were sold in wickerwork baskets intended to serve as tea cosies.

In front of the hearth there was often a coco mat or a rag rug in dark but glowing colours, and on it stood the armchairs of the cottager and his wife (she wearing a freshly laundered and starched apron, white, sprigged or spotted). The furniture usually included one or two older pieces, perhaps inherited but more often than not ousted by newer fashions from the 'big house' or the farmhouse. The chairs in Mr Moseley's cottage were a variety of the spindle back designed and made by a local carpenter. The sturdy chairs at Mrs Tye's, Little Barrington, with a single elaborately turned horizontal support, were examples of a type of which rural joiners made many spirited variations during the last century. The table was usually covered with patterned oil cloth, but when not in use it might be spread with a dark woollen cloth fringed by bobbles or tassels. At Mrs Tye's the table was resplendent with a carpet considered too good for the floor. Sideboards and 'what-nots', like the truly splendid one at Mrs Holman's, were frequently part of the cottage living-room furniture, and the occasional dresser might be quite imposing.

Cottage pictures, apart from photographs, most often consisted of Victorian oleographs or engravings. Three of the most popular subjects were *A World of Love* (a version of Edward Hicks's *The Peaceable Kingdom*),

which hung above the sideboard at Mrs Tye's; *The Death of Nelson*, which 155
adorned the walls of old Mrs Bowditch's living room; and Landseer's *Death of the Stag*, which occupied much of the wall space in Mrs Giles's two-roomed cottage at Cricklade, Wiltshire. Cottages such as these nearly always contained a few books as well, which invariably included the Bible and very often the works of Tennyson and Bunyan's *Pilgrim's Progress*. In addition to these Mrs Tye owned *Raphael's Almanac* for 1952 and 1953 and a Victorian edition of *Robinson Crusoe*. Mrs Borrick of Grasmere had *The Death of Abel* (a translation of Gessner's poem), Milton's *Paradise Lost* and *Paradise Regained*, and a novel entitled *The Spiritual Quixote*, all on a broad window ledge among pots of geraniums.

Geranium plants, sometimes accompanied by begonias or calceolaria, VII, VIII stood in almost every cottage window, and they were specimens of conspicuous virility. Through them the cottagers could watch the doings of neighbours and the approach of strangers without themselves being seen.

Cottage bedrooms were still much like those described by Victorian observers – small, rather dark, normally without fireplaces and frequently opening one into another. If the bedroom had a fireplace it was usually of a standardized design in cast iron. Bedsteads were commonly of iron with 156 brass knobs. In addition to a dressing table many bedrooms were furnished with a Victorian washstand. Lace curtains hung at the window.

There were no bathrooms in the Essex farmhouses recorded in the sales catalogues I have mentioned, and remote and modest farmhouses were still without this convenience fifty or more years later. The cottages of farmhands were always at that time without it. A tin bath was often to be seen hanging behind the outshot door, and Mrs Holman's daughter described how it was brought onto the rug in front of the living room fire on a Friday night and what a luxury it was to sit in it beside the blazing grate with the oil lamp turned low.

The privies of cottages and of many farmhouses were outside, and at the bottom of the garden of one Northumberland homestead there were three seats in a row, all scrubbed snowy white.

And this brings me to the cottage garden, which now that rural labourers have almost ceased to live in cottages and are themselves so reduced in numbers only survive here and there. For those sophisticated flowery little plots, the work of retired ladies and urban invaders of the countryside inspired by the cultivation of the cottage garden by Miss Jekyll and William Robinson, enchanting though they so often are, do not belong to the artless tradition of the true cottager. The first essential characteristic of the genuine cottage garden is that it is not primarily ornamental: its charm is wholly unselfconscious and fortuitous. The cottager's garden was originally his family's larder, and so vegetables and flowers mingle together in it in happy proximity. The little plot in front of the cement-faced cottage with the engagingly brisk air at Knapton, Norfolk, noted in the last 124 chapter, preserved all the attributes of the true cottage garden as late as 1970. The path takes the shortest way to its goal, the front door, and is lined with flowers dividing it from neat rows of vegetables, an arrangement which is repeated again and again. A bed of onions makes an unpre-

157 *Above left* Front
garden with miniature
box hedge, Eriswell,
Suffolk.

158 *Above right* Typical
cottage garden displaying
a mixture of vegetables
and flowers at Knutsford,
Cheshire.

meditated pattern among cushions of thyme, roses, Japanese anemones and
Michaelmas daisies in front of a Victorian cottage near Knutsford,
Cheshire; cabbages sprawl before a pargetted dwelling at Sibton, Suffolk,
crowding out the flowers along the path, which here is of cinders. Where
there is both a front and a back garden the cottager reserves the front for
flowers while at the back vegetables are set in rows among gooseberry and
redcurrant bushes and one or two fruit trees. Among them there may be a
rabbit hutch and a wired fowl run.

The flowers may yet be of the old-fashioned varieties – native
honeysuckle which owed its domestication to 16th-century cottagers,
Turk's cap lilies and Madonna lilies, poppies, wallflowers, pinks, violets
and primroses in their season and clematis like that festooning the cottage
146   door at Uggeshall, first developed from Traveller's joy in 17th-century
cottage gardens. Old-world roses still linger among the vegetables of the
cottage garden – moss and cabbage roses, the monthly rose and a rose
which a farm labourer of Malham called 'Glory to thee John', his name for
Gloire de Dijon.

Very often the vegetables and flowers of a cottage garden or the path and
157   the plants may be separated by a miniature box hedge, as at Victoria Place,
Eriswell, Suffolk. These trim little hedges embody the simplest form of a
clipping and shaping art in which the cottager excelled. It is an art with a
long tradition, for Gervase Markham wrote in 1614 of the square bed filled
with a design of close-cut box as one of the most ancient of all English
garden ornaments. He speaks also of hedges simulating battlements which

support the leafy figures of beasts, birds, 'creeping things and shippes'. Just such a hedge will arrest the attention of anyone approaching the Yorkshire village of Kirkby Malham by road. Rising above a dry-stone wall in front of a row of cottages, it is cut into the shape of great castellations with the green growing forms of peacocks resting upon them. The fashion for landscape gardening destroyed most of the evergreen sculpture which once embellished the formal layouts surrounding great houses, but the art lived on in the rural labourer's garden, introduced to him perhaps by gardeners who, themselves cottagers, were employed in the domains of the nobility and used their skill to enrich their own little plots. Round and massive pillars of box flank the door of a cottage at Coddenham in Suffolk, topped by small, conventionalized Christmas tree shapes on circular bases which give the little house its name – The Firs. Cocks crow from the height of tall ringed columns of yew at Sapperton, Gloucestershire; and in Warwickshire a ragged bird of gigantic proportions perches unsteadily on a swaying ringed plinth at Lower Brailes, a village dominated by shapes of living green. Dog and cat confront one another on top of a thick, exceedingly smooth hedge at Leverstock Green, Hertfordshire, while at Chipping Campden in Gloucestershire a huge symbolic cross of yew presses against a stone cottage wall stretching right up to the eaves and shading door and window with its great protective arms.

The examples of green sculpture I have just described were all flourishing in the late 1960s. But the future of cottage garden topiary is as dark as that of every other rural craft. Though yew is of faster growth than

159 *Below left* Topiary cross and trimly clipped hedges at Chipping Campden, Gloucestershire.

160 *Below right* Folly garden, Downton, Wiltshire.

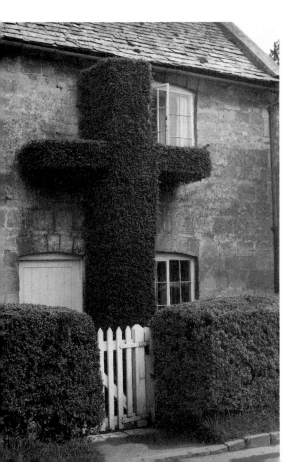

box it still takes more than fifteen years for an image like the Chipping Campden cross to reach its full sombre solidity; and it seems unlikely in our unstable, mobile society that either the new urban and urbanized owners of old cottages or the rural labourer in his council house would think of planting for a more distant future than four or five years.

These sculptures are the folk version of a once sophisticated art and the cottager also gave a final, refreshingly popular and naïve twist to another aristocratic cvmon, the folly. The gnomes and miniature lighthouses and windmills, the plaster rabbits and toadstools, the wheelbarrows filled with primroses, which were the last degraded suburban manifestation of the folly and the Picturesque, made their way to the cottage garden as communication between town and country became easier. At Madeley Court, Shropshire, where the Elizabethan gatehouse was turned into two dwellings for farm workers in the early 19th century, pixies and rabbits merely added a touch of whimsy to a cottage plot without changing its character. All too often, the cottage garden tradition is destroyed by a weak suburban Picturesque convention. But in Cornwall a lighthouse on a pebble-studded base between two identical windows in one of those tiny flower gardens against a wall, in which cottagers delight, has the visual intensity of a painting by Alfred Wallis; and at Downton, Wiltshire, 160 miniature pebble-encrusted steps inlaid with bits of china and with raised, rounded mosaics of pebbles and tiles like little cakes, leading up to a miniature pebble church amid tobacco plants, cabbages and leeks, create a composition as crazy and compelling and heart-warming as the ebullient little façade of the cottage at Wylye in the same county. 123

It is a wonderful ending to the Picturesque tradition that helped to undermine the vernacular tradition of which I have been writing and of which we have now seen the last. Old surviving farm buildings are no longer a reflection of working habits and have become objects of enthusiastic academic study; museums have been established to house old farm tools and implements and to preserve relics of the folklore and agricultural and village history of different regions. We live in a world where rural labourers have become mechanics, where the majority of farmers love profit more than they love the land, where agriculture has become an industry, farm buildings are products of the factory, and it is better not to contemplate what goes on inside them. Yet viewed in a wider context the scene is not without a glimmer of light. The influence of ecologists with comprehensive insight is daily growing. It may achieve a compromise between industry and agriculture and a general acceptance of the great metaphysical truth expressed by Bacon's dateless words: 'Nature cannot be commanded except by being obeyed.'

Opposite
161 Pargework and cabbages at Sibton, Suffolk.

Further Reading

Besides the books mentioned in the Foreword, and the contemporary sources and probate inventories quoted in the text, the following publications illuminate various aspects of the subject:

Batsford, H. and Fry, C. *The English Cottage*, 1938

Billett, Michael *Thatching and Thatched Buildings*, 1979

Bourne, George *Change in the Village*, 1955 ed.

Briggs, M.S. *The English Farmhouse*, 1953

Campbell, Mildred *The English Yeoman under Elizabeth and the Early Stuarts*, 1942

Charles, F.W.E. *Medieval Cruck Building and its Derivatives*, 1967

Clifton Taylor, A., and Brunskill, R.W. *English Brickwork*, 1977

Collins, E.J.T. *From Sickle to Combine*, 1970

Emmison, F.G. *Jacobean Household Inventories*, Beds. Hist. Record Soc., XX, 1938

Ernle, Lord *English Farming Past and Present*, 1912

Evans, George Ewart *The Farm and the Village*, 1969

Fussell, G. *Robert Loder's Farm Accounts*, Camden Soc., 1936

—— *The English Rural Labourer*, 1952

Harris, Richard *Discovering Timber-framed Buildings*, 1977

Hasbach, W.A. *A History of the English Agricultural Labourer*, 1894, reprinted 1966

Havinden, M.A. *Household and Farm Inventories in Oxfordshire*, 1966

Hoskins, W.G. *The Midland Peasant*, 1957

Howitt, William *The Rural Life of England*, 1838

Jewell, Andrew (ed.) *Victorian Farming, a Sourcebook*, 1975

Jones, Sidney R. *English Village Homes and Country Buildings*, 1936

McHardy, D.N. *Modern Farm Buildings*, 1932

Mercer, E. *English Vernacular Houses*, 1975

Orwin, C.S., and Whetham, E.H. *History of English Agriculture 1846–1914*, 1967

Salzman, L.F. *Building in England down to 1500*, 2nd ed., 1967

Smith, J.T. 'Aisled Halls and their Derivatives', *Archaeological Journal*, 112, 1955

Steer, Francis *Farm and Cottage Inventories of Mid-Essex 1635–1749*, 1950

Tate, W.E. *The English Village Community and the Enclosure Movement*, 1967

Thirsk, Joan *English Peasant Farming*, 1957

—— 'Tudor Enclosures', *Historical Association*, 1959

——, and Imray, Jean (eds.) *Suffolk Farming in the Nineteenth Century*, 1958

Walton, J. *Homesteads of the Yorkshire Dales*, 1947

West, T. *Timber-framed Houses in England*, 1971

Index

Page numbers in *italic* indicate illustrations.
New county locations are given in brackets.

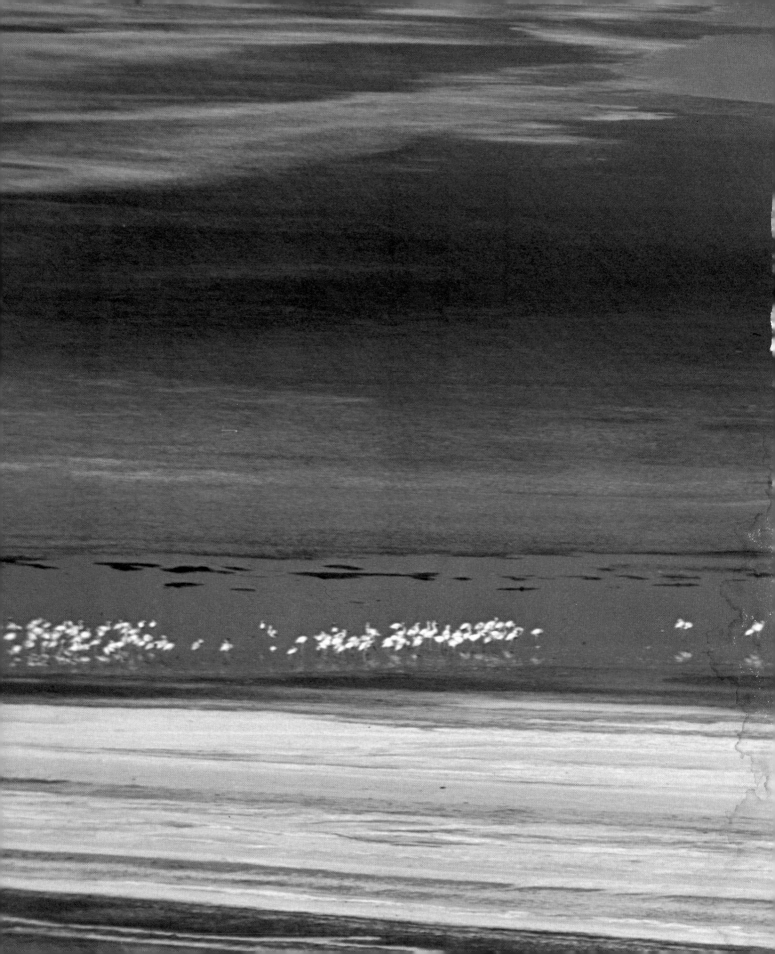

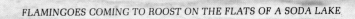

FLAMINGOES COMING TO ROOST ON THE FLATS OF A SODA LAKE

GOLIATH HERON BACKED BY PAPYRUS

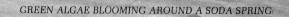

THE RIFT'S LARGEST LAKE, RUDOLF, AT DAWN

AFRICA'S RIFT VALLEY

THE WORLD'S WILD PLACES/TIME-LIFE BOOKS/AMSTERDAM

BY COLIN WILLOCK
AND THE EDITORS OF TIME-LIFE BOOKS

WITH PHOTOGRAPHS BY GOETZ D. PLAGE

THE WORLD'S WILD PLACES

Editorial Staff for *Africa's Rift Valley*:
EDITOR: John Man
Deputy Editor: Simon Rigge
Picture Editor: Pamela Marke
Design Consultant: Louis Klein
Staff Writers:
Tony Long, Robert Stewart,
Timberlake Wertenbaker, Heather Wyatt
Picture Researcher: Kerry Arnold
Art Director: Graham Davis
Design Assistant: Joyce Mason
Editorial Co-ordinator: Vanessa Kramer
Editorial Assistant: Jackie Matthews

Consultants
Botany: Phyllis Edwards
Geology: Dr. Peter Stubbs
Ichthyology: Alwyne Wheeler
Invertebrates: Dr. Michael Tweedie
Ornithology: I. J. Ferguson-Lees
Zoology: Dr. P. J. K. Burton

The captions and text of the picture essays are written
by the editorial staff of Time-Life Books.

Published by Time-Life International (Nederland) B.V.
5 Ottho Heldringstraat, Amsterdam 18

Colin Willock is an executive director of Survival Anglia Ltd., which specializes in the making of wildlife films. One of Survival's recent films, *The Flight of the Snowgeese*, won two television Emmy awards. Once assistant editor of *Picture Post*, he has written more than 20 books, including *The Enormous Zoo*, a profile of the Uganda national parks. He has travelled extensively in Africa while writing and producing Survival films. Three of his novels, *The Animal Catchers, Coast of Loneliness*, and *Hazanda* are set there.

Dr. W. T. W. Morgan, the consultant for this book, is the author of *East Africa*, a standard geography of the area. He is a graduate of London University and received his doctorate from Northwestern University, Illinois, before becoming Professor of Geography at University College, Nairobi. He later returned to England to teach at King's College, London, and is now lecturing at the University of Durham.

The Cover: Stained grey by its coating of fresh alkaline ash, the active cone of the volcano Ol Doinyo Lengai, the "Mountain of God" of Masai tribesmen, dominates the Rift in Tanzania.

Contents

A Land under Stress

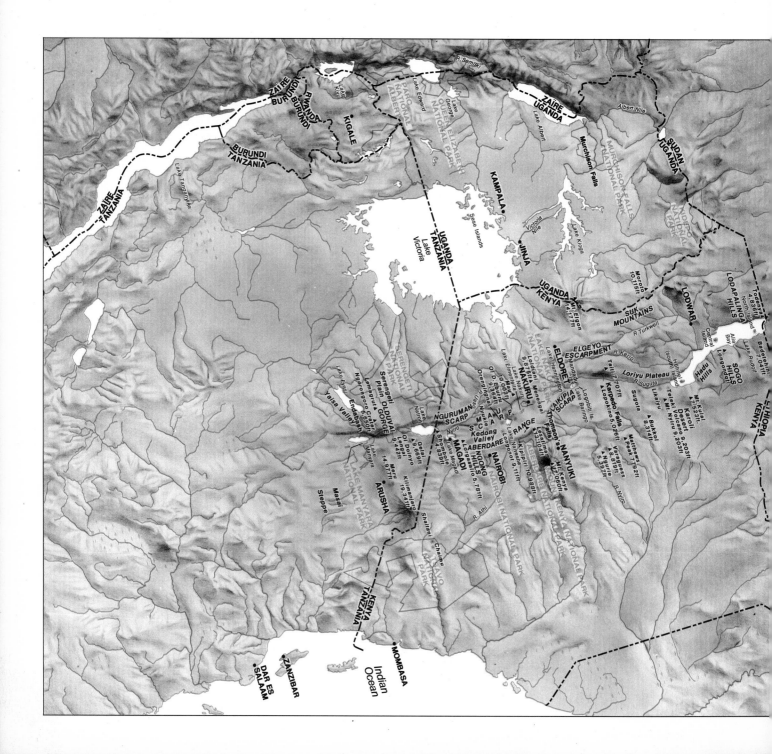

The Great Rift Valley is a 6,000-mile fissure in the earth's crust, stretching from the Lebanon to Mozambique. Its most dramatic section is in the area of East Africa indicated by the brown rectangle on the outline map (right). In the 1,500 miles between the Red Sea and Lake Manyara, nearly all of which was travelled by the author, a steep-sided subsidence (darker brown shading) cuts through the continent, mostly 30 miles across but widening to nearly 300 miles in the Danakil Depression. It was formed by violent subterranean forces that tore apart the earth's crust, causing huge chunks to sink between parallel fault lines and forcing up molten rock in volcanic eruptions. Evidence that rifting is still in progress comes from the 30 active or semi-active volcanoes (red asterisks) and from the boiling springs that bubble up sodium carbonate, turning many lakes along the Great Rift to bitter water or blistering soda flats.

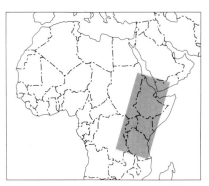

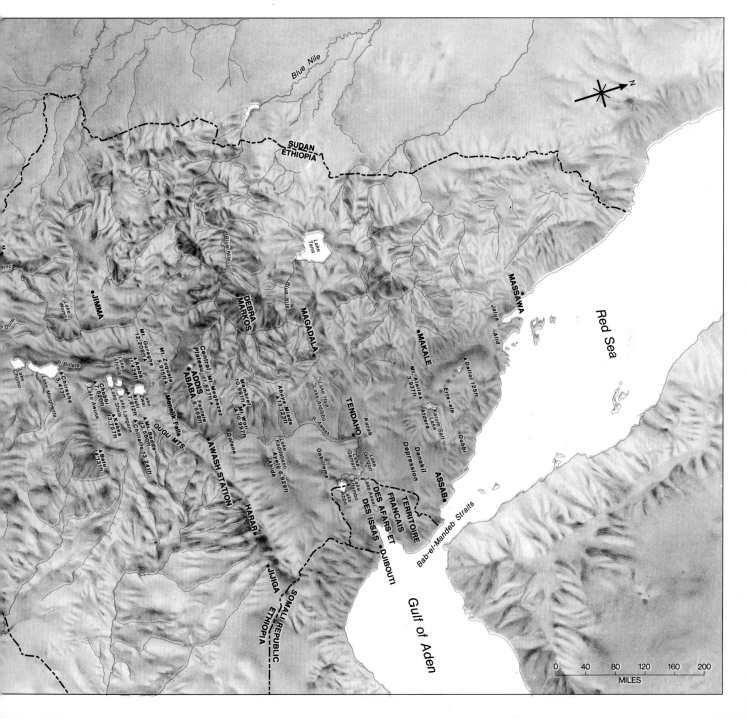

1/ A Scar on the Earth's Face

The natural boundaries of the geographer are rarely described by right lines; wherever these occur the geologist may look for something remarkable. HUGH MILLER/ *OLD RED SANDSTONE*

I first saw the Great Rift Valley during a journey north from Nairobi, the capital of Kenya. Thirty miles from the city, I came suddenly, without any warning, to the lip of a gigantic chasm. The scrub-covered slope fell away almost vertically in front of me. Spread out 2,000 feet below was an immense yellow plain, stretching into the distance. Thirty miles away, blue in the haze, I could see another almost vertical wall, very similar to the one on which I stood, rising to the same height. The whole landscape was so regular, so continuous, that it appeared almost unnatural. On either side of me, the valley wall stretched north and south in a straight line as far as the eye could see—and the distant wall did the same. There are very few straight lines, let alone parallel straight lines, in nature. Yet, as anyone looking down into the chasm would realize, only the most powerful forces of nature could have created a trench so colossal in scale.

The cliff-like walls of the valley appeared fresh and comparatively unweathered. I was unable to resist the impression that they had been formed not long ago, and that the entire valley floor had subsided from the level of the plateau in one enormous piece, like a lift 30 miles across going down a gigantic lift shaft. This is approximately what happened, not just here, but over thousands of miles to north and south. Over the last 20 million years—very recently in geological time—global disturbances tore at the continental masses of the Middle East and Africa and created a great scar down one-sixth of the earth's circumference. The part of the Great Rift Valley I first saw is a particularly dramatic point on a 4,000-mile line of subsidences between the Lebanon in the north and Mozambique in the south. From the Jordan valley, the scar runs through the ocean-filled trench of the Red Sea until it touches Africa in the low-lying Danakil desert of northern Ethiopia. From here it continues as a huge trench, rarely more than 30 miles wide, climbing and plunging through the landscape of East Africa. First it rises steeply into the Ethiopian highlands and travels south at 6,000 feet above sea level, its journey signposted by a series of lakes, the walls of the valley broken by cross fractures. Then down into Kenya, through Lake Rudolf, rising to Lake Naivasha, the highest lake in the valley, then on past the point where I had stood, through more lakes and down again into Tanzania and Mozambique until it finally peters out beyond Lake Nyasa, heading towards the Indian Ocean.

From this great crack in the earth's crust, there are other, lesser cracks that branch off: the Gulf of Suez and Gulf of Aqaba stretch out from the northern end of the Red Sea, and the Gulf of Aden from its southern end; in Africa, a lesser, western rift, containing, among others, Lakes Albert and Tanganyika, curves northwards from Lake Nyasa like the branch of a plant growing up from one side of the stem, in this case the main trunk of the Rift.

Geologists believe that some of the most recent major happenings in the formation of this great rift system took place within the last 10,000 years. Certainly there is a wealth of associated stories and legends to lend credence to the occurrence of cataclysmic earth movements within the time span of man's accumulated memory.

The Somalis, referring perhaps to a time before some major rifting occurred, claim that their ancestors travelled from Arabia to Africa over dry land, across the present straits of Bab-el-Mandeb, at the southern end of the Red Sea. The Old Testament, picking up the story, tells how the Egyptians, in pursuit of the Israelites, were caught and engulfed by the Red Sea: possibly a local arm of the sea was then in the process of formation. The Old Testament also describes an event which may have occurred at the same time, when the biblical cities of Sodom and Gomorrah, now thought by archaeologists to have been situated just south of the Dead Sea, in the line of the Rift, were destroyed by "fire and brimstone". The natives of Ujiji—where the explorer Livingstone made his base before his discovery of Lake Nyasa in 1859—tell long-ago stories about the African part of the Rift, where a great flood is said to have inundated plains rich in game and cattle, so forming Lake Tanganyika.

None of this literally earth-shattering past was investigated or even suspected by Europeans until the late 19th Century, when attention began to focus on the main trunk of the Great Rift Valley in Kenya, where my own travels were to be concentrated. Their ignorance was not surprising, for the colonial powers had barely penetrated inland from the coasts. Although Arab caravans trading in slaves and ivory had crossed the Rift on their journeys from Mombasa, on the coast, to Uganda for hundreds of years, there were no maps to be had. The first maps were not even made until the 1860s, when two amateur cartographers, T. Wakefield and Clemens Denhardt of Mombasa, drew a series based on lengthy questioning of the Arab traders. Considering they were drawn from hearsay, these maps were remarkably full and accurate, but they naturally had some notable failings. They were very poor on the location of rivers and lakes, and particularly on the actual sizes. They vastly exaggerated the extent of Lake Baringo and left out Lake Hannington. Above all, they failed to mention or depict the line of the Great Rift Valley at all.

If the map-makers were still making guesses, the geologists had not even started work—nor could they until there was more for them to go on. But now the time of the explorers had arrived. In the 1880s, a pioneering group of travellers revealed the mysteries of the East African Rift, the most pronounced section of the whole system. Although they did not draw wide conclusions from their piecemeal discoveries, they rapidly provided the missing parts of the puzzle. In 1883, the German naturalist, Dr. Gustav Fischer, became the first man to enter Masailand, as the territory of the warlike Masai tribesmen was then commonly known. He described the country stretching from the volcano, Ol Doinyo Lengai, in the south, in what is now Tanzania, to a spot just north of Lake Naivasha in Kenya, where he ran out of supplies. He had explored the line of the Great Rift Valley just beyond the point where I had first seen it. Later the same year, the Scottish explorer, Joseph Thomson, pushed further north, passing beyond Lake Naivasha where the Masai were now at their most bellicose, until he reached Lake Baringo. He was able to reveal that, far from being the enormous expanse of water shown on Wakefield and Denhardt's map of the 1860s, Baringo was barely five miles wide by 14 miles long. Meanwhile, the German explorer, Baumann, had provided details about the area around Lake Manyara in the south, beyond which point the walls of the Rift cease to be so clearly defined and the line of the valley becomes diffuse.

The discoverer of the Great Rift Valley, J. W. Gregory, remarked long before the space age that the Rift would be one earth feature visible from the moon. His prediction is borne out by this picture, taken from Apollo 17 at a distance of 90,000 miles, showing all of Africa, with the Mediterranean at the very top and the Arabian peninsula near the top. Just below the southern tip of Arabia can be seen the Y of the northern end of the Rift, enclosing the light patch of the Danakil Depression. Clouds obscure much of the valley to the south.

In 1887 came the most important discovery of all. The Hungarian sportsman Count Teleki and his gifted companion, a German artist, Ludwig von Höhnel, marched 300 miles from the coast to discover the vast lake which was still a traders' tale for Europeans. It was then called by its African name, Basso Narok. Having discovered what the African tribesmen had known was there all the time—this to me is the perpetual irony of the white man's exploration of Africa—he renamed Basso Narok "Rudolf" after the Austrian crown prince, who was his sponsor. Its smaller, marshy and even more remote companion to the north-east, Basso Ebor, he called Lake Stefanie, after Prince Rudolf's consort.

The knowledge of the size and position of these lakes, especially Lake Rudolf, the most northerly of the new "discoveries", was immensely important. Plotted on the map, they appeared as links in a connected chain leading north to the Red Sea. The first significant deduction from this new information was made in 1891 by the Viennese geologist, Eduard Suess, who had never been to Africa, but had collected the explorers' accounts on his desk. He declared that the whole line of country from Lake Nyasa in the south to the river Jordan in the north had been fractured by a connected series of earth movements. He used the contemporary geologists' term to describe the phenomenon. He called it a *Graben*, or grave. However, there was one key figure yet to come upon the scene who would explore the valley scientifically, diagnose it for what it was, and bring it to world attention. That figure was another Scot, the young geologist John Walter Gregory.

Gregory was the son of a Scottish wool merchant trading in Bermondsey, south London. He was trained to be a merchant too, but as a colleague later put it, "an overmastering bent for natural history rescued him from business and secured him for science". After studying at London University, he was appointed in 1887, at the age of 23, to the geological department of the British Museum of Natural History in Kensington. Gregory was an ardent follower of Suess and agreed with him that there was once a super-continent, Gondwanaland, which broke up to form the present southern continents. The movements that pulled the continents apart, he believed, were also responsible for tearing at the fabric of Africa and causing the subsidence of the Rift. However, it was still a theory, developed from the observations of explorers who were not experts, and Gregory now felt he must see the Rift for himself and discover empirical support for his beliefs.

In 1892 Gregory got his chance. He was asked to go as naturalist on an expedition across Somalia, and accepted the invitation with enthusi-asm. Unfortunately the journey was a disaster. Bad planning, bad Somali porters and lack of food forced the party to turn back from the interior after only six weeks, and Gregory ended up in the port of Mombasa, far to the south, with malaria, dysentery and an unshakeable determination to mount his own expedition. He decided to follow the ancient Arab caravan route inland from Mombasa. Despite repeated discouragement from Europeans, who urged him not to venture into the little known territory of the hostile Kikuyu and Masai tribes, Gregory left Mombasa on March 23, 1893, at the head of 40 men. He was accom-panied for a little while by two European officials, who gaily sent the balding, lanky Scotsman off with the refrain of "Will he nae come back again?" Gregory, suffering from another bout of malaria, wondered wistfully whether he would.

In order to diagnose Suess's *Graben* geologically, Gregory intended to adopt the geologists' standard method of discovery and make a "section" right across the valley, collecting rock samples from selected points and using them to draw a cross-section diagram of the rock strata under-lying both the walls and the floor. He knew that, if he chose a suitable spot to make the section and was successful in collecting his samples, the resulting diagram would enable him to prove to the world how the Rift had actually come about. Nothing is simple for the field geologist. Assuming that the valley floor had been created by a gigantic subsi-dence, Gregory expected to find the picture complicated by the other events which would surely have occurred during the immense time span of a geological happening. Lava streaming in from the volcanic eruptions along the fault lines at the edges as the floor sank down would have covered much of the valley floor; immense deposits of silt would have been laid down by the lakes that have filled much of the valley with water at varying times and at varying levels; different parts of the valley may have slipped to different positions. The end result of so complex a pattern of events is an intricate layering and apparent confusion of rocks which initially defies sense.

The first spot Gregory chose for his section was near Lake Naivasha, and he spent five weeks marching through Kikuyu and Masai country to reach it. On the journey, he revealed a remarkable talent for diplomacy, knowing when to yield to native intransigence and when to show tough-ness. When he arrived at the Rift, however, seeing it initially at a point close to my own first glimpse, he found that the area round Naivasha was a hotspot of Masai belligerence. The tribesmen were not only busy slaughtering Kikuyu but also harassing and even attacking any caravan or traveller who seemed insufficiently protected. Diplomacy was little use here, and Gregory was forced to move another hundred miles to the north where he reached Lake Baringo, an extremely lucky accident both for him and future geologists.

The cross-section of the valley at Lake Baringo is one of the most spectacular of all. In the east, where Gregory had arrived, the wall of the Laikipia escarpment, 7,000 feet above sea level, drops down towards the lake, ending in a series of step-like foothills. Then, ten miles from the foot of the escarpment, comes the lake with its green islands and beyond, another ten miles to the west, what at first looks like the other wall of the valley. In fact, this is a great block called Kamasia, or the Tugen Hills after the Tugen tribe which lives there. Only after climbing its crest to an altitude of 7,000 feet can one see that a further ten miles to the west, beyond the valley of the river Kerio, rises one of the most imposing escarpments of all, the Elgeyo scarp, also 7,000 feet high. Elgeyo, not Kamasia, is the western wall of the valley.

This confusion right across the valley was a godsend for Gregory, since it enabled him more easily to discover the nature of the underlying strata. Perhaps his opportunity can best be understood by picturing the countryside before the great subsidence took place. It was then level land from the plains on top of Laikipia to the plateau on top of Elgeyo, in the west. Now think of it, not as a slice of Africa, but as a broad, multi-decker sandwich. Bread, butter and fillings represent different strata composed of lavas, sediments and the hard crystalline rocks of the continent. At first, only the smooth top layer of bread is visible. Then the sandwich is cut into six segments—two large ones at the edges and four thin strips in the middle—by parallel, north-south lines. This represents the tearing and cracking of Africa. The large segment on the right stays where it is—the Laikipia plains—but the next slips down a little, splitting into smaller sections that each slip down a little more—the foothills. The third slides down a great deal further and receives some extra layers of bread and fillings on top. This represents Lake Baringo and its shoreline: the extra layers are the sediments washed into the ancient lake and deposited over the whole of its once great area. The fourth pile is the most important of all: the great block of Kamasia. Instead of sinking, it has tilted violently to the west, revealing the layers of which it consists, including the basic crystalline rocks—gneiss and schists—at the bottom. Beyond Kamasia there is a further fully subsided segment—the valley of the river Kerio—and then, finally, comes

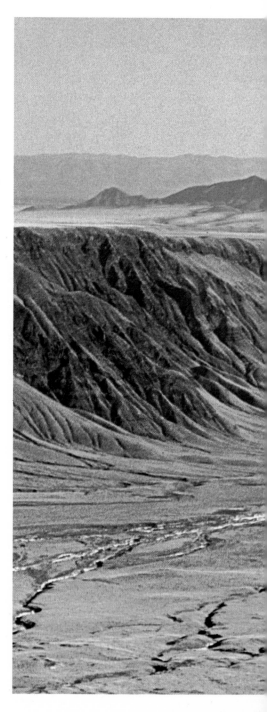

The western Rift wall, opposite Mount Lengai, towers to 1,500 feet, testimony to the great subsidence that created the plain below.

the large, stable segment on the left representing the Elgeyo plateau.

One can imagine Gregory scrambling along the precipitous wall of Laikipia with his geologist's hammer, chipping away in a state of high scientific excitement at the strata exposed when the segment of the foothills slipped. He made his base in the village of Njemps at the south-eastern end of Lake Baringo and set out on a series of rock-gathering excursions around the lake, taking samples of lavas and sediments all the way down, carefully noting where he had found the specimens and at what height. Finally, he climbed the base of the tilted mountain block of Kamasia, storing the vital information about its upturned strata. At this point he ran out of supplies and received warnings of new tribal hostilities nearby. He was forced to abandon his wall-to-wall survey before even studying the Elgeyo scarp. After traversing only half the valley, he returned to Mombasa and sailed for England.

But the expedition had not been a failure. Gregory's feat was to reach the correct conclusions without the missing data. His section of the Baringo basin, pieced together from his own information and from maps, showed the position of the strata that composed the valley floor and its walls. It demonstrated that the layers along the eastern escarpment of Laikipia closely matched those in the central block of Kamasia and in Elgeyo, the western escarpment. It portrayed the same layers in the valley floor, but as much as 6,000 feet lower.

Addressing himself to the orthodox geologists of his day, Gregory concluded triumphantly that "these valleys were not formed by removal grain by grain, by rivers or wind, of the rocks which originally occupied them, but by the rock sinking in mass, while the adjacent land remained stationary". Gregory now invented a new term in geology and gave the whole vast feature he had discovered a name to be remembered by. "For this type of valley I suggest the name of Rift Valley, using the term rift in the sense of a relatively narrow space due to subsidence between parallel fractures. Such valleys", he continued, "are known in many parts of the world, but that of East Africa may justly be called the Great Rift Valley".

Gregory wrote two books on his adventures and geological discoveries in Africa, and became Professor of Geology at Glasgow University. He subsequently travelled to the Arctic, India and finally South America where he was killed in 1932, at the age of 68, when his canoe capsized in a Peruvian river. Though little known outside his own field, Gregory nevertheless has his memorial: the Great Rift Valley itself. Even today there are a good many people, both geologists and

John Walter Gregory, who was the first geologist to explore the Great Rift Valley, led his own expedition to Lakes Naivasha and Baringo in 1893. His men nicknamed him "bulging pockets" because of his habit of stuffing his pockets with numerous rock samples.

laymen, who still refer to its main trunk simply as the Gregory Rift.

Had he been able to stay in Africa longer and travel to Elgeyo, Gregory would probably have unravelled more than he did. He did not entirely appreciate the amount of in-filling by lavas and sediments on the valley floor—sometimes as deep as a mile. Modern geologists have since discovered it is in the tilt block of Kamasia that the total geological history of the Rift Valley lies revealed, from the lavas and sediments on top down to bedrock at the bottom.

Since Gregory's day, geologists have gradually been building on his work, dating the various stages of the Rift's creation and fitting them into a global picture of earth movements. According to the latest geophysical conclusions, based on the dating of rocks along the whole of the rift system, rifting took place in three main phases: Triassic (200 million years ago), Cretaceous (between 80 and 130 million years ago) and, finally, Late Cainozoic (the last 20 million years), the period when the eastern Rift was formed. These dates coincide with the chronology of continental drift, the theory which was in its infancy in Gregory's day. In the earliest of the three phases, 200 million years ago, the great super-continent of Gondwanaland, in which Gregory believed so ardently, is considered to have been still in existence. Deep down within the earth, radioactively generated heat produced slow but immensely powerful currents beneath the surface crust, causing the solid rock of the earth's mantle to move like a heavy liquid. As the great subterranean currents rose towards the surface, they came into contact with the crust of the super-continent, where they turned outwards, wrenching Gondwanaland apart. Molten rock spewed up through the cracks as lava in volcanic eruptions and the fragments were slowly carried away to their locations as the present continents. Oceans filled the gaps.

One of these new sea areas is the Indian Ocean, and Madagascar is a piece of Africa that was torn off and carried away. Geologists today sometimes speak of the Great Rift Valley as "an aborted ocean". There, but for the grace of unfathomable underground forces, they say, should have gone a large piece of Africa east of the Rift, floating off like Madagascar. If this had happened, salt water would have filled the Rift until it resembled the Red Sea. The eastern half of Ethiopia, all of Somalia, and half of Kenya and Tanzania would have become a large offshore island. In the event a new sea was not formed.

What did happen was that during the creation of the Indian Ocean there was a great outpouring of molten rock. Much of this material must have come from beneath East Africa, parts of which subsided as a result. The creation of the Great Rift Valley began. In the Oligocene, roughly 40 million years ago, major riftings produced some of the great lakes, the forerunners of today's smaller lakes. Eleven million years ago came the main faulting, followed in the last three million years by subsidiary faulting on the valley floor and the renewal of movements in the main fractures. A bare million years ago the valley's shoulders were uplifted and yet more faulting took place on its floor. All these movements produced intense volcanic activity, as the subsidence of the floor caused the molten rock beneath to be squeezed up at the sides. This volcanic activity goes on today and is evidence of the continuing operation of continental drift. Indeed, the Red Sea and the Gulf of Aden are gradually widening and there is every reason to think that East Africa is now being torn apart and that the Great Rift Valley may well in some tens of millions of years become an ocean after all.

The feeling of a landscape on the move, constantly rearranging itself according to some unfathomable plan, is always strong in the Great Rift Valley. Unlike the plateaux either side of its precipitous walls, which mostly consist of shield rock as much as 3,000 million years old, eroded to a flat monotony, the interior of the valley is a young land. Volcanoes both active and dormant rise at intervals along its length, while steam vents and boiling springs bear added witness to the turmoil beneath. The ground is covered in volcanic ash rich in sodium carbonate, or washing soda, and this has found its way into the lakes, turning many of them bitter or transforming a few into almost solid deposits of soda. Many animals are unable to cope with such extreme conditions, but there is one notable exception: flamingoes thrive on the wealth of diatoms, blue-green algae, found in soda lakes and the millions that live in the Rift provide one of the finest wildlife spectacles to be seen anywhere.

Despite their bitterness, many of the other lakes support a large indigenous population of birds. Thousands of pelicans, egrets, herons, storks, wildfowl and cormorants, as well as kingfishers and fish eagles, can be seen here. The lakes also form staging points along one of the world's most heavily travelled bird migration routes. In early spring, small, familiar birds like swallows and wheatears fly in thousands between the towering walls of the Rift, travelling north to Eastern Europe or Russia. They are joined by storks, cranes, eagles and hawks. Many of these birds are helped on their way by the numerous thermals, currents of hot air that rise up the steep escarpments of the Rift.

The plains of the valley contain some of the last big game herds, including, at Lake Manyara in Tanzania, the highest concentration of elephants per square mile left in Africa. And, distributed throughout the valley, there is a rich variety of wild people, a fair cross-section through the patchwork of African tribes. As anyone who wishes to understand Africa must realize, tribes dictate the realities of territory, emnity and allegiance more often than the lines arbitrarily placed on the map by former colonists. In the extreme north, in the Afar triangle of Ethiopia, live the most savage people I have come across in Africa or anywhere else. The Danakil, a Muslim race possibly descended from the ancient Egyptians, are still liable to murder and castrate strangers to protect their desert home and its scanty water supplies. In the extreme south of the area covered by my travels around Lake Natron, live the tribe who most easily capture the European traveller's imagination, the ochre-daubed Masai who once harassed the explorers. Between these extremes of north and south lie the tribal lands of the adaptable Kikuyu; the Njemps, a fishing tribe close in blood to the Masai; Tugen, Samburu, Pokot, Rendille, Turkana and Galla. Each have a different tradition, language and background. Some grow subsistence crops, some specialize in hunting. Most are herders of cattle, camels or goats.

No one can fail to be impressed by the scenic contrasts of the magnificent country the tribesmen live in. In the Danakil desert in northern Ethiopia, the Rift plunges to a torrid 400 feet below sea level and the temperature soars to the infernal, while along many of its escarpments there are dense and gloomy rain forests, fed by the clouds that often cloak them. And at Naivasha, the highest of the lakes, there is often frost on the morning grass. All this richness and diversity can be found in the most pronounced section of the valley, between the Danakil in the north and Manyara in the south. That is why, in my travels, I concentrated on this 1,500 mile section. I knew that here I would find the wildest and richest scenes to be experienced in the Great Rift Valley of Africa.

Signs of Subterranean Turmoil

The Great Rift Valley is one of the most spectacular volcanic regions in the world, and also one of the least known. Most of its volcanoes are long dead and their gigantic remains now litter its course, geological corpses dominating the land that created them.

But 30 still show some signs of activity. They are the signals that deep down inside the earth, continent-splitting forces are at work along the line of the Rift. Internal heat creates titanic currents which over the ages stir solid rock like stiff treacle. These currents push up and turn outwards beneath the earth's crust, stretching it like opposing conveyor belts. In the process a layer of molten rock, or magma, is built up. When the stretching reaches an intolerable pitch, the earth's crust fractures and magma rushes through, emerging as the molten lava of an erupting volcano.

The classically symmetrical cones of the volcanoes have been built up over millennia of geological activity by the alternation of two kinds of eruption, explosive and effusive. In an explosive eruption, there is a large amount of gas in the magma, which blasts through a chimney-like vent and showers a storm of rocks, ash and molten lava around in a circle. In an effusive eruption, the magma contains less gas and flows out quietly like hot plasticine, covering the previous layer of rock and ash with a coat of lava.

Both types of eruption occurred in the Rift in the 1960s. In the Danakil desert at the northern end of the valley, there was an unusual type of effusive eruption in 1960 that filled the crater at the top of the volcano Erta-ale with molten lava, forming one of the world's rare lava lakes. Then in 1966 there was an explosive eruption in the southern part of the Rift when Ol Doinyo Lengai (opposite) blew up. Because the volcano stands in remote, inhospitable country at the southern end of Lake Natron, an arid soda lake, few people saw the eruption and no world-wide publicity attended the event. However, the roving photographer, Gerald Cubitt, climbed to the lip of the crater twice during the month of the eruption, and took the photographs on this and the next four pages. They show Lengai before, during and after the eruption, from both inside and outside the crater, providing a rare documentation of the changes an eruption brings.

Ol Doinyo Lengai, the Masai "Mountain of God", pours out lava rich in alkali during its 1966 eruption. This type of lava is black when it emerges, but is chemically unstable. Within 48 hours of coating the slopes of the 2,000-foot cone, the lava turns white, for contact with moisture in the air converts much of it to crystals of sodium carbonate—commonly known as washing soda.

Lengai's crater (above), a weird landscape of congealed white lava, simmers ominously only a week before its 1966 eruption. The photographer, Gerald Cubitt, recalled later how he saw "lava cones gurgitating blobs of molten black lava, while the ground shook with rumbles that foretold the coming storm".

On the right, Lengai is seen erupting only a week after Cubitt had left. He returned hurriedly to watch the black cloud billowing 25,000 feet into the air, raining ash over the mountain. After three weeks the volcano subsided, leaving the slopes a chiarascuro of white ridges and black depressions.

A soft mantle of green covers the outside of Mount Lengai, put on in the quiescent years before the violent explosion of 1966.

A fresh coat of caustic white ash applied during the 1966 explosion gives Lengai's sides and foothills a wintry appearance.

The Distinctive Craters

Perhaps the most striking remnant of a volcanic eruption is the crater as it appears soon after an eruption. Its original shape reveals the type of action that formed it. In an explosive eruption, like those that have wracked many volcanoes in the Danakil, escaping gases leave behind a gaping, often steaming, chimney (opposite). An effusive eruption, on the other hand, wells up inside a dish-like, neatly circular crater.

Typical of the appearance of a volcano following an effusive eruption is Erta-ale, the most spectacular of a chain of five volcanoes that appear etched in statuesque relief against the desert's flat salt plains. Erta-ale's present crater (right) was formed in 1960 by an effusive eruption witnessed by Paul Mohr, a geologist in Ethiopia. He saw a lava lake of red hot, pasty basalt fill the volcano's crater, gushing out of fissures in its sides. From this scene of elemental alchemy billowed a cloud of steam, giving renewed justification to the name Erta-ale, which in the language of the Danakil tribesmen means "fuming mountain".

A lake of white lava wells up in Erta-ale's crater during the effusive eruption of 1960.

The crater of a Danakil volcano emits steam, the main source of the explosion that blasted it open, causing its chimney-like appearance.

Aftermath of an Explosion

Soon after the eruption, a volcano loses the top of its neat cone and remains disfigured until a shroud of vegetation cloaks it in old age. The change comes about when the top of the cone collapses, falling into the space left in the volcano's substructure by the movements of rock or magma during the eruption. The collapse of the cone gives the volcano a decapitated look from the outside and determines the form of the depression inside the summit.

Known normally as a crater but, if very large, as a caldera, this depression is always many times the diameter of the original vent. The most impressive of such calderas in the Rift Valley belong to two large old volcanoes rising between lakes Baringo and Magadi. The more northerly volcano, Menengai, has a caldera shaped like a shallow soup plate, seven miles wide, with titanic chips in its rim and a jumble of immense boulders on its floor. The southerly volcano, Suswa, has an outer caldera of five miles and an inner one of three miles. This contains a lava island which at its last eruption was cut off from the sides by a molten moat.

Between these two calderas lies Longonot, whose eruption long ago caused a different but equally dramatic type of collapse: deep rather than wide. The crater is only one mile wide, but it has steep sides and bores into the earth like a gigantic cannon barrel, seeming barely to await the touch of subterranean heat before firing.

Small patches of scrub grow in the pit of an extinct crater on the shore of Lake Rudolf.

The senile volcano, Longonot, breathes steam through the foliage on its crater, just as it has done for a century without exploding.

2/ The Danakil Inferno

Dregs of water . . . were measured out among us, in Danakil, as though they had been the contents of the last bottle of some priceless vintage wine. L. M. NESBITT/ *DESERT AND FOREST*

The hottest, lowest, most inhospitable section of the African Rift lies in the far north, separated from the Red Sea only by a range of low hills. It is the scorching Ethiopian desert, the Danakil, the lowest part of which is called, in the more precise language of geographers and geologists, the Danakil Depression. Depression is an apt word, since much of the Danakil lies 400 feet below sea level, forming a great hollow of 58,000 square miles in the earth's surface. Deep down in the Depression, the surface temperature of the rock can rise to an incredible 320 degrees Fahrenheit—more than hot enough to fry a chicken.

The Danakil, sometimes known as the Afar triangle after the Afar tribesmen who are virtually its only inhabitants, is, in fact, shaped like a south-pointing equilateral triangle. Its base stretches along the Red Sea between the sea-port of Massawa in the west and Ethiopia's border with the old French Somaliland, now known as Territoire Française des Afars et des Issas, in the east. Its apex is wedged tightly into the great Ethiopian highlands where the river Awash has cut a deep gorge as it tumbles to lose itself in the desert inferno. Just west of the gorge, 8,000 feet above sea level, stands the capital, Addis Ababa. At this point the Danakil ends and the Rift narrows to a trench about 30 miles wide, in which form it continues more or less unbroken for 1,000 miles southwards to Lake Manyara in Tanzania. Almost precisely at the centre of the Danakil is Tendaho, a small settlement with an air-strip.

It was from here that I flew by helicopter to explore the triangular desert.

The landscape looks either like the end of the world, or its beginning. I have never viewed the aftermath of an atomic explosion at close quarters, but the Danakil might well be the kind of landscape such an explosion produces. The colours are those of desert and of volcanic fire: greys, whites and yellows intermingled with ochres, deep browns and ember reds. Mud-coloured buttresses and miniature mesas lie jumbled together. Glistening salt plains stretch towards towering pinnacles, also encrusted with salt. Deep green pits appear to boil and bubble. Volcanoes belch smoke or leave grey scars where the lava of centuries has cooled. Nothing but the hardiest of plants, animals and birds can survive here.

The only exception to this barren landscape is the ribbon of green fed by the river Awash as it winds its way north-eastwards across the southern part of the Danakil. The river provides the sole support for the Danakil's 200,000 nomadic Afar herdsmen. They believe that "he who controls the water controls the Danakil", and any intruders who might threaten their lonely tenure are murdered and castrated, not necessarily in that order.

The weird, primeval appearance of the Danakil stems mainly from the fact that it is still an area of intense geological activity, as its volcanoes bear witness. It is being subjected to the continent-tearing forces, not only of the African Rift of which it is part, but also of two other adjacent arms of the rift systems: the Red Sea and the Gulf of Aden. Consequently it is prone to severe earthquakes. From May to September, 1961, for example, several shocks were recorded measuring 6.5 on the Richter scale, which has a maximum of ten.

Over millions of years, this type of activity gradually created the Depression as it appears today, probably by making its central area slip down between parallel faults to form a trench. In very recent times, possibly only 10,000 years ago, part of the Danakil was under water, and extended south as an arm of the Red Sea. Later, however, the crust rose, setting up the line of hills along the base of the triangle and cutting off the Danakil sea, leaving its waters to evaporate and form the great salt plains of the present Depression.

The old fault lines are now partly obscured, but their presence is marked by the line of the Danakil volcanoes, both active and dormant, and by lurid-coloured hot springs. These, too, are a sign of volcanic activity. When surface water seeps down through the fault cracks, it comes into contact with molten rock beneath and is then forced upwards through layers of salts and minerals, emerging boiling hot and coloured according to the type of mineral compound it has passed through. Brown, yellow and red, for instance, are colours picked up from the various oxides and hydroxides of iron. As the water cools, its minerals crystallize and form coloured stalagmites, humps and mounds. Many of the salts laid down in the process provide colour in a more indirect way, forming a specialized environment for many brightly-hued species of algae.

The Danakil's geological history is still vague because its inhospitality has kept out explorers. Apart from the Afar, very few others— mainly European and American miners and researchers—have ever walked on it. One Swiss and two Italian expeditions made ill-fated forays into it in the 19th Century. They travelled the shortest route, east-west across the desert, but it proved to be extremely arduous and they either died of thirst and starvation or were massacred.

It was not until 1928 that an Englishman, L. M. Nesbitt, and two Italians, T. Pastori and G. Rosina, managed to cross the north-western part of the Danakil the long way, 800 miles from Addis Ababa to the Red Sea. Their march took three and a half months, and three Ethiopian companions, three mules and ten camels died; the rest of the 20-strong party survived, partly as a result, Nesbitt maintained, of "my habit of placing my trust in Providence".

"We started again at daybreak," he wrote in the early stages of his journey, "and soon came to ground covered with tall horny grass which appeared to be entirely dried up and parched. Yet it was not dry within. The desert colours this grass with its own ochre hue, as it colours everything else in the dismal landscape. . . . The jet-black mountains to the west were outlined by a thin rim of light, which appeared to separate them from the sky. Presently this gradually went out, and everything became merged in a single, blue-black void, engulfing the earth and sky. Only the stars hung from base to summit of the infinite vault before us."

In 1933 and 1934, one of the great English explorers of the 20th Century, Wilfred Thesiger, first traced the course of the Awash. The river rises in the highlands south of Addis Ababa. For centuries Ethiopians and Europeans alike had assumed that it flowed to an unknown outlet in or near the Red Sea, but no one had ever found its mouth. The disappearance of its mouth, Thesiger said, "has excited considerable curiosity, and many have been the theories expounded to account for the river's failure to reach the sea".

Thesiger set out from Awash Station to map the river on December 1, 1933, "somewhat hurriedly", thinking that the Abyssinian government would forbid his departure for fear of his safety. He had a caravan of

Clouds of Danakil dust swirl around a tribal hut of mats tied over a stick frame, almost obscuring the Ethiopian humped cattle behind.

18 camels, 23 men armed with 13 rifles and an official escort of another 15 armed men. For nearly six months he struggled through "country as dead as a lunar landscape", broken only rarely by oases of green. "Throughout the hottest hours," he wrote, "we crouched among the rocks, our heads swathed in cloths, wondering if we should have the strength left to continue, but nothing could shelter us from the scorching wind which drove before it a stinging cloud of sand."

Thesiger was less afraid than challenged by the Afar tribesmen's "well-merited reputation for savagery". Although he was met once, at Berifer, 70 miles north-west of Awash Station, by "a large gathering of armed warriors" who were "far from friendly", he escaped unharmed. He attempted to investigate the Afar custom of murdering intruders, and to understand it. His report to the Royal Geographical Society in London on November 12, 1934, was packed with details of their culture, carefully studied and for the most part meticulously set down. He did find it difficult, however, to speak "unblushingly" of castration. He generally called the cut testicles "trophies". An Afar's standing in the tribe, he wrote, "depends on the number of his trophies, and ten will give the right to wear a coveted iron bracelet". Nesbitt had claimed that the Afar wore these trophies round their necks, but Thesiger reported that "they actually deny this and I find it difficult to believe that their denial is based on feelings of delicacy, when they are ready to admit that they will rip open a pregnant woman and mutilate the child inside her". Those unlucky warriors who returned empty-handed from a raid, he added, were "ragged unmercifully by their more successful companions, their clothes being soiled and cow dung rubbed into their hair".

It was not until April, 1934, that Thesiger and his party closed in on the Awash's missing outlet. When they reached the sultanate of Aussa, Thesiger could see the river entering a large, swampy lake called Adabada, "White Lake", after the colour of its water. Some comparatively peaceful Afar tribesmen whom he had persuaded to accompany him assured him that Lake Adabada had no exit. But Thesiger was not convinced. He climbed a hill and saw the Awash passing through two smaller lakes before disappearing to the west. His opinions thus confirmed, he determined to press on. For five days he waded through deep swamps "infested" with pythons to reach these lakes, and spent another two days crossing a belt of "cracked and riven lava" from the volcanic Mount Jira, the heat rising "as from a furnace door".

The trail led on to a third lake, Abhebad (now called Abbe), prized by the Afar for its supposed medicinal qualities. Thesiger remained on the treacherous black mud of its bare shores for seven days, checking for possible outlets. "Shade there was none, our drinking water was hot and brackish, and regularly at sunset a sandstorm swept down upon us from the Essa mountains across the lake," he wrote. By the seventh day, he satisfied himself that the lake had no exit. He had found the mouth of the Awash, 80 miles from the Red Sea. The river simply bled to death, evaporated in the middle of the desert. On May 20, 1934, near starvation point and after enduring almost six months in the scorching heat, he reached Tajura in French Somaliland and from there sailed home.

Few Europeans have walked the remoter parts of the Danakil since then, and I can claim to be one of them. However, I must admit I walked only briefly. I did most of my exploration from a height of some 50 feet, in a helicopter. Taking off from Tendaho at the centre of the Danakil, my pilot picked up the winding Awash as it flowed strongly eastwards, perhaps 70 yards wide, between steep muddy banks. A green strip of grass and acacia woodland stretched for about 100 yards on either side. Something slithered into the water as we approached—a crocodile about eight feet long. The muddy river is alive with crocodiles, but it is also well stocked with their staple diet, catfish, and the ample supply of food may explain why the Afar tribesmen fording the river with their camels and goats, cross without apparent fear or even watchfulness.

There were swamps along the river's course now. The helicopter put up a cloud of cattle egrets, and I spotted a horseshoe formation of great white pelicans dipping their heads rhythmically as they fished. A disgruntled hippo spouted a jet of water vapour from its nostrils and quickly scuttled itself. A second hippo, with a tangled clump of the water plant, Nile cabbage, perched incongruously on its head, sank more sedately, while its vegetable bonnet floated away.

We followed the course pioneered by Thesiger, and entered the Sultanate of Aussa where the river passes through the White Lake, which since Thesiger's time has become known as Lake Gamarri. As we continued north, the lakes and riverine woodlands of Aussa were soon left behind. The banks of the Awash became increasingly bare, grey lava showing through. The pace of the river quickened as it flowed along the foot of Mount Jira. More frequent white water appeared, then gave way to placid flow again. Suddenly the Awash broke up into several streams sluggishly flowing through banks of silt. The many-channelled waterway took on the look of a delta. It must have been about here that the tiring Thesiger began to guess how the river ended.

We were flying now only feet above the mud. The air blasting in through the open door of the cockpit smelled strongly acrid. Suddenly the pilot climbed to show me what lay ahead. A great shimmering lake appeared in the heart of the desert. This was the end the Awash was hurrying to meet. Lake Abbe, as Thesiger discovered, is a huge sump from which the waters of the river are sucked up by the sun as fast as the river can deliver them.

We turned south, heading back to Tendaho to refuel, this time over gritty lava deserts. Below, it was evident that other forms of life besides the Afar eke a living from the desert. A herd of 30 Soemmering's gazelle, a desert-adapted antelope, made the lava dust spurt at each hoof-fall as they galloped away before us. Wherever sparse clumps of grass managed to take hold, ostriches appeared, and in a rocky ravine stood one of the world's rarest creatures—the Somali wild ass, much like any donkey except that it is fatter and looks fitter. After we landed and refuelled at Tendaho, we set course north-west towards the Karum salt lake at the Danakil's far north-western corner. Beneath me was real Danakil country, lacking totally the green relief of the river Awash. Here along the Rift's north-south fault line, the lava's grey surface was interrupted with yellow, red and brown stains. I could not escape the impression that they were exhudations of a boil—matter ejected from beneath the skin of the sick earth.

It was from here that I took my short walk on one of the worst surfaces in the world, not from choice, but because fuel was running low. Finding a comparatively level spot on this craggy lavascape, we touched down. As we opened the helicopter door, the heat leaped up to meet us. The air was sulphurous and had an almost metallic taste. We stepped out. The volcanic crust crunched, fracturing like toughened glass beneath our weight. Indeed there was volcanic glass everywhere, lumps of brittle black obsidian. No human being, no matter how well his feet were protected, could have walked more than a few hundred yards across this jagged lava, for it was burning hot. We were certainly not tempted. When we had poured more fuel into the main tank from cans inside the helicopter cockpit, we took off again as quickly as possible.

As we flew north towards the Red Sea coast, we followed the lie of the land downwards until we were flying nearly 400 feet below sea level. At this level we were enveloped in the blinding white expanse of the 45-mile-wide Karum salt lake, which was once part of the Red Sea. The salt is at least 3,700 feet deep. At first it was criss-crossed with cracks. It must have been wet quite recently and had then broken up as it dried.

The flat bottom of the Danakil desert, strangely lush during Ethiopia's brief but violent rainy season, glistens with water as the river Awash overflows to form a braid of narrow streamlets. The water spills down from the grassy highlands, dividing and re-uniting around patchy thorn scrub in its path.
This annual wetting sustains the trees through the year, but the grasses that make this scene so green grow only for a brief period after the rains.

Farther on, glistening patches confirmed that quite a lot of water does reach this awful place. Heavy rains fall seasonally in the high plateau 50 miles to the west and, since water is bound ultimately to reach the land's lowest point, it comes here.

To my surprise, I saw that there were dots moving ahead of us on the salt crust. They were men from a completely specialized breed of Afar who, unlike most of their tribe, are both industrious and peaceful. They work with tools and methods of biblical simplicity, in temperatures often reaching 135 degrees Fahrenheit, levering the salt from the lake and chipping it with hand-tools into rectangular bars about the size of breeze blocks. Then the camel trains carry the salt bars to market at Makale in the distant highlands.

It is incredible that men would work most of their lives under such extreme conditions, but the Afar do not see it that way, although they receive only water and bread brought by the camel trains and the equivalent of a few shillings a day for their efforts. Salt provides them with all they need, even the building materials for their huts, which are made of salt blocks; it is used as money in various parts of Ethiopia, and an Englishman, Major Robert Cheesman, a former British consul in northwestern Abyssinia, has called Karum the Royal Abyssinian Mint. The reason for the high value of the salt is its scarcity on the high plateau of central Ethiopia. Cattle raised there have either to be driven long distances several times a year to places where they can get sufficient salt in their diet or fed bars of salt imported from Karum. The Afar clearly believe they are clinching arguments about the value of their produce when they comment that salt they can eat, but money they cannot.

Beyond the salt lake we came to a landscape equally inhospitable: deep gullies bordered with buttresses, the outermost ones standing alone, like rock pinnacles detached from a sea shore by eroding waves. Could water be the agent responsible here? It seemed highly possible. The pilot banked and headed down the only lane of order in a haphazard patterning of mud cliffs, a canyon in the bottom of which ran a trickle of rust-red ooze—more water, if it could be called that, from the highlands. Minarets and pinnacles, potholes and pits, crags and cliffs lined our route. The pilot hovered over a pit of brimstone whose green surface seemed to bubble. We were at Dallol, a huge dome disfigured by volcanic upheaval and contamination. It lies in the centre of the Karum plain, the heart of the heartless Danakil.

Suddenly we emerged from the canyon between a final group of buttresses and were back again in the blinding expanse of the salt. The helicopter curved around towards Tendaho for the return flight, passing a series of volcanoes. The flanks of the first one, nameless like so many features in this desert, belched yellow sulphurous smoke. The stench reached us even in the cockpit. Then another anonymous volcano appeared, with a crater so completely circular and sides so vertical that it might have been drilled with a brace and bit. For all its brand-new symmetry, it was apparently dormant. But the next volcano we flew alongside was certainly not. One part of its lip was torn away as if by a recent explosion, and we flew near enough to spot scarlet blossoms of molten fire in the lava at the bottom of the crater.

Our last Danakil experience was somewhat different, but no less disturbing. When we neared Tendaho, we came upon a cloud of steam rising from a boiling spring. As the steam parted in the downwash of the helicopter's blades, a man was revealed. He had the features of a bird of prey. He wore a white robe with a curved, double-edged knife at his belt and a rifle held behind his head and across his shoulders, hands looped over muzzle and bit.

He was an Afar, a Danakil warrior, and there was no expression of mercy or friendship in his face. He was unimpressed both by the intrusion and the retreat of the helicopter. He appeared almost scornful of it, scornful in the knowledge that while the machine and its occupants depended on the support of fuel and spare parts to exist in the barren expanses of the desert, he, alone, was utterly self-sufficient.

A Landscape of Salt

PHOTOGRAPHS BY DR. GEORG GERSTER

The great, dried-out expanse of the Karum salt lake in the Danakil Depression was once an arm of the Red Sea, from which its vast quantities of sodium chloride—sea salt—are mostly derived. It is entirely flat for the 45 miles of its width except at the centre, where volcanic buckling has raised a cluster of strangely contorted salt hills.

For most of the year, the salt lake is compact and glistening like marble but, when drenched by the short rains of late summer, it undergoes a strange metamorphosis. The marble-like surface softens and grows dull. Then, once more exposed to the powerful sun, it begins to dry out and shrinks rapidly, both horizontally and vertically. The horizontal contraction cracks off large hexagonal sections, five to six feet across, leaving gaps between. When the desert winds blow, these gaps may be filled by grains of gypsum, dust and sand, which harden like cement. In this case, as the salt hexagons continue to dry in the sun, shrinking downwards, the thin, dividing sections of harder materials are left upstanding in ridges (right). Gradually, however, the ridges are worn down by sand storms, and the smooth surface is finally restored.

The largest hill rising from the salt lake is Mount Dallol, an oval extrusion 125 feet high and two miles long at its base. Like the surrounding plain it is a structure of salt. It started as a gentle dome, raised by volcanic pressures deep within the earth, and bears a collapsed crater near the summit as evidence of these origins. The friable salt surface was later eroded by wind and water and shaped by dying volcanic activity, in the form of hot springs, into multi-coloured crags and sharp pinnacles.

The seasonal hot springs, or fumaroles, derive their water from the highlands bordering the Danakil Depression. The water drains down through cracks in the earth's crust and is heated by molten rock beneath. It is then forced, boiling, through mineral salt beds that give it colours. The boiling water spurts out of the earth in yellows, oranges and browns—the result of oxygen acting in various ways on iron deposits in the earth.

As the water cools, the salts crystallize, forming brilliantly coloured mounds among pools of green brine. The fumaroles last only a few months. As the water dries up, they fade to dull orange, then dirty grey.

The Karum salt lake stretches away as far as the eye can see, geometrically patterned as it dries and cracks after the summer rains. In time the raised ridges will disappear under the harsh, abrasive force of the desert wind.

Hot springs create these crags on Karum's Mount Dallol, spouting iron-yellow salt solution that overnight can dry into six-foot pinnacles.

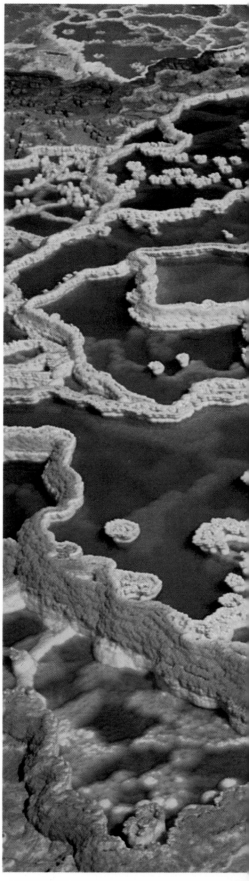

Pools of concentrated brine lie glassily
between filagreed borders of yellow
mineral salts near the crater on the top
of Mount Dallol. Both the pools and
their borders are created by the hot
springs, or fumaroles, that spew salty
water over wide areas of the hill.

When the water cools, it is trapped
by its own salts, which gradually
crystallize, layer after layer, and
turn yellow from the iron they have
picked up in the ground. As the water
evaporates and becomes saltier, it turns
progressively deeper shades of green.

Colour has faded from this grey fumarole on Mount Dallol, as it will from the other hot springs when their water supply diminishes.

Isolated chimney formations and vertical cliffs mark the ragged south-west corner of Mount Dallol. The chimneys are salt columns, up to 80 feet high. They were formed because their white caps of gypsum, a relatively insoluble mineral, diverted the eroding summer rains to the surrounding, unprotected salt, where deep gullies were eaten away.

Pinnacles of salt, chiselled by erosive summer rains, bend up from the glistening Karum salt lake (background). Their needle-like shape contrasts with the squat salt block (left in the picture) which resisted erosion because it is protected by a cap of less soluble gypsum. The ringed pattern of both pinnacles and block was formed as the salt was deposited in layers over millennia.

3/ The Fish and the Fish-Eaters

You may note that the waters are Nature's storehouse,
in which she locks up her wonders.

ISAAK WALTON/ *THE COMPLEAT ANGLER*

Between the Danakil Desert on the Red Sea Coast and the more southern parts of the Rift Valley in Kenya and Tanzania lies the central tableland of Ethiopia, a volcanic mountain mass that dominates the whole country like a lion's paw holding down a toy landscape. In the north, the Rift first cleaves its way into this mass by means of the gorge of the river Awash. The progress southward of the Rift is marked for the next hundred miles by a group of four lakes, strung out along its centre line: Zwai, Langana, Abiata and Shala. Beyond are more lakes; Awausa, Abaya and Chamo. In Kenya the line is picked up and continued southwards through a chain of still more lakes, beginning with the greatest and most dramatic of them all, Lake Rudolf.

These lakes are the jewels that the Rift wears in its belt. Most are tainted with soda, some only slightly, others to such a degree that they are sumps of nearly pure sodium carbonate—washing soda. Only two are truly fresh—Baringo and Naivasha. The soda lakes support little but flamingoes—nearly three million of them, the largest concentrated mass of wildlife in the Rift. But the fresh and nearly fresh lakes are the ones that produce the most varied fauna, a fauna that ranges from crocodiles to hippos and hundreds of species of waterbirds including vast congregations of pelicans, kingfishers, herons, fish eagles and cormorants.

For most of these birds and certainly for the crocodiles, fish is a major item of diet. The main lakes that can be classed as less alkaline and therefore able to support numbers of fish and fish-eating animals are Rudolf in northern Kenya and the group, in the Ethiopian Rift Valley near Addis Ababa, which includes Shala and Abiata. The highest concentration of fish and fish-eaters occurs in fresh and only slightly bitter lakes—with one amazing exception.

The strangest tale of the Rift's fish-eaters concerns pelicans and their remarkable relationship to a lake that contains hardly any fish at all, even though its water is highly suitable for them. This is Shala, a remote, lovely, but sometimes intimidating place. Its name in the local Galla language means "pelican", and yet until very recently Europeans had never seen more than a few isolated pelicans on the lake. The mystery was compounded by the fact that Shala contains no fish apart from a few small ones, less than a couple of inches long, that gather around springs at the eastern end. The reason for this is that the lake is too deep and steep-sided to produce fish spawning grounds. Since pelicans are known to tuck away two or three pounds of large fish a day, the sparse supply of small ones could hardly be an adequate food source for even the few pelicans that had been seen. Where then did the pelicans on Shala feed and why, if there were only a few birds there, did the Galla tribesmen call the lake "Pelican"? The mystery was solved in 1969 when a Scotsman, Leslie Brown, one of the world's leading ornithologists, and an American zoologist, Dr. Emil Urban, of the Haile Selassie University in Addis Ababa, followed up a clue from an Ethiopian biologist, Ato Berhane Tessema. In the late 1950s Tessema had discovered something very interesting on one of Shala's more remote islands: pelicans were gathering there in large numbers. Plainly the Galla tribesmen, at some time in the distant past, had had an inkling of the birds' presence and named the lake after them.

Yet the knowledge had lapsed, and there is a good reason why the pelicans remained forgotten: the islands were not only remote, but virtually unobserved. Since there are no fish for human (or pelican) consumption, there are no native boats on the lake. The Galla do not go boating for mere pleasure, and outsiders who might have done so rarely visited the lake's western end, where the islands are located. These cannot be closely examined from the shore, since they lie well out in the lake, and heat-haze and mirage prevent an observer from making out anything but vague outlines, even with binoculars.

Once Brown and Urban had got their lead from Tessema they borrowed an aluminium cockleshell belonging to the Ethiopian Game Department and rowed out towards the island from the nearest point along the shore. This journey involved considerable danger, for the lake lies in a steep-sided bowl of hills down which savage winds can rip without warning; the two ornithologists were nearly capsized by several fierce squalls. But after several miles of rowing the risk was rewarded. On a flat, volcanic island of two-and-a-half acres, they found nearly 5,000 breeding pairs of great white pelicans. Until that moment it had been a mystery where the immense numbers of great whites in the northern part of the Rift did breed.

Before they dared begin studying them, Brown and Urban took considerable precautions. The pelicans must never know they were being overlooked, lest they desert their nests and abandon the island as a breeding place. The two men quietly departed and waited until the breeding season ended; then they returned to build a permanent hide in preparation for the following year. By the time the photographer, Dieter Plage, and I arrived at Shala, Brown and Urban had finished their researches and we were privileged to have the benefit of their knowledge and the use of their hide.

We made our journeys to what had come to be called Pelican Island from the eastern shore, covering the ten miles in a rubber boat with a powerful outboard, and every trip made me slightly apprehensive. On the northern shore, the rim of the bowl round the lake rises to a ridge over 3,000 feet above the lake surface. To the south the shore slope is not so steep, but close to the water's edge it drops more severely, and, having dropped, keeps on plunging straight down to make the water nearly 800 feet deep. This fact is somehow hard to forget several miles out on that dark blue surface. I always told myself that I could drown just as easily in eight feet of water as in 800, though somehow, on Shala, the thought is small consolation.

The first day we made the ten-mile trip, the hills that form the bowl of the lake were a rich green. The water, in one of its good moods, reflected the hills and sky so that it was hard to tell where the sky began and the hills ended. Flotillas of panicky little grebes skittered in front of the boat and then, when alarmed by our outboard, dived en masse and disappeared into the depths. White-winged black terns hunted for insects. Because Shala is so high, there is less atmosphere than normal to filter out the ultra-violet rays in sunlight, and these rays, reflected off the shining surface of the lake, were fearsome. The brilliant sun burned our skin. We quickly found that to prevent our lips from breaking open we needed to use protective grease.

Pelican Island emerged out of the haze very slowly. It is flat, like an

Great white pelicans, at ease on their breeding colony on Lake Shala, reveal that the bottom half of their immense beak is made of skin. When the pelicans submerge their heads during fishing, this flexible pouch distends to an enormous size, with a capacity of over two gallons of water, and serves as a scoop for catching the fish.

aircraft-carrier. The flight deck, where the pelicans nest, is at its southern end. The carrier's superstructure, marked by a gradual rise to a height of 30 feet above the waterline, is well aft of midships. On this grows the only tree, an acacia, the sole source of shade.

A lower fantail, about 50 yards long, drops away to the north. We took no chance of disturbing the birds, and began to turn to starboard in order to come round under the stern of the island at the safe distance of about one mile. Even this close it was difficult to make out more than a suggestion of white on a place where we knew anything up to 10,000 pelicans could be nesting.

While still 100 yards off Pelican Island we were hit by a smell only too familiar to bird enthusiasts: bird droppings or, to fertilizer companies, guano. We beached and pulled the boat well up on the grey lava sand; if a storm carried it away there would be no ferry service to pick us up. Outside the pool of shade from the lone acacia, sun, stench and rock-stored heat combined in an almost physical assault. We crept along the catwalk of lava behind the colony and, as we clambered up the slope into the hide built by Urban and Brown, the noise of the colony became deafening. The sound was not unlike the grunting of hippos.

Smell, noise and heat were all forgotten as we parted the sacking-covered slits of the look-out. At least 1,000 pairs of pelicans were nesting on a rocky plateau not more than 70 yards long by 50 wide; the nearest nests were less than five yards away from us. The colony was alive with activity as the birds milled around in the ritualized movements of courtship. Nearby, four males vying for the favours of a single, coy female thrust their beaks backwards and forwards in what Brown and Urban named "group knobber display"—they nicknamed breeding birds "knobbers" after the fatty knob, about the size of a billiard ball, that appears on the foreheads of both the yellow-faced males and pink-faced females a short time before they come into breeding pitch. At some distance a single male marched back and forth, showing off to a female in the "strutting walk".

There were young everywhere. Parties of up to a dozen greyish birds nearly as big as their parents had grouped together in "pods"; some were digging their heads deep into their parents' pouches to feed on pre-digested fish, scooping food from the very bottom of the avian shopping bag. The larger young dug with such ferocity that the sharp ends of their beaks sometimes caused punctures in the pouches.

Watching the feeding process, we pondered the second mystery of the pelicans that Brown and Urban had solved. At the time only about a

Captured at the instant of landing on its return from a day's fishing, a great white pelican spreads the flight feathers in the tips of its massive wings—they span nine feet—to reduce speed and make a neat, slow touchdown among its swimming companions, two adults and two young birds.

quarter of the potential nesting strength was in residence. Even so, enormous quantities of fish were being consumed each day. Later in the season, when all 5,000 nesting sites were occupied, this colony would require over three tons of fish a day to keep it going. If none of the food was to be found on Shala, the pelicans must clearly go elsewhere for it. But where? Looking around the lake, it was hard to imagine. The only easy exit was over the comparatively low shoreline to the south, but there are no fishing lakes anywhere within commuting distance of Shala in that direction. So the pelicans must have a route over the high bowl-like rim around the rest of the lake. How did they cross this barrier? To witness the solution to this mystery, we would have to wait until next day. It was late now and the pelicans were already settling down for the night. The evening breeze was blowing the lake into a short, nasty sea and we decided to call it a day and do the same as the birds. We left the cramped confines of the hide and pitched our tent well out of sight of the pelicans on the flat "fantail" of our aircraft carrier.

Early next morning, we watched with interest to see which way the pelicans would go when they set off to collect their daily food supply. About nine a.m., groups of adults took off and flew out into the lake—in the direction of the most challenging route, over the highest point of surrounding land, the 3,000-foot high, sharply-ridged peak we had seen on our voyage out. It was easy to guess where the pelicans were heading: Abiata, a lake well stocked with fish only ten miles away, over the mountains to the north. But to fly over the intervening peak would take time, and require a great deal of energy. Shortly, the pelicans demonstrated how they dealt with the problem. They were indeed going to fly over that peak. The first groups of adults that had taken off from the island landed on the water half-way to the peak. More small parties joined them until about 50 individuals were assembled. Then, as if at a signal, they took off together and flew low across the lake to the far shore. From Pelican Island we could just see the birds against the green-blue of the mountain-side. They had stretched out now and were wavering like a rope fixed at one end and shaken violently at the other. The mystery was solved. They were searching for a thermal, a rising current of hot air. Once they had found one, they would soar, like human glider pilots, effortlessly. As we watched, the birds found their thermal and started to spiral upwards on their ride over the mountain crest.

A great white pelican weighs up to 25 pounds and on the ground it appears a ludicrously clumsy bird. Yet once it starts to soar it becomes as agile as a sailplane. The thermalling birds corkscrewed up and up

An adult pelican, regurgitating the fish it has caught in a day's hunting, opens its beak to let a chick stretch its brown neck deep into the expansive parental throat.

until they were well above the crest of the mountain. If we could have flown with those birds, we would have seen Abiata stretching out ahead. This lake is full of fish, mainly tilapia, and the pelicans commute to it daily, using these thermal escalators.

Already another party had formed on the lake to take off for the mountain. As the first group reached maximum altitude, levelled out and started its ten-mile glide down to Abiata, the second began searching for an up-current, while third and fourth groups assembled on Shala. As the air warmed and soaring conditions improved, the outward air traffic increased, reaching a peak in early afternoon and then gradually tapering off. The birds that had climbed over the mountain to Abiata did not return with their catch for 24 hours.

Around ten a.m. those that had made the fishing trip the previous day started arriving back at Pelican Island. They, too, had had to wait for the air to heat up and provide thermal escalators—but on the Abiata side of the mountain—before they could attempt the return flight. The first party's arrival was announced by a whistle like that of a turbojet, as four pelicans, at least 500 feet above the island, planed down with wings half-closed, spilling air like a team of display parachutists. They dropped their paddles as air-brakes, side-slipping as they lost height, then levelled off and glided in at high speed to the centre of the colony, clapping their great wings to reverse their thrust before touching down. A throng of large youngsters was waiting, like relatives at an airport, and as soon as the first arrival, a rosy-faced female, had landed, one of them detached itself and chased after the food-laden adult. The female made its offspring pursue it for fully 15 yards before it relented and allowed the young bird to dip deep into the pouch for fish. No matter how crowded the nesting area, each parent unfailingly recognized its own young, or maybe vice versa.

Thermals on both sides of the mountain strengthened as the morning wore on. Outward and incoming traffic increased to match. By eleven, the swish of landing pelicans was continuous, each bird followed by a light snow-fall of soft, downy feathers, torn away by turbulence.

Now that we had witnessed the Shala end of the spectacle, we decided to go across to Abiata to watch the pelicans fishing. We made the long voyage back across Shala and early next day loaded our rubber boat on top of the Land Rover, then laboured up the rocky track between hillsides spiked with euphorbia trees, their candelabra branches lit with white flower flames. As we bumped and bounced along a roundabout, 30-mile route towards Abiata, shrouded in clouds of red dust, I could not help thinking of the ease and grace with which the pelicans reached the same goal.

The last four miles were across level savannah, beside a muddy stream. In the clear African morning sky, herons, ibis and cormorants passed overhead and hoopoes looped from tree to tree ahead of us. Mourning doves and laughing doves provided the perpetual savannah background of cooing and churring. It was nine a.m. and everything was taking a last deep, cool breath before the sun beat the life out of the day. Suddenly, at a widening of the stream, the peace was shattered by a chorus of harsh chortles. A thousand birds streaked across the bonnet of the Land Rover. Then, the whole grassland for a mile around exploded with golden-yellow birds. We stopped to watch, realizing that we had happened upon a great wildlife event.

The birds were all chestnut-bellied sandgrouse. A long period of drought in the area had brought them from many miles around to the one stream whose course we were following, to a solitary shelving beach. The first parties came in ahead of our vehicle, touched down a few yards from the water on the sandy beach and then immediately took off around an acacia tree h   .f-way along the beach. It was all very orderly, with no pushing or risk of aerial collision. The chortle of birds arriving on one side of the acacia was almost blotted out by the wing-roar of those departing on the other. To stand at the edge of the beach was almost frightening. The sheer impetus and noise of the bird-flow had some of the characteristics of a jet engine. I had never seen anything quite so audibly and visibly impressive.

The four to nine sips of water each bird took are all that is needed to sustain it throughout a day of seed-gathering in the burned-up bush. I watched the male birds, those with pronounced bands on their chests, to see if they fluffed out their breasts as they drank. During the breeding season, the males trap water in specially adapted breast feathers so that they can carry water back to the young, and the young then "milk" the liquid from the feathers. But these birds were clearly drinking for themselves alone, so they could not have had young.

The traffic was easing off now. I glanced at my watch. Exactly six-and-a-half minutes after it all began, the last bird faded away against the hills and the savannah was left to two speckled pigeons. We had watched about 50,000 sandgrouse take their daily drink.

We drove on to Abiata, across grassy flats where crowned and Caspian plovers searched for insects. At last we launched our boat and set out towards the pelicans' fishing spot. This had taken Leslie Brown and Emil Urban nearly a year to discover. They had expected the birds to land exactly where they did their fishing, but in fact only a small percentage do so. Most touch down elsewhere and then swim to the fishing grounds. The most favoured spot lies where a stream flows into an area of dead trees that were killed by a recent rising in the level of the lake. This flooded woodland serves as an angling centre for all the other kinds of birds that recognize the fishiness of Abiata: kingfishers, cormorants, darters and all kinds of heron, including spear-fishing goliaths and the black herons that make a circular sunshade with their wings and catch tiddlers beneath. Each tree was decorated with the untidy, guano-plastered nests of the cormorants and darters, which had chosen to breed near the fish-market, so to speak. I came to think of this place as a waterbird city.

Into this city come the great white pelicans from Shala, arriving every morning in commuter relays. When they fish, they do so in flotillas, dipping their beaks in unison like rowers bending to the oars. They drive the fish into the shallows to be more easily caught. Of 40 or more birds fishing together, only a handful are successful each time, throwing back their heads to swallow the catch. Next day, with at least two pounds of tilapia stowed away, they will face the long climb back up the thermal escalator to Pelican Island on Lake Shala. It seems an arduous journey for the pelicans to undertake but, unlike the cormorants and darters of waterbird city, great white pelicans demand complete seclusion before they are prepared to nest. Pelican Island on fishless Lake Shala gives them precisely the privacy and freedom from interruption that they need. It is their only nesting colony in a thousand miles of the northern part of the Rift Valley.

There is far less mystery, though there are some surprises, surrounding those other wholesale fish-eaters of the Rift Valley lakes—the crocodiles. Perhaps the most surprising thing is their localized distribution. They require constant warm temperatures, so a high altitude lake such as Naivasha, at over 6,000 feet, with occasional morning frosts, is not for them. They demand sandy shores, secure from intrusion, on which the females can bury their eggs at breeding time. In modern times only two Rift lakes satisfy all these conditions. Baringo, which is full of tilapia, has a still large but decreasing crocodile population. Lake Rudolf, and the river Omo which flows into its northern end, is the main crocodile stronghold. Rudolf is estimated to hold 12,000 crocs.

This great population is mainly attracted by the lake's ample supplies of Nile perch, the largest fish found in the Great Rift Valley. A hundred-pounder is worthy of only passing comment. The great fish, bright silver, with a strange eye that hides its pupil and looks like a pale yellow glass marble, has the sharp, upstanding dorsal spines of the fresh-water perch and the sea bass. I have fished for Nile perch both with a spinning lure from the shore and by trailing a six-inch plug or large spoon from a boat. As a sporting proposition they are not so exciting as their size might suggest, especially on the tackle generally used here, which is more suited to shark. On a light rod the bigger fish fight dour and deep, but without any special display of fireworks.

The main breeding ground for crocodiles in Lake Rudolf is Central Island, a small cluster of volcanic craters that acts as a sanctuary for reptiles in the same way that Pelican Island does for pelicans on Lake Shala. It is a frightening place with a feeling of the lost world about it. There are no pterodactyls here, but crocs themselves are virtually pre-historic, for they have remained almost unchanged for 130 million years. They breed mainly on the flat and seldom-visited shores of two of its three water-filled craters, one of which is connected to the lake.

I had flown over the crater lakes before I made the choppy, fifteen-mile journey to the island by small boat. What struck me was that the water in each has a different colour: brown, green and blue. The phenomenon remains constant in all cloud and lighting conditions, so the explanation must lie in the craters themselves. Possibly, different depths or bottom formations encourage separate algal growths, but I could not be sure of this even when I finally visited Central Island.

As soon as I landed on the beach, I noticed a series of deep, sinuous grooves cut into the black lava sand by the tails of large saurians crawling ashore. On the shores of the main crater lake I discovered a strange notice. It said: "Lake A. No fishing. No shooting." It was, I believe, erected by the local fisheries officer, Bob McConnell, at Ferguson's Gulf, halfway up the western shore of Rudolf, in the certain knowledge that only a score of eyes, apart from those of the crocodiles, herons and egrets, would ever see it. It must be one of the loneliest jokes in the world.

The loneliness was made sinister by the knowledge that the crocodiles here can on rare occasion be aggressive. On Central Island and elsewhere in Lake Rudolf, they normally take little notice of humans. I have often swum in the tepid, soda-slippery waters of the lake with no more than a small element of risk. However, the rule has its exceptions. The one scientist—to my knowledge—who has spent any length of time

A Rudolf crocodile closes its jagged jaws on a dead cichlid fish. Acting as both predators and scavengers, these mighty reptiles ambush animals, usually herbivores like antelope, at the water's edge, and make short work of any carcases—like this one—that they find drifting on the surface.

doing field research into the flora and fauna of Central Island was bitten by one of his case studies, though he survived.

When crocs are around I tread with a good deal of caution, though when disturbed on land they are most likely to flee back to water. However, there is always a chance of meeting the exception, perhaps a big croc who is feeling the pangs of hunger. Crocodiles catch most of their prey in the water though they sometimes lie in wait on game trails leading to favourite drinking places to snatch a young or careless antelope by the leg. So I kept a wary eye on a ten-footer basking, with mouth open to cool himself, higher up the shore and between myself and the water. This reptile was more worried about me than I was about it. Persecution everywhere has made crocodiles extremely wary. Suddenly it raised itself on stiff legs and galloped back to the lake, entering with a crash like a torpedo. There it lay, looking like a sunken log, eyes just above the surface. I recalled hunters' tales about how basking crocs knock their prey from the bank and into the water with a lash of their tails. Even though I know there is no truth in the story—it is a physical impossibility—I gave the reptile a wide berth. There is something that defies reason about crocs.

Rudolf crocodiles are usually docile, yet for some unexplained reason, crocodiles are highly aggressive in the Omo and other rivers to the north of the lake flowing down from the Ethiopian highlands. While I was there, an 18-footer swallowed a man in the river Baro. When it was shot 24 hours later and cut open, only the legs of the victim were still recognizable. Apart from their different natures, there is one small physical distinction: Rudolf crocodiles grow a horny nodule on the belly skin, perhaps because of the lake's alkalinity (in the long run this may prove to be to their advantage, since it makes their skin less desirable commercially). But their vastly different behaviour is probably accounted for by the abundance in the lake of large Nile perch. Crocodiles are great fish-eaters and eaters of great fish in particular. A 50-pound Nile perch that is easily caught gives a fair return for crocodile effort. As a result, the Rudolf croc has far less need to dine on human prey. Faced with a shortage of fish, however, the reptile would almost certainly be as dangerous as its Omo neighbour.

The only other large population of crocodiles in the Rift is at Lake Baringo, 120 miles south of Rudolf. It has no Nile perch but great quantities of tilapia and barbus live in its fresh waters, and the air temperature at 3,000 feet is well suited to the saurians. The animals prosper in this favourable environment, and their disposition is usually even more amiable than that of the Rudolf crocodiles. Njemps tribesmen sometimes stand shoulder-deep far out in the lake, calmly fishing for tilapia while crocodiles on a similar mission swim close by.

This crocodiles' lake has a special interest of its own. The strange thing about Lake Baringo is that it remains fresh. Its neighbours to the south—Hannington, Nakuru and Elmenteita—are soda lakes, and it is surrounded by much the same volcanic countryside as they are. Moreover, Baringo has no visible outlet, through which the toxic minerals that affect its companions can wash away.

The explanation was first discovered by that pioneer geologist of the Rift, J. W. Gregory. He believed that Baringo had once been drained by a large river flowing from its northern end towards Lake Rudolf, 120 miles away. Among the many phenomena he noted was a geological difference between the two ends of the lake. On the northern shore was a mass of rocky outcrops and headlands, whereas the southern shore consisted of a sedimentary plain. When he inspected the plain more closely, he discovered that it too contained rocky outcrops, only here they had been buried by subsidence and then covered with sediment washed down from the surrounding hills. From this observation Gregory concluded that during some ancient upheaval of the Rift the whole lake had tilted, so that the northern end was raised and the southern lowered. These movements, together with the lava flows that accompanied them, cut the northern river. Gregory believed that the outlet, so essential to the lake's freshness, remained where it had been, at the northern end, but underground. He recorded that he had seen water seeping away through the crumbly lava flows there.

Today there is no sign of a subterranean outlet or even a clue to one until a place called Karpedo, 70 miles to the north. Here may lie the explanation of Baringo's freshness. In the midst of dry, hot and barren country, Karpedo is an oasis, complete with doum palms and a waterfall tumbling over a 30-foot cliff. The water steams. At first I took this steam for spray, yet the fall is not high enough to produce a spray mist. When I got closer I found that the tumbling water really was steaming. It emerges from thermal springs and is close to boiling point.

Both the heat and the very existence of the water at Karpedo hint that it flows underground from Baringo, 70 miles away. This underground link is by no means as improbable as it might seem at first. Water penetrates the complicated system of lake sediments, volcanic ash and old porous lavas on the floor of the Rift as if they were made of

With graceful precision, a fish eagle plucks a meal from the weedy fringes of its home lake. Sighting a fish near the surface, the eagle glides down, fanning its tail and slotting its wingtips to prevent stalling (below). With a snatch of the talons and a great downstroke of the wings, it lifts its prey clear (bottom), beats hard to gain height (centre) and banks away to a feeding perch (far right).

APPROACH

SNATCH

SPRINT

BANKING

STABLE FLIGHT

sponge. Moreover, the recent thermal activity beneath the Rift would heat the underground river. Nearby is an extinct volcano called Silali whose subterranean fires may still be smouldering.

The same explanation, an underground outlet, almost certainly accounts for the freshness of Lake Naivasha, 150 miles south of Baringo. Like Baringo, Lake Naivasha is fed by streams flowing in from a volcanic catchment area. Yet its waters remain beautifully fresh for the same reason. The best guess is that the all-essential leak occurs at the southern end of the lake. In the days when the level of water in the Rift was much higher and the lake far larger than it is today, an overflowing river certainly poured out from this end. The lie of the ground certainly falls away most steeply from here, descending 5,000 feet to the next lake, Magadi, about 120 miles to the south. So perhaps Naivasha's secret seepage is through the crumbly lavas in the direction of that austere, soda-encrusted lake.

At an altitude of 6,200 feet, Naivasha is not only the highest lake in the Rift, it is possibly the most beautiful and certainly the finest aviary. Here is Africa's largest concentration of nesting fish eagles, the great bronze and white birds whose cry, a spine-tingling, fluting whistle, has been called the Sound of Africa. The eagles live on the lake's thriving population of tilapia and black bass. The tilapia were introduced by Europeans when they settled in East Africa a century ago and desired good eating. The black bass were brought from North America as predators to eat the tilapia when this species grew too numerous for the lake. Since both species swim near the surface and are an ideal size for large fish-hunting birds, they quickly attracted the fish eagles. Meanwhile, other smaller fish support a thronging population of lesser predators from herons to kingfishers.

The setting that Naivasha provides for this concourse of water birds is one of the finest in the Rift. The lake is nearly circular and its fresh, crystal waters lie cupped within four mountainous walls: to the south rises the green bulk of the great volcano, Longonot; to the west, the Mau escarpment, which forms one wall of the Rift; to the north, the buttress of the dead Eburu volcanoes; to the east, the Kinangop plateau, which climbs to the Aberdare mountains and forms the eastern wall of the Rift. As Baringo is brown and bare, so Naivasha is lush and green for, being higher, it is cooler and more moist. Flat-topped acacia trees stand upon its shores; in its shallows and drifting about the lake are immense beds of papyrus; the purple lotus flowers of water lilies create an air of tranquil pleasure. But the calm can be deceptive. When the

Perched on a reed stem, a malachite kingfisher holds a live fish firmly in its bill. In the midst of its headlong catching dive, the bird was content merely to seize the fish. Now it must find a way of swallowing its prey without choking on fins and scales. With quick flicks of the head it will thrash the fish against the perch to kill it, then flip the corpse round to swallow it head-first.

rainy season's cumulus clouds bank high over the Rift Valley walls, the wind can come spilling off the heights, rushing down with the power of an unseen avalanche, whipping a smiling surface into a black fury, cratering the lake with meteorites of hail and giant raindrops. Such a wind overturns the fronds of floating lily-leaves and makes even the ten-foot-high papyrus stems bend like grass.

At first glance it seems that there are fish eagles scattered about in practically every attractive nesting or look-out tree, especially the acacias. But the arrangement is far from haphazard. Each pair of birds commands a rectangle of fishing and nesting territory that stretches out over the lake. Any other eagle fishes inside this area at its peril. Sometimes the territories lie side by side, like neighbouring, but rival, states. Even so, there is no trespassing. Moreover, since the rectangles stretch only a certain distance from the shore, the open waters in the centre of the lake are, so to speak, international, like the oceans. Any eagle can fish there. If it were not for this convention, the young birds would fare badly, since their parents will not tolerate them inside parental waters once they have become self-supporting fish-catchers. The birds' distinctive call is usually made to proclaim ownership of territory and sometimes to challenge a rival eagle. Often it is the trespassing bird that throws out the challenge, gracefully flinging back its white head and neck in mid-flight to do so.

The eagles exhibit the same elegant power when they fish, a remarkable display of co-ordinated action that I have often been lucky to watch. I was standing on the edge of Naivasha on one occasion when a male called from the top of a stark tree that had been killed by a temporary rising of the lake's level. (I knew it was a male because its cry was shriller than its mate's—the male is the treble, the female the contralto.) I saw it just before it struck at its prey. At the surface of the water, the movement of a black bass's dorsal fin had caught its attention. The eagle launched itself in a long, low, curving pass. At the last moment it threw its legs well forward, hooking talons into the fish, which weighed at least two pounds. For a fraction of a second the weight of the fish almost stopped the great bird in the air, but its flight was barely checked—some calculate that eagles strike with the energy equal to that stored in a bullet from an elephant rifle. Sheer impetus dragged the fish out of the water and, in a second, the eagle was swinging back to the trees with the fish held beneath. The bass's fins flapped feebly as it was carried, helpless, in those fish-hook claws.

The fish-eagles are the bird stars of Naivasha but they are backed by a magnificent and colourful supporting avian cast. Innumerable other birds live here as well: superb and glossy starlings; little parrot-like love-birds; green wood-hoopoes probing for insects in holes made by wood-boring bees; Nubian and Cardinal woodpeckers hammering so fast that it is a wonder their skulls can stand the vibration; lilac-breasted rollers swooping with a flash of electric blue about their wings. For brilliance they are rivalled only by a kingfisher that seldom, if ever, fishes, preferring to eat grasshoppers, lizards and insects. This is the woodland kingfisher, a nester in deserted woodpecker holes, a grey-headed, greenish-blue dandy found sometimes by water, but, as the name implies, more often among the trees. The woodland kingfishers can be seen swooping down to dead trees out in the shallows, disappearing inside the old woodpecker holes to feed their young chicks or perhaps to prospect for nesting sites.

All these tree-nesting bird species find specialized niches within the habitat created by acacias and lakeside bush. But right beside them are two quite different watery habitats, each supporting its own specialized bird population. On the lake itself, life is organized into two quite separate kingdoms: those of the papyrus islands and lily beds.

Papyrus is the plant from which the ancient Egyptians made paper, and it also formed the so-called "bulrushes" among which Moses was said to have been found. Papyrus is most certainly not a bulrush but a giant sedge, as its tough, triangular-sectioned stem shows. The plant grows in dense clumps that may resemble firm islands, but it is only necessary to set foot on them to discover that they are far from solid land. The space between the matted papyrus roots and the silted bottom of the lake is dead space, lacking sufficient dissolved oxygen to support aquatic life. Luckily for life on the lake bed, the papyrus is always on the move, sailing before the inconstant winds of the Rift, island joining with island to form archipelagos, continents and sub-continents encircling minor oceans of their own making.

The stems and flowerheads of the papyrus afford admirable fishing vantage points and cover for all manner of water birds. The malachite kingfisher makes flashing dives from the papyrus stems into gaps among the lily pads, spattering droplets of water. This bird is only four inches long, but its tiny size intensifies the brilliant blue of its body so that it becomes a glimmering gem. Another species, the pied kingfisher, scarcely seems to need a resting-place at all, for it can hover like a kestrel and does so for the same reason: to pinpoint its prey. It always seems to

An adult squacco heron rests quietly on a bending papyrus stem before resuming its search for food. For much of the day, it picks a delicate path through the waterside vegetation, patiently awaiting the movement that will betray its prey among the jungle of tangled roots and towering papyrus. Then it will pause briefly to snap up some aquatic insect or larva, perhaps even a small fish or frog.

make several fruitless dives for every tiddler it snatches from just below the surface. Perhaps its shadow gives it away.

The papyrus fulfills a different function for the herons, which know what all good fishermen know: that, to be unseen by the fish, it is vital to pick a background with which one merges. On Lake Naivasha, the papyrus stems perfectly suit the colour of the purple, grey and goliath herons. Five feet tall, the goliath is the largest heron in the world. In contrast, diminutive squacco herons can be seen crouched on the papyrus edges, waiting motionless, minutes on end, for tiddlers to swim within range. Mostly, though, these small herons hunt unseen, dining off the numerous tree frogs. Little egrets and cattle egrets share the hunting ground, clinging to the swinging papyrus stems. At lake level, black crakes creep secretively among the roots.

On the lily beds live the tight-rope artists of the lake, birds that know precisely how much weight a lily leaf will bear as they stalk across its quaking surface in search of insects and larvae. For the smallest inhabitants, weight presents no problem. The African pied wagtail is so slight that its bobbing progress does not depress a lily pad by a centimetre. For the smaller waders, too, sandpipers of many species, weight creates few problems. Larger waders like ruffs (the males) and reeves (the females of the same species) are just heavy enough to have to hurry over the lily pads if they do not wish to get their feet wet.

The king of the lily pads is the bird whose popular name sums up an evolutionary history devoted to solving the problems of travel on this swaying habitat—the lily-trotter, or jacana. It is a moorhen-sized bird, chestnut-coloured, with blue head and bill, weighing about a pound. Most of its life is spent afloat on lily leaves. It not only feeds on them, but finds safety there for itself and its young family. The ability to move freely on the lily pads depends upon its outsize feet with enormously elongated toes, the perfect adaptation to this strange environment. These feet spread the bird's weight across the largest possible area and thus the plant on which the lily-trotter trots can remain afloat. I have watched with wonder as a female leads newly hatched young across the lily beds of Naivasha. At first I did not realize that the hen had chicks with her, until I looked more closely and saw four stick-like pairs of legs hanging down beneath her closed wings. Almost from the moment of hatching, the lily-trotter's chicks are expected to accompany their mother when she walks upon the water. The moment they leave the nest, the lily pads become their natural world. But there is no shelter for them if a sudden storm, or a predator like a marsh harrier, catches the family in the open. In an emergency, the parent calls the young to her. They hop up to her side. The parent clamps her wings over them and lifts them off their feet, giving them warmth and protection. The hen moves about with her family until the moment of danger has passed. Then she simply opens her wings and releases the young to learn for themselves the art of lily-trotting.

Naivasha is perhaps unsurpassed in its softness and beauty by any of the other lakes of the Rift. Here the beauty is not just in the landscape, but in the whole wild world that awakes and returns to sleep every day. In the golden sunlight of an African morning, there is dew on the grass and occasional patches of frost, too. The purple lotus flowers of the water lilies are not open yet. There is not a sound except a fussing of coots around the lily pads. The wide lily beds silently tremble and lift above the backs of fish searching for crustacea, snails and larvae on the ceiling of their green underworld. Then a black crake tiptoes out of the papyrus and a pair of African pochard plane in, wings set and paddles down, scratching the glassy surface with their landing. Gradually, the lake assumes the throbbing vitality of the daytime.

The hour of greatest beauty is the one just before nightfall. Dusk on the equator is a rapid dimming. Long before the light goes down, the purple lotus flowers of the lily beds have closed again. Yet a Naivasha sunset grows its own blooms. Skeins of egrets, ducks, geese and pelicans blossom against the purpling dusk that clings to the Rift Valley walls. And a million tree frogs tune up to sing their nocturne.

NATURE WALK / # Through Hell's Gate

Within an almost continuous basin of escarpments and volcanic hills, left behind by the contortions of the Rift over the past 16 million years, lies Lake Naivasha, still large but much reduced from its ancient size. One of its old outlets seems to have been a narrow, dramatic serpentine pass that is now called, with some justification, Hell's Gate. The pass falls away southwards from Naivasha's 6,200-foot altitude, abutting the west flank of the great volcano Longonot, whose lava once dammed the waters of prehistoric Naivasha. In this gorge twisting through the mountain wall lie a multitude of habitats and some spectacular rock formations, an extraordinarily vivid cross-section in miniature of Rift geology and wildlife.

On an early March day, with a high-altitude haze that precedes the rainy season taking some of the sting out of the sun, I set out to follow the one-time route of the lake's turbulent escape through Hell's Gate. It would still be hot by any standards, so I wore a wide-brimmed sun-hat and carried a water bottle that I was determined not to use until my thirst really persuaded me.

Starting down the lake shore towards the pass, I walked at first parallel with Longonot, picking my way along the edge of a dense papyrus thicket. The spiked flower heads of the towering sedges shut me off from the cool world of water. I could hear the trombone solos of hippos grunting and snorting in the shallows beyond, but the great animals themselves were entirely hidden from me by the bankside vegetation. Every now and again I was able to snatch a glimpse of the water of the lake through a gap in the papyrus, where hippos came ashore to wander in search of their nightly rations of lake-side grasses.

Over the centuries, hippos have learned that it is only safe to venture ashore to seek their food after

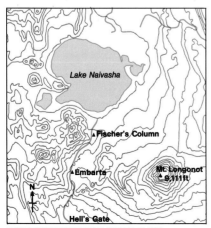

THE ROUTE THROUGH HELL'S GATE

THE VOLCANO LONGONOT ABOVE HELL'S GATE PASS

dark. They first learned the lesson in the days when Africans hunted them with spears for food. The arrival of Europeans and their fire-arms made daylight foraging even more perilous. From that moment on, they were shot for so-called sport and—with more justification—because they conflicted with farming interests. No one shoots them at Naivasha now, but the hippos still have their inborn sense of caution.

I followed one of the tracks made by the animals. Hippos are great path-makers, sometimes covering as much as 20 miles in a night. They move like bulldozers through the thickest scrub, though their trails are surprisingly narrow. There is no passing room in the tracks, and when I follow one I always hope that I will not be unlucky enough to meet a hippo coming in the opposite direction, for of all the dangerous animals encountered in the African bush, a hippo is one of the most lethal. Each jaw is armed with 30-inch ivory tusks and the mouth has the gape of an earth-grab. These monstrous weapons are likely to be used if a hippo is caught on land, for it is then a frightened animal. Its one thought is to return to the safety of the water. It weighs well over a ton, and can touch 20 m.p.h.; the result can be fatal. I was counting on the fact that the Naivasha hippos seldom venture ashore in daylight, but I was relieved to get into open country.

I turned my back on the cool lake scene of Naivasha and approached Hell's Gate. Immediately I was amidst a stand of trees whose grey bark

FEVER TREE

was peeling off, revealing a fresh surface that appeared bright yellow in the sunlight. They were *Acacia xanthophloea*, which the early European settlers called fever trees, a misnomer, and an unfair one—these acacias grow at the waterside where the settlers often caught malaria, so the trees were blamed for the disease before the anopheles mosquito had been identified as the culprit.

Beyond the fever trees, a mile-wide stretch of savannah—a yellow expanse of star grass dotted with

ANT-HOLE IN WHISTLING THORN

stunted bushes of whistling thorn—funnels towards the gorge entrance. The whistling thorn belongs to the acacia family, as do 80 per cent of the trees in the arid plains country of the Rift. But this variety has its peculiarities. On one I noted a large clear globule of sap, the first I had seen on any acacia. More distinctive of this type, however, are its dark round galls. Ants burrow into the galls and through the holes they make, the wind whistles sharply; hence the name for the tree.

But the ants also do the thornbush a service: the formic acid they secrete acts as an irritant to the muzzles of browsing animals. Thus

there is a mutually beneficial relationship between these two incongruous parties, the ants getting nourishment from the galls and, in exchange, protecting the thornbush from rhino, giraffe and antelope.

Although the country around Hell's Gate has little game—which has almost vanished from most of the heavily farmed areas on the valley floor—the gorge itself forms a natural refuge for animals, small and large. Just before I entered the savannah funnelling into it, a reedbuck with ridged, back-curving horns sprang nervously from a thick tangle of cover, giving me a far greater fright than I gave it. There were grey duiker in the undergrowth too—tiny antelopes that are almost as small as hares. The name means "diver" in Afrikaans, and accurately describes the plunging, hare-like manner in which these graceful little

STAR GRASS

THORN-TREE SAP

OSTRICHES—TWO MALES AND A FEMALE—ON THE ALERT

animals dip and scamper at speed.

Another antelope, a dik-dik, so minute that it might almost have been a toy, froze as its keen ears caught my footfall. Dik-dik, which usually weigh no more than ten pounds, will stand immobile for as long as 20 minutes if a predator such as a martial eagle, the most powerful of all Africa's eagles, should perch nearby, or cast its ominous, brief shadow as it drifts past. But I did not pose a comparable threat, so the dik-dik decided to make a run for it.

Deep now in the savannah, I saw a grey line to my right that at first appeared to be a cloud shadow. Binoculars revealed a herd of 30 zebra; their vertically-striped camouflage had blended perfectly into the mirage shimmering over the sea of yellow grasses.

On the outskirts of the main zebra herd I now spotted a small family party, the stallion a little apart and watchful over his mares. One mare had a young foal. The stallion spotted me and whistled in alarm. The mare moved in front of her foal which bucked playfully, a charming toy animal, looking like a mint humbug in his baby stripes.

The zebra were accompanied by seven ostriches, a combination that at first seems bizarre. It is, however, quite usual. The alert ears of the zebra combine in an alliance of senses with the ostriches' eyes—another example of a mutually advantageous interchange of talents. What the zebras do not hear or scent, the ostriches see. Since what alarms and threatens one species also alarms and threatens the other, each of the oddly assorted partners acts as an early-warning system for the other.

Entrance to the Gorge

To the west now, the immense guardian buttress of Hell's Gate loomed high up in front of me. I passed another thorn tree, which like many of the taller acacias had untidy clumps of dried grasses wedged in its upper branches. These are the

WEAVERS' NESTS IN THORN TREE

WEAVER BIRD

nests of a small bird, Reichenow's weaver, canary yellow and, in the male, marked by a black back and matching eye-patches. Like all weavers, it is a highly-skilled thatcher of twigs and grasses. As I watched, one of the birds alighted alongside its nest and darted inside.

If Hell's Gate was a refuge for birds and game, it was also a hunting ground for predators and scaven-gers. Death and its attendants are never far away in the African grass-lands. Leopards, eagles, civets and small cats such as serval all take their toll of small mammals. Where there is death there is a need for un-dertakers. Vultures are the principal functionaries, but mammals, like the pair of jackals that stalked boldly ac-ross my track, also do their bit. Some people dismiss jackals as slinking, skulking creatures. Per-haps they are when scrapping over a carcass with hyenas. Then they know their place. But these were un-troubled by opposition, and trotted by as confidently as handsome dogs.

The jackals had barely disap-peared from sight when a great grey bird came parachuting over the lip of the gorge, legs dangling a full two feet beneath its body. At first sight, it might have been taken for a stork. It was in fact a secretary bird, which is something of an oddity in the animal world. This bird of prey is the only species in a family known as the *Sagittariidae*.

After its apparently ungainly, but controlled descent, the secretary bird touched down and began to strut along as if the need to fly had never occurred to it. Indeed, it is fairly rare to see the secretary bird in the air. It is usually glimpsed stalking with slow, dignified gait on black legs that make the bird seem attired in plus fours. The bird's stalk is gener-ally purposeful: brushing aside the grasses, it keeps an eye open for snakes, lizards and small rodents. The one I was watching certainly did. Its hooked beak struck and came up with a small lizard. An-other time the victim might easily have been a puff-adder, for snakes, poisonous or harmless, are among the secretary bird's favourite meals.

The secretary bird in action ag-ainst a snake is unbelievably fast. The bird uses its strong legs and taloned feet to strike the fatal blows. The length of its legs seems to keep it out of harm's way. Throughout the

SECRETARY BIRD

attack it remains tensed to spring aside or to take off. The blows come in quick succession. I once watched a cobra subdued in this fashion. Quick-striking though a cobra is, it just did not have a chance. Within 20 blows the snake was dead. The bird I now watched swallowed its lizard and continued in search of something more satisfying.

Suddenly, a small rich-brown antelope with a black stripe along its flank zig-zagged across the track. It was a Thomson's gazelle. Where there is one, there is usually a party. A sweep with the binoculars disclosed a number of black spikes poking up through the grass. The spikes might easily have

THOMSON'S GAZELLES

been dead grass stems, but when they moved, they did so in pairs. They were horns. Fifteen "Tommies" were lying down, relaxing while they digested their early-morning meal. They were not exclusively a stag party, for Thomson's gazelles, unlike most species of antelope have horns regardless of sex.

By the side of the track grew leonotis, tall plants with a succession of flower-heads spaced along the stems, each flower-head sprouting slender, reddish blossoms. A small gemlike creature, a male scarlet-chested sunbird, probed the inside of the trumpets with its long curved beak. The bird was dazzlingly iridescent, the brilliant red of its throat setting off the shimmering metallic green of its head and neck. In delicacy of form and sheer brilliance, Africa's sunbirds are a match for the New

A LEONOTIS FLOWER

World's hummingbirds. Both are nectar eaters, though the sunbirds lack the hummers' ability to hover. On another nearby leonotis perched a small black and white hunting bird, a fiscal shrike. Shrikes use such look-out points to spot their victims —insects and small rodents mainly.

Suddenly, as the rock walls of the gorge began to hem me in, a sound like tearing calico burst on my ears

FISCAL SHRIKE ON LEONOTIS

and a formation of miniature black jets passed barely three feet away. They were Nyanza swifts. They climbed nearly vertically to the centre of the rock wall and then most of them simply disappeared among a hundred thousand crannies. The whole rock face was alive with shrieking swifts. It was clearly a paradise for them, for the trees and grass were full of insects, which they were busily snatching from midair. The hissing of cicadas was everywhere.

Suddenly there was a loud, yelping cry. Those swifts still in flight scattered in panic. Some dived towards the grassland. Most darted straight at the rock face at a speed approaching 80 miles an hour. In the last yard of headlong flight, they braked abruptly and miraculously found perches. But one intrepid party mobbed the source of the alarm, a black Verreaux's eagle.

The swifts need not have been so concerned by the intruder. The gorge provides food galore in the form of small mammals for this and many other birds of prey. Only a few moments before I had seen an augur buzzard hovering and then swooping on something in the grass—a mole rat perhaps, or even a wingless grasshopper like the one at my feet.

The swifts made high-speed passes within feet of the eagle's ferocious beak and talons. But the great bird soared along the cliff face unperturbed—its only concession to being buzzed was an imperious left and right bank that was more a shrug than a defence against these trivial irritants. Then the swifts returned to their insect-hawking.

The western bastion of Hell's Gate begins as a gentle, grass-covered in-

WINGLESS GRASSHOPPER

cline above a few yards of naked, vertically faulted rock. The slope climbs so steeply that, within 100 yards, the rock face is already 100 feet high. Wall and slope continue to soar until they level off at about 300 feet. The vertical columnar pattern of this immense cliff is repeated many times in the Rift. It is a fault scarp, one of the innumerable minor rendings and sinkings of the floor along the trough of the valley.

At a point that must have been midstream when Naivasha's waters rushed through Hell's Gate stands an imposing pinnacle of red rock, the isolated lava plug of a miniature and now totally eroded volcano. It is called Fischer's Column after Dr. Gustav Fischer, the German explorer who discovered Hell's Gate. At its base is a jumble of boulders.

There was a sudden scampering movement in this jumble, and I saw why the Verreaux's eagles are attracted to these particular cliffs—among the few places in this part of the Rift where they nest and breed.

A Wealth of Life

The base of the pinnacle was crawling with rock hyrax, or dassies, a favourite prey of the eagle. These

AN AUGUR BUZZARD ABOUT TO STRIKE

CLIFF ENTRANCE OF HELL'S GATE

concernedly sunning themselves.

But when the long, thin shadow of a bird of prey flicked across the grass, an old male dassie gave a high-pitched, mewing alarm call. One or two other dassies darted in alarm up the steep rock pile on feet equipped with rubber-like pads. In fact the sentinel need not have worried. For he had seen the silhouette of one of the lammergeiers, or bearded vultures, that nest in the cliffs above. A bird with narrow wings and a slender body ending in a wedge-shaped tail, the lammergeier exhibits interest in dassies only after they are dead, for it feeds on carrion.

Half a mile beyond the lonely pinnacle, the eastern wall of the gorge starts to close in. It, too, is a fault scarp, but a small one compared with the towering rock face opposite. Though Longonot was now hid-

mammals were almost certainly the "conies" described in the Old Testament. They are about the size of rabbits, and although coney is an old English word for rabbit, rabbits these creatures most definitely are not. With their short, pointed snouts and small ears, they look more like marmots. In fact the dassie, like the secretary bird, is unique. It has a special order, the Hyracoidea, all to itself, and its nearest living relative is, amazingly, the elephant.

Although dassies are preyed upon by leopards, servals, jackals and wild dogs as well as eagles, they can be surprisingly confiding with human beings. I stood dead still, and within minutes a dozen were un-

FISCHER'S COLUMN, A VOLCANIC PLUG

LAMMERGEIER NESTING RIDGE

EASTERN WALL OF THE GORGE

EMBARTA—THE HORSE

den behind the eastern wall, its work was plain to see. Much of its lava long ago streamed in the direction of Hell's Gate and overlies the earlier faulting of the scarps. Its volcanic ash is laid down in grey bands of slightly differing colours, each layer telling the story of a period of prolonged activity. Some strata are only inches thick, others three feet; the latter recording the times when Longonot was in full and lengthy eruption. The outcroppings of ash have a more rounded appearance than the rocks and lava, for centuries of torrential Rift Valley storms have softened their grey old faces.

Five miles from my starting point, the high country was becoming wilder and more barren, as were the twisting rock walls. Here, as the trail climbed, the whistling thorn trees grew taller in the dark volcanic soil. A cathedral tower of rock that the Masai tribesmen long ago named Embarta, the horse, rises from the gorge bottom. It is capped with a diminutive acacia whose wind-blown seed somehow once took root there. No matter how inaccessible or apparently hostile the environment, there are always plants that find a hold in the fertile volcanic soil.

Up to this point, the gorge was largely formed by rifting and by volcanic action. But now I reached a deep ravine cut by the action of water. From here, Naivasha's overflow must have rushed southwards with tempestuous force. There was water in the ravine's bottom now, red as blood with silt washed down by recent rains.

The last half mile of rapidly narrowing savannah yielded a bonus in terms of mammals. Six impala—a buck with lovely lyre-shaped horns and five hornless females—were munching their way towards me. Where grass gave way to thorn scrub on rising ground beneath the gorge wall, something yellowish-brown and as tall as a horse moved majestically through the red oat pastures. It was an eland, the largest of all antelope. If it were not for its long, straight, back-raked horns, the great beast, with its heavy dewlap, might easily be mistaken for a wild ox. In motion however, there is no mistaking it; even a big male of 1,000 pounds is as agile as a mustang. The

YOUNG BABOON GROOMING AN ELDER

most bovine characteristics about it are that it provides great steaks—as all hunters will confirm—and it tames in captivity remarkably easily.

A troop of baboons moved through the grass, arranged for defence as formally as a military convoy. Young, adventurous males scouted the territory ahead, while the older dominant ones stayed in the centre with females and young. If the "scouts" sounded the alarm, then the females and young would retreat and the imposing old males move up to make a barrier of fangs in front of the weaker members of the troop. This group was in a peaceful mood, for they stopped and the younger members groomed their elders' fur, picking out snags and dirt. Mutual grooming

plays an important part in baboon society. It strengthens the bonds between individuals and establishes their place in the hierarchy.

Amidst the thorn scrub grew low green solanum bushes, carrying the small fruit called Sodom, or buck, apples, and where the earth was still moist from recent rains, a cluster of butterflies—African whites,

SODOM APPLES

SUCCULENT ON VOLCANIC ROCK

FLOW-PATTERN ON LAVA

A BUTTERFLY DRINKING

only yesterday. The place where the flow stops is littered with lumps of a black, shiny substance. This is obsidian, glass fused by immense volcanic heat, so brittle that African hunters once fashioned razor-sharp spear and arrow heads from it. Primitive tools chipped from Hell's Gate obsidian have been found as far away as the Serengeti plain, 200 miles south, in Tanzania.

This great bank of black, broken lava, which was to keep me company to the crest of Hell's Gate, still two miles away, welled out of a fissure created by the Rift's complex sinkings and crackings. Its lack of weathering showed that it was of recent origin—another sign that the subterranean forces that created the valley have not yet finished altering the face of Africa.

The top of the pass was visible now, though still distressingly high

above the obsidian pile. My target was a line of wavering puffs of white—puzzlingly transient, pale clouds rising like Indian smoke signals from the distant skyline. And already, with some hundreds of feet yet to climb, I was thirsty. But over many walks in Africa, I had taught myself not to drink until the last supportable moment. This is not masochism, but common sense. One sip always seems to demand another, and the water-bottle may have to last longer than planned.

At this height, I was not expecting to see much more wildlife, but Africa is never short of surprises. From beneath a high, red earth bank came a sharp nasal chorus of cries, as more than 100 birds fired themselves out of as many holes like gleaming missiles leaving their silos. Square-tailed, with vivid red chests beneath their white chin-stripes,

swallowtails and charaxes—uncurled their probosces to probe for droplets that would provide a drink.

The scene now began to have more than a touch of the satanic about it. Were the track plunging down instead of climbing steeply along the gorge's western shoulder, it would indeed have made a suitable entrance to Hades. Rounding a turn in an ash-layered cliff, I was faced with a jumble of debris that might have been Vulcan's personal slag-heap. The path was pushed to the lip of a ravine by a bullying shoulder of lava —pale grey and reddish drippings that still seemed so plastic in form they might have oozed and glowed

OBSIDIAN, BLACK VOLCANIC GLASS

they were white-fronted bee-eaters.

Some settled on trailing roots washed out of the bank. Others darted to a ravine nearby that held water from a recent storm. It was now a breeding ground for insects and the bee-eaters were feasting. They catch the insects in mid-air with their long, down-curved beaks, which are not only precise but sharp and strong—the tools they use to excavate the nesting and roosting holes that run deep into the bank.

The rains that filled the bee-eaters' ravine had also washed out the track ahead, carving deep, yawning gullies and cutting away volcanic ash. Only the week before, the pathway had been reported intact. The immense power of water to modify the friable African soil, once the top cover of grass and scrub has been removed, could not have been more clearly demonstrated.

ERODED VOLCANIC ASH

But the rain had done wildlife a good turn. Although the top of the pass offered nothing more tempting than barren acacia and thorn scrub, small V-shaped spoor imprinted in damp mud, now preserved as it dried, showed that dik-dik had been drinking here. There were also the spoor of baboon and leopard, and antelope droppings on the path.

One of these droppings was bowling along as if powered by a tiny motor. The motor was actually a dung-beetle many times smaller than its burden. As it scuttled the ball of dung backwards—using its hind legs, with its front legs on the ground—its progress was momen-

WHITE-FRONTED BEE-EATER

BEE-EATERS' NESTING HOLES

tarily thwarted by a tree root. With a gargantuan effort, it mounted the obstacle and continued its search for a spot where it could bury the dung and lay its eggs inside the ball. When the eggs hatched, the grubs would feed on the dropping.

The cratered peak of Longonot was now well-risen above the eastern wall of Hell's Gate. Although Longonot played a major part in creating the geological formations in

DISSOTIS FLOWERS IN A STEAM VENT

this gorge, it is nevertheless young in terms of the entire Rift Valley story. A friend who flew over the volcano recently saw a steam vent inside the scrub-filled, perfectly rounded crater. Any mountain that still looks like a volcano is most certainly a newcomer here. The older volcanoes that were present when the major faulting of the valley began have long since been worn down, or have collapsed into gigantic, open, shallow calderas. Longonot still lords it over Hell's Gate, even though its rim, too, has been partially eroded and lacks the perfectly symmetrical pattern expected in volcanoes that are, geologically speaking, still infants.

The white puffs of smoke signals

on the crest were nearer and much clearer now. As I worked my way towards them, I found that the pass had saved its biggest wildlife surprise for the last uphill mile. Beyond the jumble of obsidian rose a stand of flat-topped acacias—an ideal but, in the setting, unlikely browsing ground for giraffe. Then, to my amazement, a half-grown giraffe did indeed strut across the track. Another youngster and two adults followed. Immediately, they all began to lasso the topmost acacia branches with their long, velvety tongues. It always astonishes me that those delicate tongues can work their way through shoots and branches guarded by two-inch thorns.

The Objective Achieved

Now I began to scramble up the great bank of lava. I was panting and my mouth was parched. But, at last, after a scratching progress up an acacia-guarded citadel, I reached my objective.

The ground rumbled and hissed all around. Even through rubber soles, it was hot to the feet. There was a distinct smell of fire and brimstone, a most appropriate atmosphere to breathe at the very lintel of Hell's Gate. What had looked like smoke from two miles distant was revealed as steam, bubbling furiously from a hundred tiny fissures. Incredibly, pale lavender dissotis flowers grew here, watered by the condensing vapour. And through the steam-clouds loomed Longonot, guardian of Hell's Gate and Naivasha, both of which it helped create from the red-hot vitals of the Rift.

AT THE CREST OF THE GATE, A LAVA FLOW FLANKING LONGONOT

4/ Cauldrons of Soda

*The whole deposit looks exactly like a lake which has been
frozen over with snow-ice all the winter and is breaking up
and partly flooded by the thaw in the spring.*

A. M. HARRISON/ *REPORT TO THE EAST AFRICA SYNDICATE*

To the south of Lake Naivasha, in the 140-mile stretch between the two
large volcanoes, Longonot and Ol Doinyo Lengai, lies perhaps the most
awful region of the Rift. The southern end of the trough between the two
mountains holds what to my mind are the world's most inhospitable
lakes, Magadi and Natron—two corrosive sumps of water and soda. At
first sight it seems incredible that anything could live on or near the
lakes' scum of sodium carbonate. Considering the conditions, there is a
surprising amount of wildlife at both; in Magadi, there are fish that man-
age to live in the extreme environment provided by hot springs at the
lake's south end; there are birds that live off the few fresh-water springs;
and Natron is the breeding ground for almost all of East Africa's flamingo
population—a fact kept secret by its caustic flats until the early 1950s.
  The route along which I drove southwards from Naivasha to the soda
lakes at first winds up from the floor of the Rift, climbing the eastern, or
Kikuyu, scarp. Near the top it passes close to a spot notable, not only for
its beauty, but also for its place in the Rift's history. It was near here that
J. W. Gregory gazed into the formation that was eventually to bear his
name, glimpsing "the plain, with its patches of green swamp and glittering sand and, far to the west, the long, dull grey scarp of the plateau
which forms the western boundary of the valley". The nearly vertical
walls, the thick bush just beyond the roadside, and the toylike appearance of tracks 2,000 feet below brought home to me vividly what it must

have been like for a heavily-loaded safari to climb down on foot. No matter how many times I travel this road, or how often I visit the Rift's remoter wilderness areas, I never fail to catch my breath at this prospect.

Some 30 miles further on are the Ngong Hills. Like almost all other mountains in the Rift, their origin is volcanic, and they stand in a series of peaks, their green summits rounded and softened by erosion, with all sign of their original craters worn away. Many people unfamiliar with East Africa imagine it to be a seer land, burned red and yellow, but its hills, at least, are always green.

It is hard to imagine anything much wilder—granted that I was travelling a road of sorts—than the 50-mile journey from the Ngong Hills to Magadi. As I started my descent, a man strode over the green crest to my left, wearing a red ochre robe and carrying a tall, broad-pointed spear. His hair was tied in small knots and shone with grease. I had entered Masai tribal territory, and this man, herding his cattle, was a Masai *moran*, or warrior. The plains and scrub that stretched out ahead, far down the Rift and over the Crater Highlands of Tanzania towards the Serengeti, were all his on which to graze his cattle.

On either side rose scarps of basalt, some of them 50 feet, others 100 feet or more, in height—the results of faulting within the greater fault of the main valley itself. The scarps leant against each other, like a shelf of books that had collapsed sideways. Acacias, hung with the coconut-like nests of weaver birds, dotted the countryside. Small herds of dainty, fawn Thomson's and Grant's gazelles broke cover, trotted away flicking their tails, and then stopped briefly to cast glances backwards over their shoulders. Parties of baboons crossed the path, organized for maximum protection with the older males flanking the females, which carried babies at their breasts and the larger children on their backs, jockey-fashion.

Twenty miles from Lake Magadi, the country became softer and greener where a stream, partly dried out, ran down from the scarps. More Grant's and Thomson's gazelles were grazing there, and a blossom of white in the valley bottom revealed itself on closer viewing as hundreds of European storks, searching for grasshoppers and other insects to sustain them on the long, northward migration up the Rift, over the Red Sea, through the Jordan Valley, and on to nest in Eastern Europe and Russia.

A final dusty descent beside yet another fault scarp and at last Magadi was in sight, a monstrous growth of pure soda. Lake Magadi has a weird fascination all of its own. Its predominant colour is an unearthly pink, reminiscent of some decaying confectionery, like coconut icing. Close to the edges, where minor fault scarps rise abruptly, the thin scum of water mirrors the greens, greys and sombre browns of the rocks. In certain evening and early morning lights, the surface achieves a rare beauty. At sunset I have seen its soda flats transmuted into purest gold. But in the uncompromising, overpowering heat and light of midday, Magadi is a shimmering hellscape.

There are other alkaline lakes of the Rift, of course, but with the exception of nearby Natron, they are far milder. These others are sodary because they lack an outlet for the minerals that flow into them in solution from the rivers and streams draining the surrounding country, which is rich in chemicals from volcanic ash. But Magadi's soda apparently surges up thick and caustic from the thermal intestines of the Rift. There is no other way to account for the fact that the Magadi Soda Company has been digging, dredging and sucking the native soda out since the early 1900s without making the slightest impression on the lake. All the evidence suggests that Lake Magadi is actually gaining on the miners.

No one can say precisely how Magadi performs this miracle. It seems certain that the springs that feed it well up into its bed through layers of pure soda. Even so, the source of the subterranean water is a mystery. In one sense, it might not have to flow in from anywhere: there are vast reservoirs of water stored in many places beneath the earth's surface. Perhaps a lake lies undiscovered beneath Magadi, its waters seeping upwards under pressure. One possible theory is that the hidden outflow from Naivasha might seep in this direction. The drop in elevation between the two lakes—some 5,000 feet—is certainly in favour of the theory and there is much porous lava buried in the Rift floor between them.

I drove through a settlement where freshly extracted soda dries in piles of pink crystals. The track climbs a dusty rise to a police post. Here I was required to report and write my time of arrival and destination. It was impressed on me that it was even more important that I sign out on my return. Once I had driven beyond the last worker's bungalow, only a land of hostile nothingness lay ahead of me. A Kikuyu policeman asked me what time I expected to be back from the hot springs at the south end of the lake. If I disappeared, there would at least be a record of my schedule. The country between Magadi and Natron is not an area to venture into without plenty of petrol and water.

I drove through the scrub as close to the lake's edge as I could get. Far away towards the northern end a dark spot dancing in a mirage, was, I knew, the Soda Company's dredger, sucking up the hell's brew of the lake.

As I drove southward, I came across a few flamingoes and several other species of birds, living close to the hot springs that supply some fresh water to this end of the lake. A mixture of long-billed, probing waders—reeves mainly and some little stints—wandered round the margins, while a party of African spoonbills swept methodically for crustacea with their ladle-like beaks. At one point, as I veered briefly away from the shore, thick lava dust suddenly whirled up as a pair of eland—antelope as large as oxen—burst out of the thorn scrub, easily outstripping my mere 20-miles-an-hour progress.

Where the lake ended, two arms of greyish mud ran up into the bush. The mud looked solid enough, even though it was overlaid in places with a skin of water. But I had no wish to crash through into what could prove to be stinking black ooze below. I inched forward in four-wheel drive and discovered that the softness was all on top. Extremely relieved, I felt firm ground under my wheels again and tackled the next tongue of the flats with more confidence, emerging on a wide soda lagoon that made that minor moment of tension quite worthwhile. The flats were alive with game, although the stupefying heat on the sodary mud distorted vision. Even at a mere two or three hundred yards' range, lines of zebra were transformed into legless, dancing blobs that melted and re-formed as they moved sedately across the grey horizon. Something alarmed a party of Thomson's gazelles and they galloped away, splashing up the water under their hooves. It was so hot that I almost expected to see water turn to steam as it struck the ground beside the rill from which they had disturbed it.

At last I reached the hot springs themselves and began to search for the fish I had come to see. They were *Tilapia grahami*, a dwarf species— only two or three inches long—of a very common African family. They survive, feeding on green algae that grows in the springs, in conditions of alkalinity and heat that would kill other fish. The water in which they live is almost too hot for the human hand to bear in comfort, but there are limits to the endurance of even these robust creatures. This frontier was clearly delineated: much of the bottom and sides of the springs was covered with light green algae on which the fish feed, but close to the places where the water gushed up near boiling point from the rock below, the algae suddenly became a darker green. At this point, the temperature became too high for the fish to bear and the potential source of food had remained uneaten. Unlike many animals that live in extreme conditions, however, this remarkable fish is not over-specialized to the point of vulnerability; it can tolerate great changes in its habitat. When the rains come, its pools are diluted and their temperature drops, but the *grahami* remain healthy and active.

Walking back to the Land Rover, I took a final glance across the soda flats. They were impressive, certainly, yet I had the feeling that if I were stranded on them I would have a fair chance of walking off. The lake is comparatively narrow and the soda for the most part appears reasonably solid. It will never fill me with the state of near terror generated by its awesome neighbour, Lake Natron, 20 miles south.

While *magadi* means "soda lake" in Masai, natron is the chemical word for natural sodium carbonate. Although Lake Natron is thought to be less productive of soda than Magadi, it is considerably larger—a gigantic bath, part-liquid, part-soda, ten miles wide by 40 miles long. Such a volume of crude soda must surely be delivered to the lake, as at Magadi, from underground concentrations rather than by run-off from the surrounding countryside.

To explore Natron from the ground calls for a minor expedition. For my own inspection of the lake, I decided to fly. But even this form of transport entails an element of risk, for a combination of scenery, colour and heat haze distorts a pilot's sense of level flight. My pilot, the wildlife film-maker, Alan Root, usually delighted in showing me game and scenery from a height of around 30 feet. But as we flew over Natron, he gave the surface at least 100 feet clearance, and kept a wary eye on the rate-of-climb indicator to ensure he was not descending. An unintended descent into that dreadful place hardly bears thinking about. I would hope to die immediately in such a crash, rather than perish lingeringly of heat stroke and dehydration as caustic salts flayed the skin from my body.

Natron's ability to deceive the eye derives from the area's peculiar combination of geography, chemical consistency and climate. Natron is a typical long, narrow, fjord-like Rift lake, flanked to the west by the towering wall of the Nguruman escarpment; to the north-east and south-east lie two extinct volcanoes, Shombole and Gelai. Dead centre at the south end of Natron rises the most impressive volcano of all, the still-active Ol Doinyo Lengai, the Masai's "Mountain of God".

The mountains are just one element in the spell Natron casts on air travellers; another is the character of Natron's surface. Like Magadi it is a mass of ghastly pink blotches caused by the algal growth that thrives in the otherwise deadly soda. Natron is sheltered by escarpment and volcanoes, and thus is frequently glassily calm, a perfect reflecting

Although only a few large animals populate the margins of the soda lakes, a host of hardy insects hunt along their formidable, volcanic shores. Scavengers like the mole cricket (bottom right) find a wealth of animal and vegetable rubbish to eat; earwigs even eat their own kind (far right). The toughest creatures, however, have their limits, as the picture of the dragonfly shows (top right). Overcome by heat and fumes during its low-level aerial hunting, this predatory insect has drowned in the hot, bitter waters of a soda spring.

DROWNED DRAGONFLY

MOLE CRICKET

CANNIBAL EARWIG

surface. Combined reflected images of green hills, grey rock, blue sky, all caught in its pink mirror surface, produce visual confusion enough. Add to this heat haze and mirage from a surface whose mid-day temperature often reaches 150 degrees Fahrenheit, and it is impossible to tell where lake ends and shore begins. Lengai, rising at the end of the lake, performs this double game most bewilderingly of all.

Far more experienced and adept fliers than the human pilots of light aircraft crash, to their short-lived surprise, into the waters of Natron. The ends of the lake at migration time are littered with the corpses of birds that have made precisely the navigational error of which Alan Root was aware. Deceived by topography and reflection, they descend when intending to fly straight and level. Many of the birds apparently make their fatal mistake when migrating at night. It is not hard to imagine how, in conditions of moonlight or bright African starlight, the visual disorientation can be disastrous.

Despite Natron's terrifying nature, flying over the lake on a fine, still, early morning can be one of the most sublime experiences in Africa. From two or three thousand feet, I have looked down not only on a wine-pink lake but on Shombole, Gelai and Lengai and, beyond them to the east and west, even greater volcanoes of the past. In clear conditions, Mount Meru and Kilimanjaro show up eastwards. To the south-west, the huge green massif of the Crater Highlands rises beyond Lengai.

At low altitude, even in the aircraft, I could feel the oven heat beating upwards off the soda flats. At ground level, on the lake shore, it must be like standing on the oven top itself, hotter yet than Magadi. The familiar, acrid smell of soda flooded thick inside the cockpit as we slid the canopy back for a better view. With flaps lowered, our light aircraft could fly safely at 50 miles per hour and it was possible at this speed to make out every detail. We flew slowly down the eastern shore. Where a river, the Uaso Nyiro, flows in, there is a wide expanse of fresher water. Fifteen miles down the lake, a rough track connecting Natron with Magadi comes in. It was built to serve a now derelict magnesite mine. But for this very basic track the lake would still not be accessible even to most four-wheel-drive vehicles.

From the air, game trails and the animals that made them showed up clearly. I saw zebra, oryx—large antelope whose long straight horns are said to have given rise to the legend of the unicorn—and awkward-looking, shaggy wildebeeste. An ostrich had ventured out on the firm white soda bordering the shore, thought better of it and wisely turned back. One thermal spring, marked by a steam vent, was surrounded by the prints of many game animals, including rhinoceros and lion.

Alan pointed down to a single large acacia. It had been from here, he shouted, that naturalist Leslie Brown had set out to find the breeding grounds of the Rift Valley flamingoes, and had walked alone across the Natron soda flats in an extraordinary journey. He made it back alive— though only just—to complete what is possibly the greatest epic of the Rift since the early explorers first entered the Valley.

The nesting grounds of the Rift's 3,000,000 flamingoes had long been a mystery. The Masai around Lake Natron had their own explanation. From time to time they saw fully-fledged young birds, still in their grey, juvenile plumage, standii.g in the shallows on the edge of the lake. They accounted for this by saying that the birds were hatched out of the lake itself and simply walked ashore when they were ready to fly. Who can blame them for thinking so? The world of Lake Natron is weird enough to make anything seem possible, even to scientists.

Leslie Brown, then chief agricultural officer for Kenya, was the first to employ an aircraft in the search. He found what seemed from the air to be two large colonies several miles offshore on the Natron soda flats. However, the only way to be certain that flamingoes were breeding was to approach them on foot. He marked the acacia tree over which we now circled as the nearest point to the colonies from which to start walking.

Having risen at dawn and trudged the few miles from his own camp at the foot of Mount Gelai, Brown left the grudging shade of the lone acacia, equipped with only a canvas water bottle, and started out across the soda towards the colonies. At first, the going on the hard white soda close to the edge was comparatively good. Then he began to break through the crust into the thick, stinking, black ooze just below. Leslie Brown is immensely strong and, as a wildfowler brought up on Scottish estuaries, he understands the mechanics of walking on mud. But no estuary mud ever matched this. Beyond the hard stuff, a half-mile of shallow water waited. This was where he quite rightly expected trouble. A scum of pinkish water littered with the bodies of dead locusts overlay softer soda. As the water gradually deepened, the soda became mushier until his feet sank into foul-smelling sulphurous mud beneath.

Now every step in that intense heat dragged energy out of his body. He struggled across the shallows, confidently expecting to walk the rest of the way to the colony on the hard white floes he could see ahead. Here, the soda had formed itself into polygonal plates with raised edges, looking like giant water lily leaves. The soda lilies were, in fact, brittle in the extreme. He was soon crashing through and floundering about once again. The mud below was drier but more glutinous and the effort of extracting one gumboot often buried the other foot even deeper. At one point he was on all fours but he dared not stop for fear of sinking and becoming immoveably stuck. A further crisis followed: when he drank from his canvas water bag he found the soda had impregnated it. The water was bitter and made him retch, but he drank nearly all of it before it could become any worse.

When he finally gave up his attempt to reach the colony, he had few reserves of strength left for the return journey. He later recalled his journey back: "Then began a frightful treadmill. Crushed by disappointment, and far more exhausted than I knew, I had to make my way back across the two hundred yards of sticky mud before I could reach the shallow water where conditions would be easier. The full weight of my fatigue seemed suddenly to strike me like a blow and I realised for the first time that I would be extremely lucky to escape alive. I had reached the little soda island only by putting out all the effort of which I was capable, driven by the spur of enthusiasm. Now I must cover the same ground starting from extreme exhaustion, in the hottest hours of the day, and without any spare water. I knew that I could succeed only if I husbanded carefully the last remnants of my strength. And so I set out, but the mud forced me to continuous racking effort. I found I could take five or six steps before I was brought up short, plunging in the filth and gasping for breath. At each halt I could only allow myself a momentary respite, for I sank slowly into the black foul mud beneath the crust, and I dared not sink too far for fear that I would be unable to wrench my boots free again.

"So it went on—five or six steps, reeling with exhaustion and barely able to see in front of me, so that I even lost the clear black trail of my outward passage and could think only of steering generally towards the bulk of Gelai. And this was just as well, for by some strange quirk of fortune I struck a slightly easier patch of going where, once, I actually made about ten yards between halts, treading delicately along the raised crust of a soda ridge. So great was the relief at this break in my enforced rhythm of struggle that it seemed as if Providence was lifting me bodily and helping me through.

"If I had not been a strong man and an experienced mud-walker I should be there yet, the flesh dissolved from my bones and the skeleton stuck in the mud. It was partly the thought of the beastliness of this way of dying, and partly anger at my own stupidity, that kept me going.

Suffice it now to say that after two hundred yards or so of appalling struggle I found the mud growing wetter. I knew then that the worst was over, that I was coming to the part overlaid by water and that I should escape."

When Brown at last reached hard, white crust again, he took off his gumboots, which were filled with crystalline soda, to find his legs raw with red blisters that turned black in the air as he watched them. He was still faced with a seven-mile walk back along the shore to his camp and the 45-mile drive back to Magadi. He lay more or less unconscious for three days in the Magadi Soda Company's hospital and spent a further week swathed in bandages. The legs took six weeks to recover and finally had to be repaired by skin grafts.

In 1957, Leslie Brown assaulted Natron again, and this time reached a colony of breeding flamingoes by walking over comparatively firm brown mud at the Gelai end. But then he vowed never to set foot on the lake's dreadful surface again.

He confesses that he was always nervous when flying across Natron. I certainly was. At one hundred feet, should the engine fail, there is simply nowhere to go, except in. Even as I looked down on the strange pink whorls of soda on Natron's port-wine surface, I was listening tensely to the engine's beat. Alan banked the plane away at last. We set course towards the western Rift wall, the Nguruman Escarpment, climbing the first heavily treed step and then pulling up sharply to clear the final scarp. We banked and looked down into dense green gullies. Natron was far away below, pink, beautiful and enticing once more.

Caustic Swamps and Bitter Waters

Through the aeons of the Rift's shiftings, the history of the lakes that formed in many of the valley's troughs and depressions has been as troubled as that of the land that created them. Rivers feeding and draining the lakes have changed course or disappeared and the chemicals in the land around them have been renewed with every eruption of lava and ash from beneath the earth's crust. As a result, many of the lakes that originally held fresh water have been spoiled by the intrusion of mineral salts, washed in by rain from volcanic slopes or welling up from springs. The most abundant of these is a water-soluble alkali: sodium carbonate, known as soda.

The soda affects the lakes in two ways, making some bitter but drinkable and encrusting others with thick beds of nearly pure alkali, so that any water that accumulates on top is reduced to an acrid, poisonous film. The outcome depends on the nature of the water supply and on whether or not the lake has an outlet. An outflowing river bears soda away, but in the absence of an outlet, water is lost only by evaporation, which leaves the soda to concentrate until it dries out completely.

The lakes that lie in the deepest, hottest trough in the Central Rift—Magadi and Natron—are the Rift's greatest tracts of soda. They lack outlets and nearly all the water that reaches them is already very alkaline: much of the run-off from the surrounding hills passes through the effluvium of Ol Doinyo Lengai, an active volcano so rich in alkali that even its crust is white. The springs nearby contain up to two per cent in solution and soda surging from below pockmarks the lakes' margins.

Magadi and Natron are arid, caustic heat traps; only 16 inches of rain fall on them each year, but over the same period 130 inches of water evaporate. Under the circumstances, it is hardly surprising that they support little wildlife. Flamingoes that feed on soda algae are the only large animals fully adapted to these extreme conditions.

By contrast, Lake Rudolf supports a wide variety of fish and the birds that prey on them. Its shores partly consist of volcanoes, and soda does, therefore, enter it by run-off. However, fresh water from the river Omo dilutes the lake and so the soda does not become significantly concentrated by evaporation. Rudolf's waters thus remain within limits that allow life to flourish.

Cracking and buckling in the intense tropical heat, the soda flats of Lake Magadi surround a shallow puddle of alkali-saturated water.

A view northwards over Lake Natron in the dry season reveals white "tide marks" of crystallizing soda alternating with dark ooze of the lake bed. During rains the lake rises, but wherever the water is shallow it becomes heated by the sun and evaporates quickly to leave ridges of soda. The lake is supplied by alkaline springs below its surface and by streams flowing over soda-rich soil, like the one at the bottom right entering from the direction of the volcano Gelai.

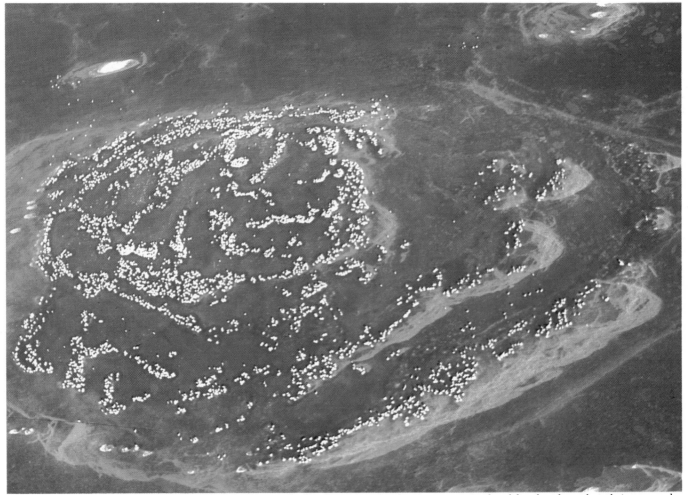

Swirls of hundreds of flamingoes appear white against the lurid surface of Lake Natron, stained red by the algae that thrive on soda.

White, soda-rimmed craters pock-mark the surface of Lake Natron where bubbles of liquid or gas have burst upwards through its crust.

Along the south shore of Lake Rudolf, the extinct cones of Nabuyatom (foreground) and Abili Agituk jut out into the water, which they have helped contaminate with soda. Although the lake is bitter, it supports many forms of life, particularly an immense bloom of algae that changes the colour of Rudolf from sky blue to jade green according to the amounts of sunlight and wind.

Snaking into the middle of Lake Rudolf, the fresh-water river Omo flows towards the camera between its own raised banks, or levées. These and the bird's-foot delta in the foreground are accumulations of debris and silt, carried out into Rudolf by the fresh river water, which is comparatively light and therefore flows over the top of the denser soda solution already in the lake. The debris is deposited as the river current gradually slows down, and builds over the years into firm ground.

5/ Flamingoes by the Million

Lesser flamingoes are rather remote beings inhabiting a world only they can inhabit with enjoyment.

LESLIE BROWN/ *THE MYSTERY OF THE FLAMINGOES*

Imagine a river of flame fifty yards wide and three miles long. From it rises a continual grumbling, growling murmur. As I approached across the powdery grey soda flats along the shore of Lake Nakuru, 100 miles northwest of Nairobi, the growl increased to a roar. I saw flames in the carpet of fire flickering in uneasy movement. As if my approach were fanning the conflagration, the wave of red curved suddenly outward into the lake. A few yards closer to the water's edge and the pattern broke up into individual tongues of fire.

Each flicker was a flamingo running in panic to take off. At this moment, the flamingo was grotesque, a creature out of *Alice*, a suitable butt for Tenniel's pen. The webbed feet stamped the surface to foam as the scarlet wings beat for lift. Such an alarm, raised by human intrusion, is sometimes purely a local one. But often it proves infectious, so that the ripple runs at least part way through an immense throng of birds, stretching as far as the eye can see along the water's edge. Ten thousand flame-pink birds may suddenly be poured into the blue bowl of the sky.

Though the take-off is anything but graceful, after only a dozen paces a miraculous transformation takes place. Each bird, so clumsy in earth-bound motion, has become, in flight—and it is impossible not to reach for some technically aerodynamic comparisons—a miniature jet aeroplane. The comparison is not an exact one. The wings of a supersonic jet are set back towards the tail. The flamingo's wings are mid-set, perfectly and equally dividing trailing legs from reaching head and neck. In front of the wings, the image of a streamlined super-jet is more exact. Even the heavy, downpointed bill bears its resemblance to the aircraft's nose, lowered for a landing.

Whatever else lives and breathes throughout the length and breadth of the Rift Valley, the greatest faunal success story belongs to the flamingo. There are about five million flamingoes, belonging to six different species, in the entire world. Of these, at least three million live on the lakes of the Rift. There are only two species in this vast gathering and their names exactly fit their physical appearances—the greater and the lesser flamingo. Apart from differences in plumage and beak they appear similar in formation and colouring, but they represent the extreme ends of the size scale of the flamingo family, one standing almost six feet tall, the other being about half that height. The four intermediate species all come from the New World. Of the three million African birds, perhaps 50,000 are greaters, the rest lessers. They range the length of the Rift, wherever there are sodary lakes. I have seen them in huge numbers all the way from the Danakil Depression in Ethiopia to Lakes Manyara and Eyasi in Tanzania. Despite their wanderings, there is only one place in the Rift that can be considered their true home—Lake Nakuru. On this one small lake, barely four miles by six, it is often possible to see more than two million flame-pink birds.

Nakuru has been called the greatest bird spectacle in the world. It well deserves its title. Most of its shore was gazetted a National Park by the Kenya Government in 1961, the remainder in 1968. The Park is a narrow strip varying between a mile and a few hundred yards wide that runs beside the lake for most of its circumference. Joined to it is the Baharini Sanctuary, a lovely area of shoreline and acacia woodland that was once the farm of John Hopcroft, a young Kenyan who has dedicated his land and his entire efforts to the study and protection of Lake Nakuru and its birds.

What draws flamingoes in such huge numbers to Nakuru is food: diatoms, the blue-green algae *Spirulina*, in incredible concentrations that also support populations of brine shrimps and other small crustaceans. The soda-saturated water produces this rich food supply faster than all the flamingoes and other water birds can extract it, at an estimated rate of at least 200 tons per day. One reason for this abundance is the chemicals in the water. The other is the lake's location. The algae, like all green plants, need sunlight. Nakuru is set close to the Equator, at 5,767 feet, where year-round it is bathed in the ultraviolet rays comparatively unfiltered at high altitudes and beneficial to plant growth. The source of food, consequently, is there for the getting.

The snag is that while the vegetables in the broth are nourishing in the extreme, the liquid of the soda soup itself is lethal to the birds. But the evolution of a sophisticated pumping and straining process has ensured that the flamingo hordes have no need to drink the broth to get the vegetables (when they need water, they drink from fresh springs around the soda lakes). In ecological terms they have found themselves a niche that no other animal occupies. Their success is measured by the size of their population.

How the flamingoes take advantage of the food in a toxic soda soup can be seen by closely watching a batch of lessers feeding just offshore. The lesser's bill, a dark carmine red that looks almost black except at the tip, provides the specialized tool needed. Internally the flattened surfaces of both upper and lower bills are covered with fine hairs, lamellae, which interlock to form a sieve when the bill is closed. This strainer can retain particles as small as 1/1250 inch. In addition a line of bristles along the bill opening prevents pieces of food larger than 1/50 inch from reaching the sieve itself. The feeding birds suspend this ungainly, but superbly efficient, apparatus upside down in the water. The bill is submerged almost to the nostrils. What happens then cannot be seen from shore: the water is sucked in and out of the closed bill as if by a pump, the piston being the bird's tongue, moving up and down inside the closed beak.

While the vegetarian lesser flamingoes pump algae from the lake, the greater flamingoes feed on the crustaceans in much the same way. They use a rather coarser strainer, consisting of bony plates rather than filter hairs inside the beak. Quite often greater flamingoes employ an additional technique of their own to extract food from the mud, paddling in the silt to dislodge the minute forms of life embedded in it.

The detailed techniques of flamingoes' feeding methods are difficult to observe, but some other characteristics are spectacularly obvious. Probably the most striking of all flamingo acts is their massed courtship display, which sometimes continues for weeks or even months on end. The behaviour—indeed the whole question of flamingo breeding—is mysterious. They often display, but they do not necessarily follow through and nest, for they do not breed every year.

Whatever starts this behaviour off, once begun, it rapidly gathers momentum until suddenly there are thousands of birds displaying in the

A catastrophe that overtook flamingoes in 1962 is documented in these two pictures. The lesser flamingoes, which usually breed in the soda shallows of Lake Natron, were driven by floods to the soda-saturated Lake Magadi, nearby. Just when the eggs were about to hatch, Magadi's shallows became too dry and many birds deserted their nests (top). Chicks that did hatch became encrusted with soda anklets (bottom), and although wildlife field workers helped to free some 10,000 of them, thousands more died.

midst of thousands more who appear totally unconcerned. Probably most of the disinterested ones are not yet ripe for mating. Some experts say that flamingoes are not sexually mature until they are seven years old.

The ritual is an unbelievably noisy one. The displaying birds parade up and down, jammed closely together; heads raised and stiff-necked, they march and countermarch in a continuously moving column. In Leslie Brown's words: "The whole looks like some strange composite monster with a thousand legs, with the legs and the necks moving rapidly all the time, while the bodies remain at one level and seem to float along in a block." Sometimes individuals stop to fluff out their feathers and then suddenly drop their heads as if their necks have been broken. Some, on the outside of the displaying group, suddenly stand bolt upright and shoot out their wings. And then the clamorous, weirdly intricate tribal dance continues.

The actual breeding does not occur on Nakuru. Though the courting is done here, and nests are often built here and on other lakes, the flamingoes invariably abandon them and, for reasons not yet understood, resort to Lake Natron, 150 miles to the south, to mate and lay eggs.

It was here that Leslie Brown observed something over half a million pairs at their nests. These they build by squirting or ladelling wet mud into a volcano shape, which then dries and hardens in the sun. These nests are built far out on the mud and soda flats of Natron, and are peculiarly subject to disasters. In November and December of 1957, for instance, Brown recorded that 200,000 nests were washed out by rising water. And in 1962, the whole flamingo population of East Africa was threatened by a catastrophe of huge proportions.

Drought followed by floods in Natron had so oppressed the flamingoes of the Rift that they were forced, for the first time in memory, to try to nest on the forbidding soda flats of Lake Magadi. But the concentration of soda in Magadi proved too much for the birds. Wildlife filmmaker Alan Root discovered that the youngest chicks, too small to move about much, were becoming trapped in deposits of pure soda that formed round their legs like lumps of concrete. Alan and his wife, Joan, began a rescue operation. With a few helpers, they broke away the chicks' soda anklets by hand, and, when this proved too slow, chipped them off with a light blow from a hammer. Soon the East African Wildlife Society, the World Wildlife Fund and even the British Army based in what was then Tanganyika sent money and reinforcements. At least 10,000 chicks were eventually saved by releasing them and by driving them into areas where the soda concentration was lower.

It may be tempting to suppose that the Rift's flamingoes had never before made the error of nesting on Lake Magadi, but this is very unlikely to be true. The same combination of drought and flood that had denied them their traditional nesting grounds on Natron for two seasons running must have occurred many times previously in the changing history of the Rift. As proof, a fossilized soda anklet was recently found similar to those worn by the young birds in the Magadi débâcle.

So stunning is the flamingo spectacle on Nakuru that it is easy to overlook the lake's other bird life. Four hundred species have been recorded around the lake, though none is as well adapted to the sodary environment as the flamingo. Fishing fleets of great white pelicans communally trawl for their living, drawn by the fish recently introduced into the lake as an anti-mosquito measure. (The fish are the same *Tilapia grahami* that have so successfully adapted to the hot springs of Magadi.) Neat little shoveler ducks swing their large spatulate bills, sweeping up the algae and trapping it in lamellae similar to those inside the flamingoes' beaks. Several species of waders bob and strut in their search for molluscs, insects and crustaceans. And marabou storks, that sometimes prey on flamingoes, parade ominously on the lake's shoreline.

If there is a bird of more evil omen than the marabou in the length of the Rift, I have yet to meet it. Not even the griffon or the hooded vulture approach the marabou in physical meanness of appearance. Long ago, someone—it must have been an Army officer—christened these great birds Adjutant storks. There is certainly something in their speculative, parading gait reminiscent of a critical Regimental Adjutant inspecting a parade. Even this comparison seems to take too kindly a view of the character concerned. To me it far more resembles the character of an undertaker, hands held behind back and obsequiously hidden in the tails of a rusty old frock coat.

This funereal image is certainly closer to the storks' wholetime occupation and pre-occupation, for they are not so much hunters as funeral directors and grave-robbers. Their main living is from the dead. In this they resemble vultures, but they have certain anatomical limitations. The marabou does not have the vulture's talons, nor its powerful, ripping, hooked beak. Yet the beak that nature has provided the stork with is powerful in quite a different way. It has the power of a pick-axe combined with the grasping ability of an outsize pair of long-nosed pliers. This means that, when tackling a large mammal carcase, the marabou has to wait for other scavengers to open up the corpse before it can probe and reach for the soft interior tit-bits. But the beak is also a formidable weapon with which to strike living prey. At Nakuru, young flamingoes sometimes provide the marabous with just such victims.

One day on the grey soda flats I watched predatory marabous in action. Dense parties of young flamingoes, perhaps six months old—pale, greyish, their immature plumage not affected by the carotene pigments in the algae that give the adults their soft pink colour—were grouped together in the water. Several marabous stalked about on the beach with an air of studied disinterest. Their pink throat pouches—whose purpose, by the way, no ornithologist has yet satisfactorily explained—wobbled obscenely. Suddenly one marabou took off and flew low and straight towards the flamingoes.

A marabou on the ground is both macabre and grotesque. It is, however, a magnificent and accomplished flier, able to soar with the best, while in level flight its ten-foot wing-span provides it with handsome acceleration. It was halfway to the flamingo group before they reacted. There was no time for those in the centre of the closely packed throng to take off. The birds began to stampede through the shallows. The marabou pressed on into the middle of the pack. It was as if the great stork had marked down one weak or injured bird and was determined to have this one alone. If this were true, then the marabou had remarkable eyesight to be able to detect its victim's failings in the first place, so dense was the assembly of flamingoes.

The end of the chase was near. Many of the flamingoes had at last succeeded in taking off. The marabou kept on and on, skimming down to run in for the kill through the lashed-up water. A few devastating blows with that pickaxe bill quickly finished the job. Those birds that escaped pitched a few hundred yards up the shore. And there another marabou strutted, perhaps awaiting its own opportunity for attack.

The Flamingoes' Sodary Home

The alkaline waters of the Great Rift Valley's soda lakes are fatal to most living creatures, yet in the shallows of many such lakes—especially Natron and Nakuru—millions of flamingoes can be seen apparently sipping the lethal broth.

The explanation is an unusual evolutionary adaptation that allows the flamingoes to get food from the soda solution without ingesting the corrosive liquid. There are two species of the birds: the lesser, which eats bluegreen algae growing near the water surface, and the greater, standing head and neck taller, which sifts the bottom mud for tiny molluscs and crustaceans. Both depend for survival on their highly specialized bills, which are similar in design.

The flamingo bill is heavy and awkward-looking and bends abruptly downwards halfway along its length. The bird uses it like a ladle, feeding with its head upside down so that the "bowl" points in towards its legs. Opening the beak slightly, it sucks in water or mud by swaying its head from side to side and pumping with its tongue. A system of bristles on the inside of the beak excludes large, unrequired objects. A further network of finer bristles lies flat during this operation, but when the sodary liquid is expelled, the bristles are erected to trap the food particles, which can then be safely swallowed without the soda.

Both food supplies in the soda lakes contain canthaxanthin, a substance very similar chemically to Vitamin A, which turns the flamingoes pink. Away from the lakes they fade to white and in zoos they are fed synthetic canthaxanthin in order not to disappoint visitors. Strangely, pink is a colour often at odds with their surroundings, a contrast that might seem to make them easy prey for predators. But there are only a few predators of flamingoes, such as the marabou stork, and even it attacks only fledglings or weaklings.

The flamingoes take full advantage of their specialized niche. In the Rift, with its many soda lakes, there are more of them than in any other place on earth. In any one lake at any one time there may be two million flamingoes or more—mostly lesser flamingoes, which outnumber the greaters by as much as 200 to one. That number can remove up to 11,000 tons of algae from the water a month. The fast-growing algae can more than keep pace with this loss, and for the flamingoes the lakes remain an undiminished cornucopia.

Sleeping flamingoes stir with the early morning sun and begin to feed. Night and day they remain in the alkaline waters, their webbed feet supporting them on the soft mud. The lake acts both as their source of food and as a protection from most predators. An occasional fledgling may fall victim to a lance-billed marabou stork, but otherwise the only casualties in a flamingo colony are eggs or chicks in nests that can be reached over firm ground by enterprising, prowling animals such as hyenas or jackals.

In a breeding colony of greater flamingoes, the canopy of ruffled plumage and the forest of legs provide a secure home for the chicks.

A greater flamingo chick receives a parent's preening; soon it will be pushed out for a Spartan upbringing in adolescent colonies.

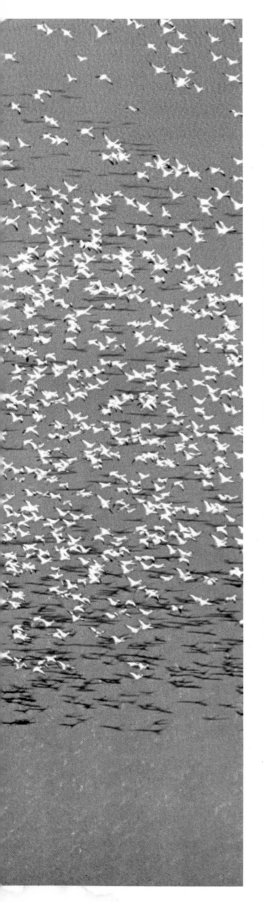

A great cloud of lesser flamingoes takes to the air (left), necks outstretched to counterbalance their long legs. Like many other waterfowl, they may well be unable to fly at all when they moult in the breeding season. Luckily, their breeding quarters are invariably on a soda lake, where there are few predators.

Gawky and vulnerable, lesser flamingoes run through the shallows (above) and beat their wings for take-off. It is a dangerous moment. A marabou stork that chooses its moment can easily intercept a weak one as it scrambles to escape into the air, knock it into the water and there peck it to death.

Mirrored in the lake, lesser flamingoes huddle in a tight group to prevent breezes disrupting the calm water that is ideal for feeding.

With their heads in the characteristic upside-down position, a pair of lesser flamingoes suck and sift algae from the calm soda shallows.

Flamingoes plane through the morning mist to join their flock on Lake Nakuru, while cormorants seem to act as sentinels in the trees.

6/ People from the Past

I felt as if we had stumbled on a race that had survived
simply because Time had forgotten to finish them off.

JOHN HILLABY/ JOURNEY TO THE JADE SEA

Most of the Rift, even the most brutally hostile parts of the Danakil
Depression, have for many thousands of years supported a complicated
pattern of tribes—Bantu peoples, Hamitics, Nilotics, Nilo-Hamitics.
Some of these are hunting peoples, others agriculturalists, many semi-
nomadic pastoralists, who rely on their cattle and goats. The Masai, who
range along the Rift in southern Kenya and Tanzania, are perhaps the
warrior pastoralists best known to the outside world. Today, even the
Masai are beginning to feel the pressures of so-called civilization. One
must look farther, to the remote and forbidding areas, to find tribes who
are virtually untouched by the 20th Century. In the parched landscape
that surrounds the shores of Lake Rudolf, several tribes, ethnically
widely different, eke out existences so primitive that they seem
survivals of the Stone Age. (The term "Stone Age" is not quite accurate
when applied to these people, since even the most remote tribes know
about metal, though they have not produced metal tools themselves.)

The region around Lake Rudolf, the 195-mile long inland sea discovered by Count Samuel Teleki in 1887, is one of the most severe and
uncompromising, though often beautiful, wildernesses in the entire Rift
Valley. Very little grows along the lake's sandy, sterile western shore,
except where a rare fresh-water spring wells up and produces an oasis of
doum palms. Few large wild animals survive there. The eastern side is
quite different. A harsh rocky ledge is relieved by stretches of vivid

green reed bed, where zebra, oryx, lion, hartebeeste and waterbuck come to drink. But beyond the reeds stretches a country of pitiless dryness, gullied and eroded, with sparse scrub breaking up the grey volcanic earth and yellowish lake sediments. At the southern end of the finger-shaped lake, the water laps on the cruellest desert of all, a countryside of volcanic rocks bordered by sheets of knife-edge lava.

Yet in past ages, Rudolf was neither waterless nor barren. Its shores were teeming with wild animals including prehistoric elephants, three-toed ancestors of the horse, and game animals similar to those we know today. And by a strange irony it seems likely that here, where man now has to struggle for survival, some three million years ago hominids—early men-like creatures—took a vital evolutionary step along the path that led to *Homo sapiens*. Palaeontologists agree that, although Lake Rudolf and adjacent parts of the Rift may not necessarily be the only—or even the earliest—womb of mankind, this area has strong claims for primacy. Peking, Java and South Africa all have rival sites, backed up by fossil clues. But none of these geographical competitors has yet produced anything like the abundance of evidence that early, tool-using man evolved in what, today, seems an unlikely corner of the world.

The reason may simply be that 16 or more million years of unique geological history have created ideal conditions in the Rift Valley for preserving and revealing evidence that has been lost elsewhere—conditions ideal, first for fossilizing ancient bones, and, second for uncovering them by erosion or making them relatively easy for scientists to unearth. The past was encapsulated by the volcanoes that have played so active a part in the Rift's history, spewing out chemicals, such as calcium carbonate, that help turn bones into fossils. At the same time rifting created a chain of lakes whose levels rose and fell with the amount of rainfall. Some lakes were deepened by further faulting, and then obliterated by the lava flows that followed, while new ones were created by subsequent earth movements. Each new lake and each new lake-level laid down fresh layers of sediment, forming a complicated inter-layering of lava and sediment to capture and preserve bones until further upheavals brought them to light again, lifting up long concealed layers and exposing them to erosion.

It was here that the oldest hominid skull yet discovered was found by a young Kenyan anthropologist named Richard Leakey, son of celebrated parents, Louis and Mary Leakey, who had already uncovered much of early man's history in the Rift, notably in Tanzania. It was they who in the 1960s discovered the bones of a creature 1.8 million years old in Olduvai Gorge. Theirs was the oldest hominid find until 1972, when near Koobi Fora, at north-east Rudolf, Richard Leakey came upon a shattered cranium with genuinely humanoid characteristics simply lying on the surface in the grey-brown fossil beds. It appeared to have been washed out by recent rains. There is no problem about dating such finds—it is done by analysis of the traces of potassium argon gas found in them—especially if the bones have been fossilized in volcanic soil: Leakey's skull was 2.8 million years old.

Though the precise status of the skull has not been determined, and it is registered simply as "1470 man" by the National Museum of Kenya, scientists are in no doubt about the accuracy of the dating or that "1470", whose braincase was nearly as large as that of later ancestors of man, is indeed the earliest precursor of *Homo sapiens* yet found.

We can be reasonably sure how the owner of this skull looked and behaved. It is probable that he belonged to the same species as the hominids of Olduvai—*Australopithecus boisei*. These "men" stood under five feet tall, possessed low foreheads, bulging eyebrows and brains no bigger than that of a gorilla. Their molars were twice the width of our own, which suggests grinding teeth suited to a vegetarian diet. Most experts, including Leakey, believe that the Australopithecenes came to an evolutionary deadend and never made the all-essential leap to tool-making which led to the genus *Homo*, culminating in ourselves. Yet hundreds of stone axes and cutting tools have been found in the same area, so who *was* making stone tools on the shores of Lake Rudolf just over two and a half million years ago? There are many secrets locked up in the accumulated sediments of that wild and remote lake to which the key has yet to be found.

The scattered tribes that now live along Lake Rudolf's shores use techniques for living that are often not greatly different from those of the early hunters. The modern environment cannot support large numbers of land mammals, either animal or human. For peoples who are pastoral, with social organizations based on communal grazing land and water supplies, the problems of living in a region where rainfall is erratic and grazing land sparse are almost insuperable. Most of the tribes have been forced to become nomadic or semi-nomadic, with land held in common and individual ownership restricted to a man's herd of camels, cattle, sheep or goats. Surprisingly, only one tribe makes ends meet by fishing in the well-stocked waters of Lake Rudolf.

The lake is kept reasonably fresh by the river Omo, which flows in from the north through one of the strangest-looking deltas I have ever seen. It varies in extent according to the rainfall hundreds of miles away to the north on the Ethiopian high plateau, but its most unusual feature is the continuance of the river Omo three or four miles out into the lake, between high banks or levees. This canal-like formation, so regular that it appears almost man-made, is constructed by the river itself. As the Omo arrives, powerful and fresh, at its journey's end, the lighter, fresh water of the river floats on the heavier, sodary waters of the lake. As it thrusts into Rudolf, the river carries its sediments with it. After a short distance, the sediments at the edge of the Omo's current sink, building the first walls of the parallel levees. The river flows on between these banks, building an extension of the canal system for itself as it goes. Presumably there must be a limit, dictated by wave action, to this extending part of the delta, but there is little visible sign of destruction.

The three tribes that occupy the delta and the meander belts that stretch for 50 miles back to the Ethiopian and Sudan borders probably number not more than five or six thousand all told. These, the Desenech, the Bume and the Mursi, are the kind of ethnic mixture one would expect to find at a point sufficiently far north in the Rift to feel the strong tribal surge that sub-Saharan Africa has experienced from the Nile and Ethiopia. They are tall, dignified people, peaceful and stable enough within their own tribal frameworks, but fierce in defence of their territories and in their occasional raiding ventures on other tribes.

The Nilotic peoples—the Bume and the Mursi—probably come as near to the untouched primitive life as any people in Africa. Their bee-hive huts, very similar to those of the Danakil, 700 miles north, have a framework of bent saplings over which are laid hides or grass mats. The whole edifice is highly mobile, yet the village clusters of several hundred huts, interspersed with granaries built on stilts, are largely sedentary. The entire village is usually surrounded, like a walled city, by a single fence or even rings of barbed-wire-like, thorn defences, designed to keep stock in and enemies out.

Their farming is basic in the extreme, providing the village granaries with subsistence crops of sorghum, millet, beans and poor quality tobacco. Frequent bush fires suggest that they appreciate the value of regular burning to control old growth and encourage new, but, despite the sporadic flooding of the delta, they seem to know nothing of irrigation. They have, however, learned other uses for water: when flying low over the delta I have seen fishermen in dug-out canoes, a sophisticated form of water transport unknown throughout the length and breadth of

Turkana tribesmen wait patiently for fish on the shores of Lake Rudolf. When one of them spots a fish, he plunges his upside-down basket into

the water, trapping his victim against the lake bottom. He then puts his arm through the meshes and threads its gills with a reed.

the lake. The probable explanation is that the river provides them with trees large enough to be hollowed out with fire and axe.

The eastern shore of the great lake belongs to desert nomads, peoples of mainly Galla descent, Galla being the principal ethnic group of central and southern Ethiopia. It would take a whole faculty of professors of ethnology to sort out the precise tribal ancestries of the Rendille, the Kerre, the Banna, the Bachada, the Amarr, the Arbore and the Borana—north-east Rudolf peoples all. The most striking of these tribes are the Rendille, tall and proud people who wander the areas in which Richard Leakey made his great anthropological finds. They are camel people—it is said that, when a Rendille dies, his brother mourns him with one eye and counts his camels with the other—and are of warrior stock, given to tribal raiding.

But eastern Rudolf holds a greater menace than the Rendille: brigands, or the Shifta as they are known. The Shifta move in bands, like renegade Red Indians of the Old West, ready to kill and rob anyone whom they can outnumber or surprise. In 1965, a band of Shifta moved in on a small outpost called Loiengalani, at the south-east end of the lake, where some Europeans lived, and murdered three people, including the tourist lodge manager and a priest.

The two tribes I know best, however, are the Turkana, who live on the western shore, and the El Molo, sometimes called The Impoverished Ones, who are down at the southern tip. The Turkana are a jet-black people, with a majestic air that is utterly in contrast with the plight in which they now find themselves. Nomadic grazers of cattle, camels and goats, they have been increasingly hemmed in by the growing pressure on the land. In pre-colonial days, when they needed more space for their herds, they simply went out and seized it. They were cattle-rich—able to dole out as many as 40 head, plus other valuable goods, as a bride-price. But for the past century, because of rigidly defined tribal boundaries set up by the colonial government, they have been forbidden to expand their territory. At the same time, medicine has raised the population and veterinary services have tended to increase the survival rate of tribal cattle. Nomadic pastoralists seldom kill or sell their stock. To them, cows and goats are visible evidence of wealth and status. So there are more people and more stock and less food and grazing available. Not only that, but the landscape suffers from over-grazing; grass and scrub disappears, hooves cut up the topsoil, and erosion sets in. Thus, paradoxically, modern aids undermine the area's remaining resources.

Although there are now some 169,000 Turkana, about 13 times the number of Rendille, they have only a little more than twice the territory, and about one-third the number of camels and cattle. The situation is grave, and made even more so by the Turkana's insistence on the freedom of individual decision. The number of water holes, for instance, is extremely small. Yet the Turkana refuse to work co-operatively. There is no collective effort either to regulate or increase water stores.

Since 1962, the Kenya government has made great efforts to convince at least those Turkana who live closest to the lake to make the transition from their traditional pastoral life to that of fishermen. But to people who relish the taste of millet, blood and milk, fish is hardly a palatable substitute. There is an even more serious psychological problem: a man with no cattle is a man with no status. The Kenya Fisheries Department's programme has therefore moved along only haltingly. Fisheries' officers began by trying to teach the Turkana in the area of Ferguson's Gulf, halfway up Rudolf's western shore, to use boats and outboard motors. But water life is so alien that of 500 trained on the boats, only 200 stuck to fishing on a commercial basis. The rest returned to pastoral life within three years, and when an officer visited them to see how the experiment was progressing he found that many boats had been turned upside down and raised on stilts as dwelling places. Even the few who have continued to fish on a commercial rather than a mere subsistence basis regard the lake with awe and venture off-shore timidly. When the water is calm, handline or spear fishermen will kneel on rafts made of two palm logs bound together and, paddling with their hands, go out as far as several hundred yards. But no more. Their caution is justified. Rudolf is a lake of sudden gusting winds that come tearing out of the desert country to the north east, whipping up waves that can knock the life out of a small dinghy, let alone a dugout canoe or a palm-log raft.

So most Turkana prefer, if fish they must, to use another method taught them by the Fisheries people—gill-netting. They stand naked, lithe and black as obsidian, heaving nets and stone-weighted handlines into the breakers. Their feet do not appear to feel the heat stored in the yellow sand. Their primitive handlines are armed with forged steel hooks supplied by the Fisheries Department. And with these they bring in some truly giant Nile perch. I once watched a Turkana land one that comfortably topped the 100 pound mark, but that was no record. These fish, delicious to Western taste if not to the Turkana palate, often weigh as much as 200 pounds.

One form of Turkana fishery owes nothing to superimposed modern technology. I have stood at dusk on the shelving sandy shores and watched a reddish-yellow, will o' the wisp light dance along the reeded edge of a lagoon. Its glow catches the features of a Turkana as he stoops quickly towards the water. He bends and pauses and the light dips with his movements. Then he stands fully upright again. The light flickers a few paces closer along the shore, and the actions are repeated. I see now that the light comes from a smouldering bunch of dried reeds, a primitive torch used to attract fish. The Turkana's other hand holds a hemispherical, open-work basket made of bound saplings. In the hope that the light has lured to the surface fish who lurk among the reeds, he dips the basket at random, pausing each time to feel inside. At the seventh dip, his groping hand withdraws a small wriggling tilapia. Here is a method of fishing linking modern man to his Stone-Age ancestors.

Compared to the Turkana, the El Molo, living on the barren, pumice-strewn ridges at the southern end of the lake, are in a pitiable state. Beyond the great barrier of grey volcanic slag that hems them in, the ground drops away to a desolate frontier where no man lives, the Suguta Valley. Unlike the Turkana, the El Molo have always been fishers. The literal translation of their name is The People Who Live by Catching Fish. The tiniest and most depressed of all Rudolf's communities—numbering only about 270—they live in ragged round little huts made of grass and bits of driftwood that are so low that even their diminutive inhabitants must stoop to enter them.

Dr. John Hillaby, the English naturalist, visited them in the early 1960s, and felt as if he had been carried back into pre-history. "Rotting fish remains littered the ground; naked babies snatched at the flies; a few sticks upheld tattered nets. The impression was Neolithic."

Time has certainly wrought little change in their lives since Count Teleki first discovered them where they still are today, in the area of Loiengalani. At that time they lived exclusively on a little island just offshore, called Lorian, on which they had taken refuge from marauding tribes, especially the Turkana. Some of them still live on the island, ferrying their goats across to the mainland on rafts and feeding their few scrawny cattle on weeds dredged up from the shallows of the lake with their hands. But most have now returned to the mainland.

The El Molo pole about in the shallow edges of the lake on palm-log rafts, either spearing or netting fish. But unlike the Turkana, they are superb fishers. As harpooners of perch they are magnificent. There is something heron-like about the poise of an El Molo as he stands motionless with the quivering spear of hardened thorn root, detachable barbed tip attached to fibre line glinting as the sun strikes the metal. That metal tip is about the only concession that the El Molo, who not so long ago fashioned their harpoons from bone, make to the 20th Century.

South of the El Molo, and Loiengalani, where the ground drops away past razor-back bare hills into a nightmarish landscape of utter desolation, life seems almost to stop. There are no tracks across the southern end of the lake except ghostly-seeming trails picked out between lava boulders and knife-edged ridges by Turkana herdsmen. The winds that howl down the eastern shore of Rudolf mount in tempo throughout the early afternoon, increasing in violence into the night and finally exhausting themselves just before dawn.

It is in the no less hostile Suguta Valley, the "salt steppe" just to the south of this volcanic barrier, that Richard Leakey, flying his own light aircraft, has pinpointed strata that he hopes will yield some of the most dramatic traces of early man yet found.

At present there exists a break of ten million years in the hominid fossil record. There are no relics from this entire period except for a single crown of a nine-million-year-old molar found in the Tugen Hills near Lake Baringo. But layers of sediment and lava which Leakey glimpsed from his aircraft suggest that they may hide fossils that will bridge the gap. If such fossils are found, they will confirm Lake Rudolf's greatest irony. A place once lush enough to be the cradle for mankind has now been reduced by climate, geological change and animal grazing to a wilderness where man has to struggle to survive at all.

Into the Dark Continent in 1887

Count Samuel Teleki von Szek, a Hungarian sportsman, geographer and wildlife enthusiast, set out from Pangani on the east coast of Africa (map right) to work his way into the interior in January 1887. By that time, many of the dark continent's mysteries had already been plumbed. Lakes Victoria Nyanza and Tanganyika had been pinpointed and Lake Victoria identified as the source of the Nile.

But challenges remained. Teleki's companion and the chronicler of the expedition, Lt. Ludwig von Höhnel —from whose journal the engravings on these pages were taken and the text adapted—wrote, "our idea was to penetrate the then quite unknown districts on the north of Baringo, as yet unvisited even by native caravans, and in which some geographers said there was one lake, whilst others thought there were two big sheets of water".

For 22 months, the explorers penetrated jungles, swamps and lava-strewn volcanic plains in style. They travelled with a massive caravan that contrasted sharply with the improvised small-scale expeditions

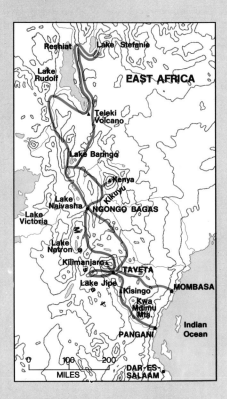

mounted by most European explorers. The party, financed by the Count himself, included some 450 porters, six guides and assorted translators, and was weighed down with 470 loads of trade goods for bartering with the Africans.

Although they made valuable observations on geology, geography and ethnology, they also spent considerable time satisfying their "hunting zeal". With the wanton passion that characterized explorers of their era, they shot everything from small fowl and antelope to hippopotami and elephants. Early in the trek they encountered their first leopard (opposite) which, in von Höhnel's bland words, "brought forcibly before my mind the fact that I was in Africa".

Though harassed by unfriendly natives, by extremes of temperature and by shortages of food and water, they ascertained that there were indeed two lakes. These Teleki named after Crown Prince Rudolf, heir to the Austro-Hungarian Empire, "who took the greatest interest in the expedition", and after Rudolf's wife, Stefanie. The expedition ended in Mombasa in October 1888.

FIRST ENCOUNTER WITH A LEOPARD

With Teleki to Rudolf

COUNT SAMUEL TELEKI VON SZEK

The first stages of our march quickly taught us how hot and thirsty one can become in East Africa. Worst of all was the terrain known to the natives as *nyika*—an uninhabited, barren, waterless, bushy steppe. The glare from the red laterite soil was terrible, and the dust was fearfully deep. The footprints of wild beasts proved that there was plenty of big game, but we shot little until we approached Mount Kilimanjaro. One morning, after almost three months, we set out in high spirits, for we expected to have our first glimpse of the snow-clad peaks of the mountain. The view was at first shut out by the heights jutting across the valley between the Kisingo and Kwa Mdimu mountains. But when these were left behind there was nothing to impede our vision. The whole valley was now spread out before us; on the west rose rugged mountains, gradually increasing in height. In the wide plain stretching to the east, we could see Lake Jipe, which looked like a narrow streak of light.

On this day Count Teleki had started earlier than the caravan, so as to do some hunting. He almost had more than he bargained for. Besides a successful double shot at two impala, he barely missed stumbling over a leopard. He had seen one in the high grass, but it disappeared too quickly for him to fire. Almost immediately he heard a growling nearby, and saw some animal approaching through the long grass. Thinking it was a wild boar, or something of that kind, he changed his rifle for a shotgun and fired. There was a rolling over and over in the grass, and then he saw the paws of a great leopard. He seized the rifle again; but the danger was past.

HORNS OF SLAUGHTERED BUFFALO

Some of his pellets had fortunately found a vital mark, and the animal lay dead.

The immediate neighbourhood of Lake Jipe, where this incident took place, is haunted by lions and leopards, giraffes, hyenas, ostriches and other wild creatures, which come down to the water to drink, so that it is a very paradise for the hunter. The lake itself abounds in crocodiles and hippopotami, as well as catfish and perch.

After almost three long months, only a few hours' march now separated us from the first goal of our journey, the forest-girt village of Taveta. Often the very sound of the name had acted like a magic spell upon our men, filling them, weary and worn as they were, with fresh hope, fresh energy. It was no wonder that now we were so near it we were all intoxicated with delightful anticipation! How much we might hope for in the beautiful quiet forest, into the depths of which we tried in vain to peer from the hill near the lake! What peace, what rest in the shade of this African paradise, beside murmuring streams, after our long tramp across arid steppes!

A Well-Guarded Entrance

As we neared the village the vegetation became greener and more luxuriant, the trees grew higher and closer together, the undergrowth denser and the parasites more numerous. At last we were utterly immersed in the dark, humid shades of the forest. The trees rose many feet above our heads, casting their long dark shadows across the path. Many a trunk lay right across the track, which wound in and out and backwards and forwards. We had to stoop and twist, to creep and crawl in single file, in order to avoid the many impediments in the way. Suddenly there was a shout of joy at the sound of distant firing—the signal that the head of the caravan had

A GERENUK

reached the entrance to Taveta, a door made of tree-trunks, closing the pathway to the settlement.

And now, like rolling thunder, the sounds of the firing of guns echoed on every side, startling hundreds of birds and terrifying the apes, which had been peering at us at close quarters. When the village door had been opened and we had made our way on all-fours through the narrow entrance, we could see better. The path led between tall hedges of banana-palms and across

MARABOU STORKS AND VULTURES COMPETING FOR A RHINOCEROS CARCASE

numerous little rivulets. Idle natives gazed at us in friendly fashion, whilst the women at work in the little wood-encircled fields paused to shout their greetings to us as if we were old friends: "*Yambo, Yambo, sana! Sabalcheir! Uhali ghani? Habari ghani?*" and so on, which meant, "Good day! God bless you! How are you? What's the news?"

As we intended to stop in Taveta for a long time, our first care was to get our camp in order. Some of the men cut away the weeds, while others dragged the tree-trunks and palm-leaf ribs with which to build the huts. In a few days we were the owners of a complete village, fitted out with stables for the donkeys and goats, a workshop and a kitchen.

The Local Inhabitants

We soon got to know the people of Taveta well. Every shady corner of our clearing was usually crowded with a chattering mob offering their wares for sale: fish, bananas, tobacco, honey, potatoes, sugar cane and now and then a hen. The first impression the Tavetans make is that they are extremely primitive, but nearer acquaintance proves that, like most of the tribes living near the well-organized Masai, they more or less closely resemble those handsome, semi-nomadic pastoralists.

This similarity is not surprising, for some 40 years ago the Tavetans were joined by a considerable number of Wakwafi, a branch of the great Masai family which had been decimated by civil war and dispersed. Deprived of their cattle, they had been forced to give up their accustomed pastoral life and were now scattered all round Masailand as tillers of the soil.

In Taveta, only the young copy the Masai style of costume in servile imitation. The young men, as a rule, wear only one garment—like the Masai. It is a short mantle of hairy goatskin of brownish red cotton stuff, which covers the left side of the body, and is fastened on the right shoulder. Now and then, they add a kind of leather apron to sit on that hangs down the back. Their hair is generally twisted into a number of thin, spiral locks that fall low on the forehead, sometimes down to the eyes. At the back it is lengthened with a plait of bark fibre which resembles a pigtail. The lobes of the ears are artificially widened, and decked with ornaments made of iron or brass wire, beads or iron chains. A few ornaments—bracelets around the wrists and ankles, mostly made of twisted wire or strips of leather sewn with beads—complete the costume. On the right side they wear a short, straight sword with a broad blade and on the other side swings a finely decorated wooden club.

The girls wear a petticoat of tanned and dressed goatskin, which sometimes hangs down below the thighs. The upper portion is often quite prettily trimmed with beads. They are particularly fond of neck ornaments, and sometimes wear necklaces made of more than 100 strings of beads twisted together; and the usual

MAN OF TAVETA

bracelets and anklets of brass and iron. In the widened lobes of their ears they insert a piece of fresh banana-leaf rolled up like a quill, or a round bit of wood. Both young women and men smear the nude portions of their bodies with a preparation of red earth and fat. In our eyes this presents a most terrible appearance; but to their fellows, a thick layer of grease gives them a delicate finish.

The older women wear, in addition to the petticoat, a second garment that partly covers the upper portion of the body; and some few ancient dames have lately adopted the cotton drapery, wrapped tightly about the bust in the style of the women of Zanzibar. One much-admired ear ornament worn by married men and women consists of thick brass wire wound in spirals till it forms a circle about four inches in diameter. Since these coils are too heavy for the lobe of the ear, they are partly supported by a band that rests upon the neck.

Circumcision is universally practised. Boys generally retire to the forest afterwards for a time, whilst girls, on whom a somewhat similar operation is inflicted, remain secluded for a month in their huts. If a stranger approaches, they hide their faces. The mothers of the girls smear their faces with streaks of red and white.

TAVETAN MARRIED WOMAN

From Taveta we made several excursions to visit the chiefs of two nearby tribes, the Chagga and the Meru, and to Mount Kilimanjaro, which Count Teleki climbed to over 15,000 feet. Then it was time for us to move on from Masailand.

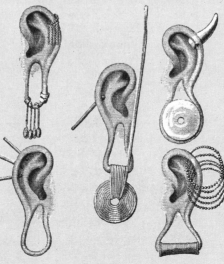

KIKUYU EAR ORNAMENTS

On August 27 we reached Ngongo Bagas, the spring of Bagas, an important camping place on the borders of Masailand and Kikuyuland. We had come to a vital stage in our journey. We stood upon the threshold of Kikuyuland, on the eve of a time full of trial and adventure.

Into Kikuyuland

Before our arrival, little was really known about the land or the people and countless tales were afloat of their fierceness and hostility. A caravan from Mombasa, it was said, had tried a few years ago to enter Kikuyuland from the east, and had been destroyed. Since then no traders had dared venture within range of the Kikuyu's poisoned arrows.

Fortunately an old Masai woman, named Nakairo, who was held in high esteem by the Kikuyu, happened to be in the camp, and she offered to be our intermediary. It is noteworthy that women on both sides are always perfectly safe in spite of the constant feud between the Masai and Kikuyu men. Knowing this we appointed the old lady to be our diplomatic agent. Although frightened by the white faces at first, the Kikuyu soon began to bring food and sell us their produce.

This people's lively, restless temperament is an indication of their relationship to the great Bantu stock. But physically they resemble the

ORANGE-FLOWERED SENECIO JOHNSTONII

Masai. Though they are seldom above medium height, they are well built, muscular and strong.

We only traversed the southern portion of the land inhabited by the Kikuyu, and as far as we can tell it stretches to the eastern base of Kenya and north to the equator.

To Mount Kenya

Our camp was not particularly beautiful scenery. About 100 paces off in a shallow ravine was a swamp overgrown with waterlilies and rushes, to which snipe and cranes came down now and then, whilst the croaking of frogs was continuous. Otherwise the district seemed deserted alike by men and animals.

We pitched our tents facing Mount Kenya, so that we might look at it whenever the cloud canopy that generally shrouded it from view was lifted. Count Teleki was pressing on with his preparations for the ascent of the mountain and started on the morning of October 17 with five guides and 40 porters, leaving the rest of us behind in camp.

After his departure, it rained heavily. Woods and fields, which had been so dry and dreary-looking, were bursting with fresh life. It must, however, have been different in the lofty regions where Count Teleki now was. The mountain was continuously shrouded in gloomy clouds and heavy snow extended down the slopes. I was very anxious for the Count's return, but I need not have worried. His trip was perfectly successful. He ascended Mount Kenya to a height of 15,355 feet—all but the last two or three thousand feet—and ascertained the nature of its crater and slopes.

In his climb, he met many zebras, elands and water-bucks, some longtailed apes and a leopard. "From nearly every cleft of the mountain," the Count reported, "flowed a little brook on the swampy banks of which grew various plants, some resembling the *Senecio johnstonii*, which bear large orange flowers." At 13,100 feet the Count saw the last animals of any size: a humming-bird, a pretty thrush-like bird and a hairy, tailless marmot.

After several months of journeying, from October 1887 to March 1888, we approached Lake Rudolf. There was a mighty mountain mass looming up before us. We hurried to the top of the ridge, the scene gradually developing until a new world spread out before us.

CRANES NEAR MOUNT KENYA

RARE OLEANDER-LIKE TREES

For a long time we gazed in speechless delight, spell-bound by the beauty of the scene. Our men, equally silent, stared into the distance, then broke into shouts of astonishment at the sight of the glittering expanse of the great lake which seemed to melt on the horizon into the deep blue of the sky.

The next day, after working our way through plains covered with black streams of lava, and dotted with craters from one of which clouds of smoke rose, we finally stood upon the beach of the lake. The beautiful water stretched away before us, clear as crystal. The men rushed down shouting, to plunge into the lake; but soon returned in bitter disappointment: the water was brackish! What a betrayal!

After several days, always in fear of hunger and thirst, we marched through a district where large herds of elephants lived. Several fell victim to our guns. Three we had wounded sought refuge in the lake, but by morning only one remained. So the Count sent three men out in our canvas boat. They were either to shoot the animal, or to drive him ashore. The boat circled the quarry, but the elephant did not budge an inch, no matter how many bullets struck his body. Suddenly, he charged furiously, and the men jumped

A WOUNDED ELEPHANT DESTROYING THE EXPEDITION'S BOAT

overboard. In the twinkling of an eye he was upon the fragile craft, which he seized with his trunk. He shook it, crushed it, tossed it about, and then contemptuously flung it aside. Finally, he marched with slow and stately steps through the water and disappeared behind a peninsula in the shoreline.

Making Friends with the Reshiat

After a month on Rudolf, we were full of delight at beginning our last march by the lake. We were off early, our men crying "Hurrah!" and "*Haya ugali!*" as they shouldered their loads. We would have shouted ourselves if previous experience had not taught us caution. But in spite of the assurances we had received of the friendliness of the Reshiat, the local tribe whom we were about to meet, we preferred not to make ourselves too much in evidence.

After an hour's walk we emerged from the wood that stretched westward, and came upon a stretch of ground strewn with human skulls and bones. This seemed ominously warlike. But a little later, we found ourselves amongst numerous herds of oxen and donkeys. The animals were grazing unguarded—a sure sign that the natives were peaceful.

This was perhaps the most interesting day of our whole journey, for we were now face to face with a perfectly unknown people. And the way in which these natives, who had hitherto lived quietly far away from the rest of the world, received us was so simple that we could not get over our astonishment. First came a party of ten or twelve warriors, and behind them a group of some 60 or 80 men, who advanced fearlessly. They paused every now and then, but evidently not from nervousness, for they allowed the women laden with food to approach.

The chief of the village, a tall, slim man of about 50, recommended a camp site where we should be little bothered by mosquitoes and should have a pool of rainwater for drinking.

They sold us warm milk, beef, corn and tobacco, and our men got *ugali*, a stiff porridge, twice every day. Many supplemented this with fish and mussels, of which there were quantities in the lake, and with soft, sticky red berries. We encountered several kinds of fish, including one extraordinary species that resembled a snake, but with a coat of stiff, armour-like scales.

Our men now being fairly restored to health, we were once again seized with a longing for new discoveries and fresh experiences.

To Lake Stefanie and Back

After about a week's march eastwards from the northern tip of Lake Rudolf, and led by two guides who had only a vague notion of where the next sheet of water might be, we discovered a lake which we christened Lake Stefanie. It was shallow, barren and too brackish to drink, and surrounded by volcanic debris. We met no natives, and being short of supplies, left almost at once.

On the morning of April 25, we pushed on along a path running parallel with the lake in a westerly direction. On this march the Count came upon a group of crocodiles, which rushed headlong for the water; not, however, before one of them had been shot dead.

As we marched further, we made the disagreeable discovery that it had not rained during the last few days. We obtained a little water by digging the next day, but no more after that. So we were compelled to do the whole of the march from Lake Stefanie to the village of Reshiat in four days. The last stage was no less than 25 miles, and we achieved it between daybreak and sunset, with only one short interval for rest.

The Homeward Journey

On the evening of May 27 we returned to our camping-place of March 12. Although we had only marched for 14 days since leaving Reshiat, and eight rhinoceroses with one zebra had been added to our stores of food, not one of our men had a scrap of their rations left.

We pressed on along the shore, reaching our old camping-place at the southern end of Lake Rudolf on the evening of May 31. We had done the 235 miles in 16 days of 90 marching hours, whereas the same distance had taken 28 days going up. The fears of food shortage with which we had started southwards had not, most fortunately, been realized. So far fate had been kind to us, and, full of fresh hope, we set off for far-distant Mombasa.

THE CAMP AT THE SOUTHERN END OF LAKE RUDOLF

7/ The Elephants of Manyara

Elephants breed in that part of Affricke which lyeth beyond the deserts. . . . Wonderful is the wit and subtiltie that these dumb creatures have and how they shift for themselves.

PLINY/ HISTORIA NATURALIS

My journey down the Rift began in the Danakil desert, as stark and inhospitable a landscape as anywhere on earth; it was appropriate that it ended with a complete contrast: a visit to the lush forests and savannah of Manyara, 80 miles south of Lake Natron.

The area below the escarpment at Manyara is possibly the most luxuriant place in the whole East African Rift. Its soil grows anything from elephants to bananas, from rhinos to pawpaws. Much of the area is a National Park, one of the few actually in the Rift. But it nevertheless represents Africa at its wildest, as anyone who has lived under canvas and worked down there will testify. I once came back to my tent after a few minutes' absence to find that four lions had sacked the place and dragged all the bedding out into the open. The sheets were still wet with saliva and jagged with tooth marks. The park itself—30 miles along Lake Manyara's western shoreline—and the surrounding area is also the one place in the entire valley where large numbers of elephant roam. It has an average of 12 elephants per square mile, the greatest concentration of elephants in Africa.

The park, bordered on the east by the alkaline waters of Lake Manyara, runs on its western side up into the Manyara escarpment. Other escarpments may be higher but few have the magic of Manyara. The tree-covered, often nearly vertical slope plunges down, sometimes to within a few hundred yards of, and seldom more than four miles from, the lake shore. The scarp is fissured by a series of twisting gorges. Between these, forested buttresses project into the savannah beneath. I have flown down some of those gorges with Alan Root who has often been forced to bank the plane at an angle of 45 degrees to negotiate the next turn. In places, these ravines are barely half again as wide as the wing-span of the aircraft. It makes for interesting flying.

On one occasion we took a gorge unknown to Alan. Several flat-topped huts hanging on the face of the chasm proclaimed that Sonjo tribesmen lived there. The Sonjo, an agricultural, Bantu-speaking people, comparatively light in colour, once lived in terror of the dark-skinned, warlike Masai and so built their homes underground to hide them from raiding warriors. The need has receded but a remnant of the tradition remains. The huts from whose roofs we raised the red dust were, I noticed with what eyes the hair-raising flight left me for anthropological observation, half buried in the soil. These Sonjos had evidently never seen an aircraft before. When we bellowed through their pass, they took to the cellars, as did their chickens and, I believe, one goat, almost as if the Masai had taken to the warpath once again.

Observations from the ground are somewhat less nerve-racking but equally informative. Driving from the escarpment on the rough road down to the forests and plains below, it is easy to see why so many elephants and other animals live there. The road runs into an area of well-watered forest. Many streams, clearer than the purest trout streams, run down from the escarpment just here and so maintain a constant and fairly high level of ground water. Springs well up throughout the forest. Water is generally an element to beware of in Africa. Close to habitation and, especially when slow-running, it is almost certain to contain human effluent, one of the carriers of bilharzia parasites which eventually attack liver and intestines. But no menace hides in this pure water. It is perfectly safe to bathe in it, drink it, and eat the succulent water cress that grows alongside it, planted years ago by some European with memories of English high teas and summer salads.

The forest itself evokes memories of Tarzan. It is green and cool. Among its trees, the magnificent figs and African mahoganies are taller than English oaks and beeches and far more luxuriant. The savannah just beyond the forest grows many kinds of acacia, notably *Acacia tortilis*, and also *Acacia clavigeria*, the stinkbark, whose aromatic scent is to elephants what aniseed is said to be to dogs. Near the lower part of the scarp, one tree dominates by size and stature, *Adansonia digitata*, the baobab. Several African tribes believe that the baobab is the home of night spirits. One legend declares that God was angry with the tree and planted it upside down. Its trunk is bulbous, and its branches do have an upside-down look. Baobabs are soft-tissued, fleshy, and frequently full of holes excavated by birds and small mammals. They support and offer temporary home to everything from eagles to arboreal snakes. At night they are visited by bats that help to pollinate their ghostly white blossoms. Big-eyed bush babies creep around their branches in the dusk. It is small wonder that the baobabs have found their way into legend as the homes of ever-active night spirits.

The luxuriant forest supports a rich variety of animals. Lions lie idle along branches, cooling in the breeze and escaping the attentions of biting flies. Baboons shake themselves from the trees like ripe fruits. Blue Syke's monkeys swing and leap, using the creepers as trapezes. A heart-stopping crash and tearing, close at hand, announces elephant; the dense ground cover makes it impossible to see how many, even at 30 yards. Nearby in a small open space, a black rhino cow, wallowing in a spring, snorts and throws its head from side to side, searching with its nose for what may be an enemy and deciding in the primeval darkness of its mind whether it should bother to charge or not. Black rhinos, as unstoppable once in motion as a runaway locomotive, are totally unpredictable. Fortunately they are also short-sighted. Often they cannot focus clearly on the target and thus lose at least 50 per cent of the opportunities for throwing their one and a half tons about.

Where the springs cease, the dense forest ceases also. More open savannah begins. It, too, is amazingly green, and its scattered stands of trees are usually in leaf before the rains start. The run-off from the escarpment makes its influence felt here, even if not in quite such an obvious way. The soil, brought down over thousands of years from the highlands, is ready to grow practically anything.

Among the trees of the savannah, *Acacia tortilis* is the one Manyara elephants like to eat before all others. *Tortilis* is a beautiful flat-topped tree. Just before the rainy season it blossoms with white flowers that baboons appreciate, and in the dry season it is hung with yellow seed pods to which elephants are addicted. At that season the Manyara elephants go on an *Acacia tortilis* binge, butting the tree trunks with their four-ton bulk until the acacia sheds its pods in golden rain. An elephant's trunk is a remarkably precise instrument. It can pick up an acacia pod with a delicacy matching that of a sunbird selecting a single blossom from which to sip nectar.

An alert group of impala browses through lush undergrowth around Lake Manyara. The impressive horns of the male are mainly for courtship show: these graceful antelope rely on keen noses and wide ears for early warning of cheetah or leopard. Once alarmed, they scatter in a jumping, jinking retreat.

Though the elephants do much to destroy their acacia habitat, they also perform a vital role in its regeneration. Their predilection for the tree's fruit—a single elephant may contain in its intestines at any one time more than 10,000 *Acacia tortilis* seeds—provides *tortilis* with easily its most effective method of propagation. Unlike other trees, such as the sycamore which relies on the wind to disperse its seeds or the oak which enlists the burying activities of squirrels, *Acacia tortilis* is regenerated through the guts and droppings of elephants. There are two schools of thought about how the cycle works, but both conclude that unless the seeds pass through the elephants' alimentary canals, they are unlikely to germinate. One theory places emphasis on the elephants' stomach. It compares the seed to a time-bomb whose firing mechanism is at "safe". If it simply falls from the tree to the ground, the seed is considered to be unarmed and does not explode into life. But, just as some time-bombs are detonated by the action of acid eating away a fine copper wire to release the firing pin, so *Acacia tortilis* is said to have its own detonation mechanism—the acid in the digestive juices which eats away the seed's outer casing. By the time it reaches the ground encased in a dropping, the seed is fully sensitized and ready to germinate. A more recent theory argues that the key factor is the movement of the animal. According to this, the seed is unlikely to germinate in the shadow of its parent tree. What counts is not the eating away by acid but the dispersal of the seed to places where there is adequate light.

I have seen the Manyara bush littered with the nine-inch bulbs of dried elephant droppings from which the small, pea-like leaves of *tortilis* shoots are already emerging. The process of regeneration at Manyara is continuous and lively, but by no means sufficient on its own to keep pace with increasing demands from the elephant population.

To me, elephants are certainly the most impressive wild animals left in the world. At Manyara, there are some individual animals I am never likely to forget, individuals I learned to know in the company of 27-year-old Dr. Iain Douglas-Hamilton and his wife, Oria, who had then already spent five years studying the behaviour and movements of every elephant among the 500 or so that live in Manyara.

The work was essential for the elephants' own preservation. Here was a dense pocket of the largest land animals in creation living free, or almost free. Hemmed in by the steep wall of the Rift to the west, with the lake shore to their east, they have only this narrow, albeit extremely fertile band of country to call their own. At times, particularly during

Many animals of the Rift are so elusive that often the only signs of their presence are the footprints left in the soft mud of waterholes. A massive paw mark (top left) testifies to the silent visit of a leopard by night. The tiny hoofprin (top right) was left by a dik-dik, an antelope the size of a fox, and the slightly larger though similar one (bottom left) by a stately gazelle. Four long fingers and distinct nail marks identify the firm imprint of a baboon (bottom right).

LEOPARD

DIK-DIK

GAZELLE

BABOON

the dry season, they must leave it to find food elsewhere, following age-old migration routes up the Rift wall into the forests on top. Man closes the borders to north and south with farmland, cutting the routes. In the north, beyond the rich ground water forest lies the village of Mto-wa-Mbu ("the river where the mosquitoes live"). Here the red soil grows bananas and could grow any crop the local citizens cared to plant. To the south there are farms again, farms originally wrested out of the bush by the strength and capital of Europeans, who were given a concession to cultivate this land on the frontier of elephant country. The elephants, naturally, are no respecters of such frontiers and the farmers shoot them in defence of their hard-won crops.

In this way Manyara's elephants mirror the universal problems facing all wild elephants left in the world. If they follow their traditional migration patterns in search of food, they will clash with man and in all probability get shot. If they are forced to stay where they are, they may eat themselves out of food. Such ecological disasters have already happened in other parts of Africa. Once the trees go, everything else, grass, soil, a way of life and of living for most large wild animals is likely to follow. Only the wrinkled face of erosion remains. It was Douglas-Hamilton's task to consider this unhappy juxtaposition of interests and, if possible, come up with a solution.

To study how elephants fit into their environment it is necessary to understand their social structure, migration patterns and details of fecundity and age. This had been attempted before, in other elephant crisis areas such as Murchison Falls Park, in Uganda, where 12,000 elephants confined inside 1,500 square miles have left hardly a tree intact; and in Tsavo, in Kenya, where exactly the same environmental tragedy is being enacted. In these studies, research into the elephants' social behaviour had been attempted by shooting and dissecting whole family herds. This drastic procedure was partly justified by the clear need to reduce the population and thus protect the depleted food sources, but mainly because it seemed the only way of arriving at some scientific conclusions. But at Manyara, the soil is so productive that if the elephants' requirements, in terms of population distribution, freedom of movement and birth rate, are understood in time, culling may never be necessary. It was essential, therefore, to find out how the elephants lived and moved and what could be done to preserve their living space as a sound ecological unit.

Douglas-Hamilton resolved that he would perform the whole study, no matter how long it took, without killing a single elephant. First, he and his wife had to devise a method of recognizing every cow elephant—cows are the basis of elephant society. They proceeded to build up a file of recognition photographs, close-ups that gave details of individual characteristics, even down to small notches and tears in the ears. Since the elephant fully extends its ears only when it is making a threatening demonstration, this usually meant persuading the beasts to make a charge at close quarters. Then Douglas-Hamilton had to condition the different family units to know and accept him so that he could move among them, sometimes on foot, for observation.

Next Douglas-Hamilton needed to know the distribution of age within elephant groups, a goal achieved by laboriously estimating the age of each elephant in the forest. There is a direct relationship between height at the shoulder and age. The only problem was how to gauge the shoulder height of a wild African elephant. Douglas-Hamilton built a photographic height-finder. Two mirrors at the ends of a long metal arm reflected their twin images through a prism to a 35mm camera. Each elephant photographed therefore appeared as a double image. From this double image he was able to calculate—in the same way as an artillery range-finder determines distance—shoulder height to within the very fine limits of an inch either way.

Gradually, the dossier on Manyara elephants accumulated until every cow was known, logged, photographed, and given a name, so that the habits and movements of it and its group could be followed throughout the year. The structure of elephant society is a matriarchal one. Possibly this is more in evidence here than anywhere else in Africa. Under stress conditions—when food is short, for instance—the family groups spread out and individual members scatter. At Manyara, despite the pressure of over 500 elephants on a comparatively small habitat, there is seldom real shortage and the family groups keep together, under the rule of the matriarchs. (Bull elephants, despite their fearsome reputation in fiction, are not masters of their fellows but noisy cowards that trumpet, scream and false-charge on principle but very seldom mean it.) The senior cows, however, are something different.

The most impressive matriarch at Manyara at the time of my visit in 1973 was Boadicea, as Douglas-Hamilton had named her. She was certainly the most imposing elephant I ever met. Boadicea was about 45 years old, of enormous height and beautifully proportioned. Her ivory, though not especially thick or heavy, was long and symmetrical. She was totally in command of her large group of 20 or so beasts, including several small calves. Lesser matriarchs like Diana, with a broken tip to one tusk, Virgo, a one-tusked elephant from birth, and the enormous Right Hook, relied on Boadicea for leadership and protection.

I accompanied Douglas-Hamilton as he studied Boadicea. She never once took her eyes off us, and when we approached close in our derelict, open-topped Land Rover, charged with a display of ferocity that frightened me very much. Boadicea commanded the full repertoire of vocal and visual intimidation. Her first demonstration, at a range of around 50 yards, was to shake clouds of dust off her ears. Then, as we got closer, she rushed towards us at great speed, trumpeting and growling, head down, trunk down, tusks lowered to hook the enemy if he did not turn away. "Elephants have spent a few million years perfecting their threat charges", Douglas-Hamilton commented; "they mean them to be impressive".

The daily routine of Boadicea's unit is typical of life in an elephant cow herd. While the matriarch takes over all responsibility for leadership, lesser ladies perform nursery chores. Females approaching sexual maturity, and those just past it, can frequently be seen waking up young elephant that have fallen asleep in the grass and failed to realize the group is moving on. Discipline is impressed on the young, especially young males, from an early age. A calf that tries to push in at the small holes, which elephants dig in dry stream-beds, to allow water to filter up through the sand, is liable to be slapped, pushed with a leg or rump and often sent sprawling to make it learn its place.

The cows communicate a good deal within the group with a language of deep rumbling growls made in the throat. They may also communicate with what is called a kinship group, usually composed of more distant blood relations, which are likely to be cruising the bush in their own loose formation half a mile or so away. A group's reaction to alarm signals from the matriarch in charge is enough to discourage the most redoubtable enemy. The cows form a phalanx—tusks flailing bushes, heads swaying, the air torn with screams and growls—or, when caught on open savannah, frequently make a defensive circle. Calves are tucked in, hidden by clouds of dust stirred up by the restless shuffling of a forest of adults' legs. I personally would be willing to face such a gathering in nothing less than a tank.

Bulls live a quite different life. At Manyara, adult males are frequently to be found along the lake shore, either singly or in small bachelor parties. The largest all-male group I have encountered is ten. Sometimes

An elephant applies the full force of its trunk and tusks to fell a small tree, and so reach the succulent foliage above. Elephants are constantly ripping off branches and bark in their quest for food and moisture, and they often destroy large numbers of trees in times of drought when there is little nutritious vegetation remaining on the ground.

a pair of bulls can be seen 150 yards or more out in the lake, pushing and shoving at each other in the manner of playful bathers, their tusks gleaming white in the water like the newly cleaned teeth they are. And, as they press along in water three or four feet deep, the bow wave they throw up is blue-green with the familiar diatoms that multiply so abundantly in an alkaline lake.

Play-fighting between bulls starts at an early age. It is a vital activity that establishes their place in elephant society, their precedence over other bulls when it comes to food, water and sex. The first play-fighting is little more than a nursery romp that takes place within the herd and is often broken up by the cows which, like mothers and grandmothers everywhere, know when enough is enough. I watched a Manyara cow stop a prolonged fight between two largish bulls, perhaps ten-year-olds, and a precocious youth half their size. This infant had nothing to do with the original scrap but, whenever the action seemed about to slow up, intervened with a butt or two at one of the principals to get them going again. In the end a large adult cow strolled across and pushed the three apart simply by walking straight through them. Whether the smallest calf was its offspring or not I don't know, though I suspect it was. Anyway, the cow reassured the calf by putting a maternal trunk in its mouth, that most touching of elephant gestures.

At puberty, around 13 years of age, the young bull's days with the female family group come to a close. The male becomes a nuisance and its biological function must soon be fulfilled elsewhere. It turns into a rover, free to wander and mate with any cow, from any group that will accept it. Acceptance depends on his achieving sufficient status. For the last few years of group life the maturing male is increasingly chivvied by the cows until even its bullheaded nature begins to take the hint. It is not wanted. The umbilical cord stretches, but for some time does not break. At first it hangs around within sight of the heaving backs of its former family unit as they roll across the bush like a flotilla of grey battleships, hull down on the horizon. Gradually, the distance lengthens. Play-fighting with other outcasts of similar age and weight continues. The male jousts with the young knights it meets on its travels and the challenges are offered and met with more serious intent as time passes. I have heard the clash of ivory upon ivory on occasions from a half a mile away, long before reaching the scene of the battle. It seems incredible that more damage is not inflicted in these contests. One often sees elephants with body sores made by tusk wounds. But eyes, surely the most vulnerable part in a frontal attack, seem never to be harmed.

*Lake Manyara's 500 elephants are
divided into small, closely-knit family
groups, led by the strongest, most
experienced cows, a system that
provides a secure matriarchal
framework for calves, sick herd
members and adolescent bulls as they
prepare in play-fighting for a future
away from the herd.*

MATRIARCH THREATENING TO CHARGE

CALF SEEKING SECURITY

PROTECTIVE GROUP AROUND SICK ELEPHANT

YOUNG BULLS SPARRING

Much of the detail of herd life can be learned by close observation on foot and in a skilfully handled Land Rover. Iain Douglas-Hamilton has built up his picture of the Manyara herds mainly by these methods. But a wider picture of elephant group movement over a period of, say, a year can be obtained only by telemetry—tracking the bleep-bleep signals emitted from a small transistorized radio transmitter attached to the animal concerned. Telemetry in wildlife study is now a well-established method and has been practised on everything from peccaries to rhinos. The co-operation of a large and dangerous animal, necessary for attaching the transmitter, can be obtained only by darting it—knocking it out with a hypodermic syringe-dart filled with anaesthetic and fired from a gun. Not more than 20 minutes later it must be injected with tranquillizer to bring it round. The tranquillizer counteracts the anaesthetic to prevent prolonged immobility, which could damage an elephant in a number of ways. The sheer weight of a collapsed elephant on its lungs and rib-cage is one hazard. Another is the effect of sunlight reaching the retina of the eye through a dilated pupil that can no longer react to bright light. In addition, the elephant can no longer flap its ears—an action that helps dissipate body heat—and it may suffer heat-stroke.

Douglas-Hamilton decided that the easiest way to keep tabs on the annual peregrinations of a cow herd was to fix a radio to a recently evicted young bull. Since the bull would move where the herd moved, without being part of the herd, it would be an exact indicator of their wanderings. To have darted one of the cows, Iain reasoned, would have been unnecessarily dangerous, if not impossible, since the attendant matriarchs would be unlikely to leave the distressed animal. Much more than the risk to himself, Iain was concerned about the disturbance caused to the herd by such a darting. The experiment was to demonstrate dramatically how true this assumption was and how closely knit were the family groups of Manyara elephants.

The first part of the experiment went according to plan and produced the results expected. By tracking radio-carrying bulls on foot and in his own aircraft, Douglas-Hamilton was able to show how the wanderings of several herds were related to the availability of food. But he had a limited number of transmitters and so had to dart each bull a second time when he wanted a radio back to transfer it to another animal. It was one of these second dartings that caused an incident illustrating the close social ties and loyalties evolved for the mutual protection of herd members, relationships extended even to an evicted bull.

The bull in question belonged to a herd supervised by a very large matriarch called Sarah, whose appearance was all the more intimidating because the last 18 inches of her tusks were crossed. But the selected male was apparently on its own and when Douglas-Hamilton found it wearing the desired radio, he darted it according to plan. The animal staggered off under the influence of the drug and Douglas-Hamilton prepared to wait the usual 20 minutes for the anaesthetic to take full effect. Only a few minutes had passed before there was trumpeting and crashing of bushes. Presumably the darted bull had made some alarm call, for Sarah and four senior females of her group had come to the drugged bull's rescue. Here was a first-hand demonstration of what might have happened had Iain chosen to dart a member of a cow herd. But if this turn of events was potentially dangerous to a human researcher, it was an immediate and far more serious threat to the bull. If Sarah and her companions continued to guard the bull—and there seemed no earthly reason why they should change their minds—there would be little chance of injecting the tranquillizer that must follow darting within a very short time if the animal is not to suffer serious damage. Iain had no spare darts so there could be no question of injecting the tranquillizer from a safe distance.

Sarah and her attendant cows, seriously distressed, tried to lift the partially unconscious bull to its feet. It weighed well over a ton and so their efforts were, not surprisingly, in vain. Douglas-Hamilton now made several attempts to approach on foot with a hyperdermic full of tranquillizer. Each time he only just escaped Sarah's charge. She would probably have smashed him to pulp had she not stopped short to return to the unconscious bull.

Finally, he got back into his Land Rover, drove it into the centre of the furious cows and just had time to inject half a dose of tranquillizer into the bull before Sarah charged, driving her tusks first through the radiator and then up and over the bonnet, demolishing the screen and steering wheel and narrowly missing Douglas-Hamilton. To avoid those crossed tusks he lunged back so hard that he broke the Land Rover's seat from its anchorage, a feat of some desperation, not to say strength. The vehicle, impelled by Sarah's tusks, shot backwards at around 20 m.p.h. and hit a tree. Mercifully, Sarah withdrew at this point, plainly under the impression that such an application of force had killed her enemy. Iain was still not satisfied and took advantage of her withdrawal to run in on foot and inject the rest of the antidote. The bull recovered and made off—very much alive, but with the precious radio still attached—a testimony to the elephants' corporate family sense.

The Manyara elephant research project, though special to the region's particular problems, has widespread application to the tragic situation in which elephants find themselves all over Africa. And it has led to two solutions, one of which has already been put into use.

After radio-tracking showed how dense the elephant concentrations are at the north end of the Park, where Mto-wa-mbu farmers grow bananas, a special elephant delicacy, Douglas-Hamilton set out to protect the banana *shambas* from the elephants—and the elephants from the *shamba* owners. He put up a single-strand electric fence, similar to those used for controlling cattle on farmland. At first the matriarchs tore the trial fence down. But they soon learned that the mild shock they received at the tip of their trunks was distasteful and a sensation to be avoided. Today, a stout, three-strand electric fence guards the banana frontier. Though a few smart elephants find that they can outflank the defences by walking a mile or two round the end of the wire, the effectiveness of this deterrent is enhanced by the fact that the elephants have to ford a stream between forest and bananas immediately before they reach the wire. The shock—though still a relatively mild and harmless one—is that much more convincing because the elephants are still wet from their crossing.

An electric fence works only where the frontier to be guarded is a relatively short one, as here in the north, for the wire has to be patrolled two or three times a day to check for breakages. At the southern end, the situation is quite different. Here again, radio-tracking has pointed the way to a long-term answer.

To the south lie the farms allocated to European farmers in the late 1950s. At that time, conservationists questioned the wisdom of anyone trying to farm with 500 wild elephants as next door neighbours. Nevertheless the farmers went ahead, cleared the virgin bush and planted coffee, pawpaws, maize and millet, which prospered in the fertile soil below the Rift wall. And the elephants, as expected, came to help harvest the crops and, as expected, got shot. More damaging to the elephant herds than a few casualties was the location of the farmland athwart their migration route to the wall of the Rift. Only a few trails are left open and as a result these five-ton animals climb tracks more suited to the agility of baboons in order to reach 90 square miles of rich forest, the Marang Forest Reserve, that lies over the crest of the Rift and supplies food when their home grounds are overgrazed during the dry season.

Dr. Douglas-Hamilton's work has made the importance of this migration route plain to all. Now there is some hope that Tanzania will be able to buy those farmlands back. If this happens, wild animals, will, for once, have won. Manyara will have become a viable ecological unit of plains and forest which can more than contain the highest concentration of elephants left in Africa.

One of the steepest of these remaining paths into the forest rises close to a place called Endabash, where a waterfall cascades hundreds of feet from rocks above. This track taxes human legs and stamina. Yet the huge animals climb it in order to enjoy the forest beyond the crest. It is a magic place to visit, but one to be approached with caution. The bush is thick and it is an excellent spot in which to surprise—or bad spot in which to be surprised by—elephant. The elephants of Endabash are of an unpredictable nature. So many of them have been shot, or at any rate shot at, they may take any human to be an enemy.

Manyara is a fitting place at which to end my journey down the Rift Valley wilderness. Though in a geological sense the Rift continues southward, its nature from here onwards is very different. Geologists can follow its progress, but it no longer retains the unity that makes the stretch from the Red Sea to Tanzania so fascinating.

It is as if the underlying grain of Africa has changed. Like an old and gnarled piece of timber, the cracks in the Rift do not always run true. And if two terms sum up the Great Rift Valley they are precisely those: old, old as the green hills of Africa and gnarled as only 20 million years of earth history can make it.

The Moment of Fear

The "balance of nature" is a phrase much used by nature lovers, but in fact nature is never in balance. Always some influence is at work depressing the scales on one side or the other: climatic change, geological upheaval, a new evolutionary advantage that allows one species to thrive at the expense of another. The Rift Valley has known many such changes in its 20-million-year history. Yet recently, in the latest blink of time's eyelid, one pressure above all has weighted the scales against wildlife there–the hand of man.

For thousands of years, African tribesmen lived more or less in harmony with the elephant and the buffalo, the lion and the antelope, taking only what they needed for survival and what they could get with spear or arrow. But in the late 19th Century, British and German explorers introduced the firearm and indulged in massive slaughter: for sport, for trophies, to make way for agriculture, or for gain. The European remorselessly hunted and largely shot out the Rift's great herds of game. Those animals that remain have learned to avoid mankind, and in doing so have discovered a reaction that they never knew before: fear.

The hand of man is of course res-

ponsible for the remarkable portraits on these pages; and although it is man's harmless camera rather than his weapon that is aimed at the prey, the subject of the portrait in each case has been caught at that moment of fear as it reacts to the alien presence with understandable caution, stealthiness or abrupt retreat.

Thus the gerenuk raises its long neck cautiously to browse among bushtops, its ears straining to locate the source of the camera's click. From an even loftier viewpoint, giraffes pause, immobile and suspicious at the photographer's intrusion. A herd of restless, ever-moving gnu panic and stampede, stirring clouds of dust from galloping hoofs.

The ponderous hippos have learned that in daytime they are safe only in the sun-silvered waters of the lake. The jackal slinks by the photographer to disappear hastily in the golden grass. Splashing waterbuck and leaping eland rely on speed to give man a wide berth. The lion caught in the lights of a passing vehicle, or even approached in daylight, will quickly retreat, knowing by bitter experience that man's arsenal of weapons—and therefore man—is the greatest danger to the wild inhabitants of the Great Rift Valley.

A NERVOUS GERENUK PEERING FROM THE BUSH

GIRAFFES IN STATELY SOLITUDE

FLEEING WILDEBEEST

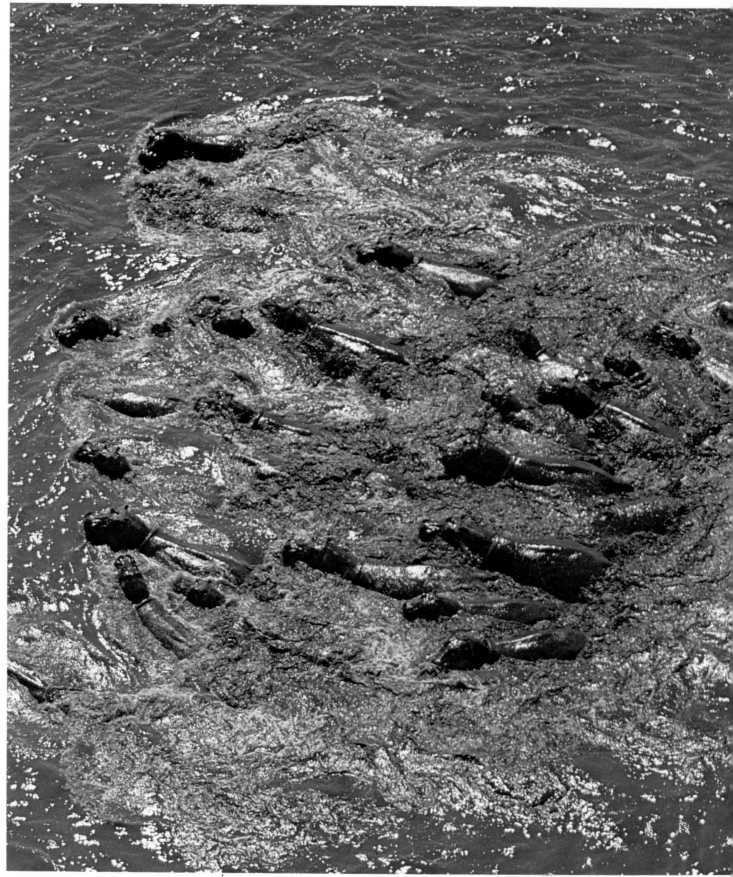

HIPPOS SWIMMING IN FORMATION

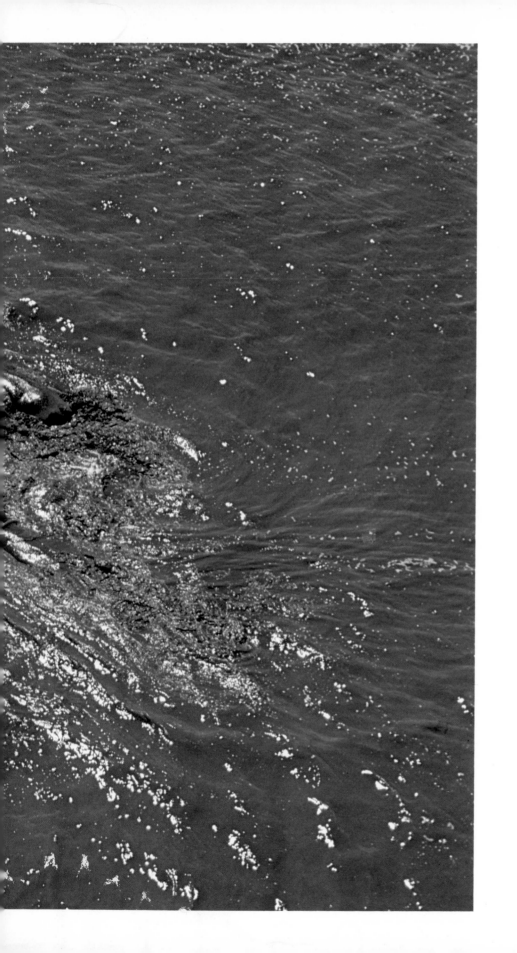

A JACKAL STALKING ITS PREY

A SPLASHING WATERBUCK

AN ELAND IN MID-LEAP

A HUNTING LIONESS SURPRISED BY A CAMERA FLASH

Bibliography

Alexander, T., "The Wandering Continents", *Nature/Science Annual*. Time-Life, 1970.

Astley-Maberley, C. T., *Animals of East Africa*. Howard Timmins, 1960.

Beadle, L. C., *Inland Waters of Tropical Africa. An Introduction to Tropical Limnology*. Longman, 1973.

Beckinsale, R. P., *Land, Air and Ocean*. Camelot Press, 1966.

Brown, L., *Africa: A Natural History*. Hamish Hamilton, 1965.

Brown, L., *The Mystery of the Flamingoes*. Country Life Books (The Hamlyn Publishing Group Ltd.), 1959.

Chapman, A., *On Safari*. Edward Arnold, 1908.

Cole, S., *The Prehistory of East Africa*. Weidenfeld and Nicolson, 1964.

Cox, R., *Kenyatta's Country*. Hutchinson, 1965.

Drury, G. H., *The Face of the Earth*. Penguin, 1959.

Edey, M. A., *The Missing Link*. Time-Life Books, 1972.

Fryer, G. and Iles, T. D., *The Cichlid Fishes of the Great Lakes of Africa*. Oliver and Boyd, 1972.

Fuertes, L. A. and Osgood, W. H., *Artist and Naturalist in Ethiopia*. Doubleday, 1936.

Green, T., *The Adventurers*. Michael Joseph, 1970.

Gregory, J. W., *The Great Rift Valley*. John Murray, 1896.

Gregory, J. W., *The Rift Valleys and Geology of East Africa*. Seeley, Service and Co., 1921.

Hemingway, E., *The Green Hills of Africa*. Penguin, 1972.

Hill, M. F., *Magadi*. The Kynoch Press, 1964.

Hillaby, J., *Journey to the Jade Sea*. Constable, 1964.

Höhnel, L. R. von, *The Discovery of Lakes Rudolf and Stefanie*. Longmans Green, 1894.

Holmes, A., *Principles of Physical Geology*. Nelson, 1965.

King, L. C., *Morphology of the Earth*. Oliver and Boyd, 1962.

Leaky, L. S. B., *Olduvai Gorge, 1951-61*. Cambridge University Press, 1965.

Luther, E. W., *Ethiopia Today*. Oxford University Press, 1958.

Mackworth-Praed, C. W. and Grant, C. H. B., *Birds of Eastern and Northeastern Africa (2 Vols.)*. International Publications Service, 1960.

Marcus, H. G., *The Modern History of Ethiopia and the Horn of Africa: A Select and Annotated Bibliography*. Hoover Institute, 1971.

Mohr, P. A., *The Geology of Ethiopia*. University College of Addis Ababa Press, 1964.

Moorehead, A., *No Room in the Ark*. Hamish Hamilton, 1959.

Morgan, W. T. W., (ed.), *East Africa: Its Peoples and Resources*. London University Press, 1969.

Morgan, W. T. W., *East Africa*. Longman, 1973.

Nesbitt, L. M., *Desert and Forest*. Jonathan Cape, 1934, Penguin, 1955.

Richards, C. G., *Count Teleki and the Discovery of Lakes Rudolf and Stefanie*. Macmillan, 1960.

Tazieff, H., *South from the Red Sea*. Lutterworth Press, 1956.

Thomson, J., *Through Masai Land*. Low, Marston, Searle & Rivington, 1885.

Williams, J. G., *A Field Guide to the Birds of East and Central Africa*. Collins, 1963.

Williams, J. G., *A Field Guide to the National Parks of East Africa*. Collins, 1967.

Younghusband, E., *Glimpses of East Africa and Zanzibar*. John Long, 1910.

Acknowledgements

The author and editors of this book wish to thank the following: Anglia Television, London; Dr. William Bishop, London; Suzie Bower, London; Christopher Chant, London; Members of Staff of the Foreign Office Library, London; Dan Freeman, London; Derek T. Harris, Los Angeles; Imperial Chemical Industries, London; The Magadi Soda Company, Northwich, Cheshire; Alan and Joan Root, Kenya; Members of Staff of the Royal Geographical Society Library, London; Donald Simpson, Librarian, Royal Commonwealth Society, London; Dr. Emil Urban, Addis Ababa; Dr. G. E. Wickens, Royal Botanical Gardens, London; Members of Staff of the Library of the Zoological Society, London.

Picture Credits

Sources for pictures in this book are shown below. Credits for pictures from left to right are separated by commas.

All photographs are by Goetz D. Plage, from Bruce Coleman Ltd., London, except: Cover–Lee Lyon from Bruce Coleman Ltd. Front end papers 1, 2–M. R. Stanley Price from Natural Science Photos, London. Front end paper 3, page 1–Klaus Paysan. 4, 5–Lee Lyon. 8, 9–A. J. Dean from Bruce Coleman Ltd. 14, 15–Map by Hunting Surveys Ltd., London. 19–National Aeronautics and Space Administration. 23–M. R. Stanley Price from Natural Science Photos. 24–Royal Geographical Society, London. 29–Dr. Ian Gibson from Robert Harding Associates, London. 30 to 33–Gerald Cubitt. 34, 35–Dr. Georg Gerster from the John Hillelson Agency, London. 36, 37–Gerald Cubitt. 41–Lee Lyon. 45–Lee Lyon. 49 to 59–Dr. Georg Gerster from the John Hillelson Agency. 71–Norman Myers from Bruce Colman Ltd. 82–Map by Hunting Surveys Ltd. 94–Colin Willock. 101–Jane Burton from Bruce Coleman Ltd. 107–A. J. Sutcliffe from Natural Science Photos. 108, 109–Lee Lyon. 110–Leslie Brown from Ardea Photographics, London. 111–Lee Lyon. 112, 113–W. B. Bishop. 114, 115–Douglas Botting. 118–Peter Hill. 123–John Moss from Colorific Photo Library Ltd., London. 124–Leslie Brown from Ardea Photographics. 125–Jane Burton from Bruce Coleman Ltd. 127–Douglas Botting. 128–Mark Boulton. 129–Douglas Botting. 130, 131–C. Weaver from Ardea Photographics. 136, 137–Mirella Ricciardi, *Vanishing Africa*, Collins, London. 142–Map by Hunting Surveys Ltd. 143 to 151–from *Discovery by Count Teleki of Lakes Rudolf and Stefanie* by his companion Lieut. Ludwig von Höhnel, 1894. 160–Iain and Oria Douglas-Hamilton. 162, 163–Iain and Oria Douglas-Hamilton. 169–John Dominis. 170, 171–Horst Munzig from Susan Griggs, London. 172, 173–Lee Lyon. 174, 175–Teleki-Baldwin. 177–John Dominis. 178, 179–Jane Burton from Bruce Coleman Ltd.

Index

Numerals in italics indicate a
photograph or drawing of the subject
mentioned.

XX

Colour reproduction by
Printing Developments International Ltd.,
Leeds, England—a Time Inc. subsidiary.
Filmsetting by C. E. Dawkins (Typesetters) Ltd., London, SE1 1UN.
Printed in Holland by Smeets Lithographers, Weert.
Bound by Proost en Brandt N.V., Amsterdam.